IT
TAKES
CHUTZPAH

IT TAKES
CHUTZPAH

HOW TO FIGHT FEARLESSLY
FOR PROGRESSIVE CHANGE

Senator Ron Wyden

GRAND
CENTRAL

NEW YORK BOSTON

Grand Central Publishing
Hachette Book Group
1290 Avenue of the Americas, New York, NY 10104
grandcentralpublishing.com
@grandcentralpub

First Edition: January 2025

Grand Central Publishing is a division of Hachette Book Group, Inc. The
Grand Central Publishing name and logo is a registered trademark of Hachette
Book Group, Inc.

The publisher is not responsible for websites (or their content) that are not
owned by the publisher.

The Hachette Speakers Bureau provides a wide range of authors for speaking
events. To find out more, go to hachettespeakersbureau.com or email
HachetteSpeakers@hbgusa.com.

Grand Central Publishing books may be purchased in bulk for business,
educational, or promotional use. For information, please contact your local
bookseller or the Hachette Book Group Special Markets Department at
special.markets@hbgusa.com.

Print book interior design by Jeff Stiefel.

Library of Congress Control Number: 2024949255

ISBNs: 978-0-306-83587-2 (hardcover) 978-0-306-83589-6 (ebook)

Printed in the United States of America

LSC-C

Printing 1, 2024

⤳

To the memory of my mom, Edith,
my grandmother Helen,
and all the strong Jewish women in Germany
in the 1930s who saw clearly the Nazi threat
so badly underestimated
by their husbands and sons.

Without them and their courage
I wouldn't be here to write this book.
And the most important women in my life,
Lilly, Ava, and Scarlett who make me kvell
every day, and especially Nancy, whose love
and strength is my constant inspiration.

CONTENTS

HOW TO FIGHT FEARLESSLY FOR PROGRESSIVE CHANGE

January 6, 2021, was a terrible day.

History may show that November 18, 2022, was even worse.

Everyone knows about January 6. It was a noisy, public attempt—embraced increasingly by Republican leaders—to prevent the peaceful transfer of power between elected Presidential Administrations for the first time in American history.

Few know about November 18. It also was an attack on our democracy, but more subtle. On that day, a shadowy religious organization filed a lawsuit before an obscure, Christian nationalist Federal judge who had been groomed by the far right to undermine the U.S. Constitution's guarantees of civil rights. Although constructed specifically to eliminate American women's freedom to obtain safe non-surgical abortions—a freedom I had helped secure 30 years earlier—their new courtroom gambit is aimed to undermine the legal principles that support virtually every other national civil right established during the past hundred years. Freedom of speech, food safety, child labor prohibitions, gay marriage, even the right to buy contraceptives or to marry someone of a different race, all are now threatened by the operatives who carried out this scheme.

The January 6 coup failed. For now.

The November 18 coup might yet succeed.

Which is why—on February 16, 2023, after months of growing horror as the legal scholars I consulted validated my fears—I took to the floor of the U.S. Senate to expose the renegade jurist and stop the coup against the Constitution.

It was a wet, dreary day in Washington, DC. But inside the United States Capitol, I was heated and I was clear.

"His name is Judge Matthew Kacsmaryk," I told my Senate colleagues, introducing many for the first time to the conservatives' newest would-be insurrectionist. "A lifelong right-wing activist. A partisan ideologue. An anti-abortion zealot who was hand-picked by Donald Trump and the Federalist Society to feign impartiality on the bench and deliver favorable rulings on the cases his fellow right-wing ideologues funnel his way.

"In a matter of days," I warned, "he will issue a ruling on a case so absurd and meritless that it did not deserve a single breath of argument in his courtroom....If we allow it, Kacsmaryk's ruling could deal the next devastating blow to the right to privacy in America, and the right of all women to control their own bodies. Not just in Texas, but in all 50 states."

On the surface, I had only one instrument to play: my voice, performed before a half-empty chamber and a C-SPAN viewership in the low triple digits. Underneath my vocals, though, I had an entire orchestra and a well-arranged score. After 50 years as a citizen-activist, I knew how to mobilize backup players across the political, media, and advocacy landscape and give them room to riff, especially when you need a bigger audience than the one in the room. And when you're taking on

The New Establishment—which today isn't the dense military-industrial complex of my youth that had killed tens of thousands of young Americans by waging an unnecessary and unwinnable war in Vietnam, but a MAGA infrastructure that had bent the Republican Party to its will, corrupted the judiciary, and confirmed a theocratically sectarian U.S. Supreme Court majority—you need a bigger audience.

My counsel to my Senate colleagues on February 16 was succinct and, to traditionalists, shocking. "Here's what must happen if and when Judge Kacsmaryk issues his nationwide injunction," I said. "President Biden and the FDA must ignore it."

⌐

It takes gall for a senior United States Senator to call on the rest of the Government to ignore a Federal judge, one of the pillars of our democratic system. But when the system is being abused and twisted to do wrong—to harm people you have taken an oath to serve—there is no other option. This was not a decision I took lightly, but it was the culmination of a life spent showing up, working hard, and trying every day not just to do good, but to do right.

My name is Ron Wyden. I am Oregon's senior Senator after 43 years in Congress. I'm the second most senior Democrat in the U.S. Senate. I chair one of the Federal Government's most powerful bodies, the Senate Finance Committee, which oversees taxes, trade and tariffs, Social Security and Medicare, health policy, and the overall economic well-being of the United States. I've written laws that injected $1 trillion in new wealth into the global economy, improved Americans' access to quality health care, stopped malfeasant insurance companies from abusing the elderly, and begun the overdue process of reversing deadly climate change. I am the ultimate insider.

My name is Ron Wyden. I am a child of immigrants. At the ripe age of 25, I was one of the first full-time activists for senior citizens in the United States. By 27, I was among the nation's youngest authorities on Medicare. I got to Congress by defeating an entrenched, disengaged incumbent in my own party's primary, 38 years before another determined young insurgent, Alexandria Ocasio-Cortez, did the same, uncommon, feat. If I can do it, and she can do it, you can do it. I am the consummate outsider.

My name is Ron Wyden. Every day I get up and try to fix the world— a vocation we Jews call *tikkun olam*. But you know what? If you're reading this book, then regardless of your race, religion, or background, *tikkun olam* is your occupation, too. So I'm going to show you how to fix your world, and if you've got the enthusiasm for it, how to fix *the* world, too.

This is a book about how I've shown up every day, played the long game, and learned some important lessons about defying convention, disavowing received wisdom, upending old dictums, and charting new pathways that can contribute to better lives. And it's a book about helping you do exactly the same thing, across every dimension of your own life, to make your school, your workplace, your volunteer organizations, your community, and our nation a more elevated and effective place, using the same tool—the only tool, really—that I've had at my disposal throughout my 52 years in public life:

Chutzpah.

Chutzpah is the indispensable instrument for improving America. Like any instrument, it's not there just to make noise—it exists to achieve objectives, to harmonize otherwise random notes, to make beautiful things happen. Chutzpah requires the orchestration of instruction, observation, practice, and collaboration to bring goals to life. Learning and applying the music of chutzpah transformed me from being a diffident kid whose only dream was to play pro basketball into being a cheerful and determined combatant on behalf of American ideals. If you're willing to become part of our larger ensemble—if I can enlist you in the Chutzpah Nation—you can use your inner chutzpah to make the United States and the world that accommodates us happier, healthier, and greater.

In recent years, the perception of chutzpah has been misappropriated and warped by loudmouth Donald Trump and his enablers in politics and the media, who engage in what my Chief of Staff calls "self-aggrandizing f*ckery" and pass it off as chutzpah.

Chutzpah isn't about having a big mouth. It is a learned skill that allows its practitioners to self-confidently embrace the possible, despite the odds. Chutzpah doesn't require a noble purpose, just a positive one. After all, Steve Prefontaine was just a kid from Coos Bay, Oregon, too short to make his high school's starting football and basketball teams, who, with homegrown chutzpah and some terrific coaching, effectively invented the modern sport of long-distance running. In our complex, cacophonous culture, important goals, especially civic goals, are impossible to achieve without some combination of vision, ideas, partners, processes, and—yes—the voice and the audacity that willing and prepared *chutzpadiks* bring to everything we do. (While *chutzpadik* is traditionally used as an adjective, I think the times call for its use as well as a word for good people who use their chutzpah to change the world.)

Fundamentally, chutzpah is about applying a set of rules I've learned during my half-century in public life. Cheekily, I call them Ron's Rules of Chutzpah—guidelines that enable individuals and groups to achieve beneficial objectives.

The 12 Ron's Rules of Chutzpah are:

1. If you want to make change, you've got to make noise.
2. In a world where everyone thinks and acts for the short term, always play the long game.

5

3. Leading is coaching: You've got to bring people and ideas together around a shared goal.

4. Show up every day prepared to play.

5. There are two equally important paths to progress: Start good things and stop bad things.

6. Embrace the unscripted moments.

7. Ideas are the seeds of change; find them and plant them wherever and whenever you can.

8. Pay attention to your friends, because they can be far more unpredictable than your enemies.

9. Don't push rocks up hills. Push boulders. They will fall back on you, but you'll gain the strength to get to the top.

10. Be a principled bipartisan: Work with anybody who is serious about moving forward.

11. Compromise isn't about horse-trading bad ideas for each other; it's about blending good ideas together into a whole that's better than the sum of its parts.

12. Political capital doesn't earn interest and is worth nothing if you don't spend it.

Ron's Rules of Chutzpah are for anyone who's ever asked themselves: Do I have the...guts?...stamina?...self-regard?...conviction?...charisma?...vision?...to knock on the next door and the next and the next (whether it's to sell Girl Scout Cookies or get petitions signed to build a traffic light at a dangerous intersection)?...to absorb the sass, accept the challenges to my intelligence, deal with bullies, and combat hidden agendas?... to pursue goals that might not resonate with everyone, that might make me unpopular, no matter how important I know them to be?

If you've ever asked yourself any of the above questions (and you have) and you're still standing (and you are), you've already got chutzpah. I want to offer you guidance about how to polish that raw chutzpah and deploy it to do good in the wider world—to make great things happen amid the obstacles every and any organization will throw in your way. I want this book to be a handbook for achieving goals, a sort of management guide for life itself.

My playbook isn't typical in the U.S. Congress. In fact, it's made me an inside-outsider, in a way that some of my colleagues have found confounding. After all, I wrote the law that, in the words of one eminent scholar, "created the Internet"…yet I've written the toughest tech privacy legislation on offer, which would jail tech CEOs who abuse our rights. In a Government allegedly paralyzed by partisan gridlock, I routinely team up with deeply conservative Republicans to pass legislation, without sacrificing my equally embedded progressive principles.

It all makes sense. In telling the stories of these legislative efforts and the life that spurred me to take them on, I hope to illuminate Ron's Rules of Chutzpah in ways that will encourage you to take on the system; build *better* systems, institutions, and laws; establish new customs; and experience the sheer thrill and delight of shaping a better future for your families, tribes, neighbors, communities, and nation.

Of course, I have an ulterior motive.

I hope that, by showing the universally applicable life lessons of chutzpah, I can persuade you to engage in serious political action to stop the United States from falling into the abyss of fascism, what George Orwell called "a boot stomping on a human face, forever," a bottomless pit in which the only thing that matters is how rich you are and how much power your wealth can buy. I want you to join my passionate crusade to fix the world, to assure a future where Americans will remain free and able to lead healthy, safe, private lives where we can choose our own futures without a heavy-handed Government telling us what we're allowed to think, say, be, and do.

Let me also tell you why I'm not writing this book.

I'm not writing this book to grease my run for President of the United States. It's a fantastically interesting job that I *don't* want to do. In fact, I long ago declared myself the Senate's "designated driver"—the person who won't ever succumb to the intoxicating fantasy of being *The Leader of the Free World*—so that I could freely raise the ideas and advance the legislation the nation needs, but which would be poisonous in a sound-bite-driven Presidential campaign. Reducing health-care costs, shoring up Medicare and Social Security, closing the massive loopholes that enable billionaires to avoid paying taxes, and reining in the surveillance state from tracking law-abiding Americans—if you're running for President there are political reasons not to address these issues, and I have liberated myself from that straitjacket.

Which gets me back to the reasons I *am* writing this book.

First, for millions of Americans, Congress might as well be Mars, for all the connection they feel it has to their daily lives, and I want to rebuild that connection. To the extent citizens even consider the Congress, it's because all the nuttiness of recent years makes it look like a poorly produced WWE wrestling match overpopulated with grifters and gamblers, political-machine hacks and idiot nephews, glory hounds and womanizers.

I won't try to convince you that those impressions are wrong. We're all flawed—those who put themselves out there to run for office are inherently flawed. That said, this untidy legislature is responsible for the body of laws that has allowed America to grow and thrive, to maintain the liberties established at the founding and to build on their foundation, and to respond to changes in technology and economics by fostering innovation and resisting the power of established interests. For all its defects, the U.S. Congress has managed this complicated tango with history and our diverse citizenry far better than any other legislature in any other democracy—the indecorous mudslinging, stuntsmanship, and blather notwithstanding.

The second reason I'm writing this book is to show the links between the Jewish American experience in the 20th and 21st centuries and the principles that underpin American democracy. These have been central to my life for all my 75 years—a life that would not have been had my parents not fled Nazi Germany in the 1930s and been welcomed as refugees into the United States.

There are two Jewish concepts in particular on which I'll focus, one cultural and one rooted in ancient liturgy, both of which I've already referenced.

The cultural concept, of course, is chutzpah—which to me is shorthand for the individual's self-confident, against-the-odds embrace of the possible. True, you need your voice, its amplifiers, and its echoes; as my mother (all Jewish mothers in the 1940s and '50s, and '60s) used to say, "You got a mouth—use it!" But successfully applied chutzpah requires other ingredients, notably ideas, people, process, and goals—particularly the second Jewish concept, the religious goal of *tikkun olam*, which literally means "to repair the world." *Tikkun olam* is the reason you see Jews, although less than 3 percent of the U.S. population, more fully represented in the leadership of civic organizations, NGOs, the law, and journalism. Our religion *requires* us to be worldly and engaged; we are raised to want to make things better. Without a sense of *tikkun olam*, you don't have chutzpah.

The third reason I'm writing this book is to explain how my own chutzpah and the concept of *tikkun olam*, inherited from my parents and nurtured by my friends and colleagues, have come together to drive the four greatest passions of my life aside from my family: civil rights, health care, the environment, and innovation.

These are not new nor novel issues.

In his most famous State of the Union speech, in 1941, Franklin Roosevelt artfully articulated a set of principles he called the Four Freedoms—freedom of speech, freedom of worship, freedom from want, and freedom from fear. Those four freedoms remain at risk in the United States and the world today, as much as they did when Nazi Germany and Imperial Japan were attempting to force their malign will across the globe. Today, though, some of our worst threats come not from foreign enemies, but from within. In practice, the four freedoms manifest themselves now a bit differently than when they were first articulated. The freedom of speech today is the freedom to speak your mind or read what you want without risk of Government intrusion or direction, like Florida's pernicious "Don't Say 'Gay" law. The freedom of worship is the freedom to believe what you choose, to make your own health-care decisions, and to vote, without coercion, sanction, violent opposition, or religious zealots gaming the legal system to deny these rights. The freedom from want today is most paramount in our ongoing need for all individuals and families, regardless of their financial situation, to have access to health care without being bankrupted, so everyone can exercise the opportunities America offers. Freedom from fear is clearly represented in Black Americans rising up to reject the specter of police violence that has haunted their lives; in all citizens' desire for safe communities; and in the freedom to live in a world that is not polluting and poisoning itself into rapid annihilation.

That's why Donald Trump is important.

Donald Trump demonstrates how you can use a malicious imitation of chutzpah for evil ends. He has warped the Republican Party and made principled compromise on important national issues infinitely harder.

Historically in American politics, we agreed on the most important public problems but disagreed on how to solve them. Sadly, the impulse in the Trump Party is to disagree that problems even exist if they don't match the Leader's own baleful needs, and to invent non-existent problems where his agenda requires it. Instead of addressing inflation, Social Security and Medicare solvency, global warming, energy security, and continuing job growth, all we hear from him and his MAGA minions is how they're beating up on folks who might be different than you and me, and beating down any institution that might question those attacks.

Donald Trump's four years in office were a disaster. The President suffered from a predisposition toward cruelty. He was aided and abetted by an Administration stocked with ideologues, yes men, and aspiring fascists. The Republican Congressional leadership that controlled both houses seemed incapable of doing anything other than to say, "Yes, sir." But he and his malignant MAGAtts can be beaten, as we showed when we determined to use all the levers of Government to halt Americans' slide into economic disaster during the deadly coronavirus pandemic.

By mid-March 2020, millions of Americans were being told to leave their jobs and go home to stop the spread of Covid-19. The economy was grinding to a halt. Congress responded by preparing the emergency Coronavirus Aid, Relief, and Economic Security (CARES) Act. In its first draft, Senate Republican leader Mitch McConnell showed how little compassion he had for working

Americans by devoting only eight lines in the 247-page bill to the plight of the unemployed. His one concession to the 11 million people tossed from work because their companies had shut their doors or simply couldn't afford them was a proposed requirement that states let the unemployed apply for benefits online. Most of the rest of his bill showered tax breaks on his big business allies.

McConnell put together a series of bipartisan task forces that were charged with assuring the bill covered all the necessary bases but which were really meant to rubber stamp his deficient proposal. As the ranking Democrat on the Senate Finance Committee, I was co-leading with the Republican Chair Chuck Grassley one of those task forces, whose chief aim was to tackle ballooning, Covid-caused unemployment. This was my opportunity to repair a hurting world.

My concept of the long game is having a closet of ready-to-wear public policies that can be taken off the shelf, shown in public, and, if the stars align, passed. The Wyden *tikkun olam* closet contained fixes to outdated laws and regulations, so that when the need for them was urgent, we could move quickly. Repairing a broken down unemployment insurance program had long been near the top of my list. State unemployment offices were plagued with hopelessly out-of-date computers, and the laws virtually ignored gig workers, the self-employed, and independent contractors.

Mitch McConnell's empty proposal, coming in the midst of extraordinary national pain, was my opening to present one of the unemployment insurance fixes I'd prepared more than a year earlier, well before Covid struck: guaranteed payments to the unemployed from the Federal Government, managed through but otherwise divorced from the individual states' unemployment insurance mechanisms.

In our task force meetings in the Dirksen Senate Office Building, I tussled with two Trump Cabinet officials, the obstinate Secretary of

Labor Eugene Scalia and the mostly quiet Treasury Secretary Steve Mnuchin, who were there with multiple members of their departments' staffs. Scalia, as deeply conservative as his late father, the Supreme Court Justice Antonin Scalia, made it clear from the outset that his priority was a minimal package that was devoid of systemic reform (he never even mentioned the word), and focused instead on McConnell's big business tax breaks, which Scalia contended would trickle down and provide relief to those in need.

The centerpiece of the Democrats' agenda was a temporary, 100 percent wage replacement package that would get unemployed workers what they needed to pay for rent, groceries, and essentials during the darkest days of the quarantine. At that moment we had no idea how serious the pandemic would become—whether it would kill 5 percent or 0.005 percent of those infected. But what we did know was that if people had to show up at work to pay rent and put food on their families' tables, they were going to show up, Covid or no, potentially exposing themselves and their kin to disease and death. The idea that working people were going to risk their families' lives out of economic necessity should be anathema to any public servant. Scalia fought me for hours, claiming the states were largely incapable of calculating a worker's previous wage and for that reason my wage replacement concept was a pie-in-the-sky fantasy.

So I asked Scalia: Wasn't it correct that in response to the 2008 recession that Congress provided temporary supplemental payments of $25 to unemployed Americans? His staff agreed this was correct. I then said to Mnuchin and Scalia that their staffs' admission proved my key point: The Federal Government was capable of sending out supplemental weekly benefits of a set amount. The only issue that remained was to determine the amount. The Trump Administration officials and their staffers sullenly agreed.

I asked for a short recess in the talks so I could add Covid-specific details to the proposal I had developed more than a year earlier. When we reconvened, Scalia made it clear that if we were going to add a relief package to the bill, he cared only about two issues: keeping the amount of the benefit as low as possible to stay within Federal budget guidelines, and having the payments last for as short a period as possible. I countered with what I called rough justice: a four-month-long, $600 weekly benefit—the difference between what an average worker would make on the job, and how much that worker would receive in unemployment benefits.

Impossible, the Administration officials replied—that would break the budget!

My crackerjack Finance Committee staffer Rachel Kauss and I embraced this unscripted moment. We each pulled out our cell phones, launched our calculator apps, and held them up: The $600-a-week four-month payment to the Covid-displaced scored well within budget limits. Mnuchin, the Trump Administration's chief CARES negotiator, broke with his colleague Scalia and agreed. The relief package was added to the bill.

On the Senate floor, a furious Mitch McConnell and his Callous Caucus attempted to strip the benefit from the CARES bill. Resurrecting arguments that Republicans had made 90 years earlier opposing the very concept of unemployment insurance, Nebraska Republican Ben Sasse argued that our relief checks would incentivize laziness among the working class. "Health aides and grocers and people doing local delivery, garbage men, lots of important industries in America have median wages which are lower than what would happen under the unemployment benefits portion of this bill," fretted Sasse.

Their objections failed. A handful of Republicans joined

unanimous Senate Democrats, and late on March 25, 2020, the CARES Act passed, extending unemployment benefits to 39 weeks, and leaving intact the four-month, $600-a-week extension. From the Wyden policy closet, we also got coverage for gig-economy workers and contractors previously ineligible for unemployment insurance; subsidies to help small companies retain employees they otherwise might lay off; and loans and loan relief for small and midsized businesses.

"This expansion of aid to the unemployed did double duty. It alleviated hardship, letting laid-off workers continue to pay rent and put food on the table. And it supported overall spending much more effectively than those stimulus checks, most of which were probably just saved," concluded Nobel Prize–winning economist Paul Krugman. "Who deserves credit for this very good policy? A recent *Times* article describes Steven Mnuchin, the Treasury secretary, as the 'architect' of the CARES Act and the bill as a 'victory' for Trump. Actually, however, the crucial unemployment provisions were devised largely by Senator Ron Wyden, Democrat of Oregon."

Although he may not have meant this to happen, Trump compelled millions of people to understand the imperative to engage with the world around them. By generating a kind of national nervous breakdown, Trump forced the United States to recognize and reject the torpor that first settled on us in the 1970s, when the protests against the Vietnam War gave way to the Me Generation's self-involved impulses and became more devoted to myriad forms of personal expression than to solving the world's problems. Trump has shown us that, on a personal level, the core of the self-centered individual is hollow, unhappy, and unlikeable, and that such self-centered hollowness, unhappiness, and unlikability, when resident in our leaders, can literally tear communities, even whole countries, apart. He reminds us every day about the stakes. That politics matters. That one voice, backed by chutzpah, can make a difference. That mixing it up in public can make big things happen. But instead of Trump's wanton, pathological destruction of norms and institutions, imagine that it's *your* voice mixing it up. Imagine that you're deploying your voice not to persuade people to hate Muslims, people with disabilities, immigrants, women, and poor seniors, but to create a better local school system or build a senior citizens program for your neighbors or develop respectful neighborhood policing that makes communities safe.

If I, the once-aimless son of divorced refugee parents turned bookish wanderer turned unmonied activist turned United States Senator, can, in ways small and large, fix Medicare, help reverse climate change, and inject a trillion dollars into the economy with a 26-word law, think what you can do in your town. And even if you're not able to engage directly, think what my like-minded colleagues and successors in government will be able to do with your guidance and encouragement. And, oh yes, your votes.

Progress not only remains possible, it is real, and it happens every day. I will show how and why. I am determined the United States will surmount this moment of stress in our Constitutional system, as we've overcome earlier tensions.

All it takes is chutzpah.

ONE

MAKING PRODUCTIVE NOISE

t's August 2023. I'm in my Chrysler, piloted by a young staffer to a meeting in Corvallis, beautiful Corvallis, a college town located on the site of an ancient Native American settlement at the convergence of the Willamette and the Marys Rivers. We'd departed from my comfortable craftsman house in Portland's Eastmoreland neighborhood, a leisurely 10-minute walk from Reed College. I'm in the front seat; with my gangly legs, I avoid back seats like the plague.

Although we've got an hour-and-a-half before we get to Corvallis, there's no freedom to peruse the morning's newspaper. Social media already is throbbing with scores of news and news-esque items, any one of which I might be hit with when I step outside. I'm fielding calls and SMS messages about Medicare and the Middle East, homelessness and affordable housing (big issues in Corvallis!) from staff, advisors, and my merry band of kibitzers in DC, Salem, and the rest of the country. Politicians have always been tripped up by "gotchas," but these days the game is particularly frenzied, non-linear, and relentless.

I take time to thumb some quick notes into my iPhone. The radio is playing softly. A Talking Heads oldie comes on. *And you may find yourself living in a shotgun shack...And you may ask yourself, "Well, how did I get here?"*

I smile. How did I get here? Simple: chutzpah.

Chutzpah is mother's milk for Jews, especially Jews who came here as immigrants or were reared by immigrant parents. Our heroes are *chutzpadiks*. Al Jolson, born Asa Yoelson in Seredzius, Lithuania, had the chutzpah to believe a poor cantor's son could become a massive Hollywood star. Sandy Koufax, née Sanford Braun, in Borough Park, Brooklyn, had the chutzpah to assume that a skinny kid with exactly one season of college baseball under his glove could pitch in the major leagues (and later the chutzpah to tell his pennant-winning Los Angeles Dodgers employers that he would not play in the World Series on Yom Kippur). Jewish kids like me in the 1950s and '60s, we inhaled these stories.

Our anti-heroes also were seemingly infused with chutzpah. Jolson's fictional doppelgänger, Sammy Glick, the amoral protagonist of Budd Schulberg's 1941 novel *What Makes Sammy Run?*, filled with "driving ambition and frenzy and violence," lied, stole, and plagiarized his way to Hollywood's pinnacle. The real-life mobster Benjamin "Bugsy" Siegel was fabled for founding the gambling mecca Las Vegas. Furtively, we shared these stories, too, wondering, can chutzpah be both good *and* bad?

I understood chutzpah because it saved my family and gave me life. My grandmother Leni was brazen enough to leave her wealth behind and lead her husband and child out of Germany. Her son Peter, my father, all joyful cheek, had zero doubt he could shape-shift from "my Berlin incarnation to my New York self" and become a globe-trotting U.S. journalist, one who would even dare to tell Americans things they didn't know about their own history.

But to paraphrase a famous advertising campaign from my youth, you don't have to be Jewish to have chutzpah. It courses through American history. What was Franklin D. Roosevelt, a jaunty "traitor to his class" who oversaw the New Deal that lifted millions of Americans out of Depression-era poverty, if not a *chutzpadik*? Or FDR's cousin Teddy, charging up San Juan Hill to the Presidency, where he took on the "malefactors of great wealth" and launched the modern era of financial regulation to check corporate power? Definitely a *chutzpadik*. Abraham Lincoln, born in a log cabin, overcoming his own insecurity to stump the nation with one goal—to end the sin of human slavery in these United States? A *chutzpadik*. What were Sam Adams, Benjamin Franklin, and Alexander Hamilton, hell-bent on overthrowing a despotic, distant king and creating a Government devoted to life, liberty, and the pursuit of happiness, if not raging, extravagant *chutzpadiks*?

I also have come to understand that American Government is replete with political anti-heroes who look like they're deploying chutzpah to advance destructive objectives. Wasn't Strom Thurmond applying chutzpah when he set the record for the Senate's longest filibuster, standing up live and arguing (thankfully, unsuccessfully) for 24 hours and 18 minutes to prevent the passage of the Civil Rights Act of 1957, the bill that granted Federal officials the authority to enforce Black Americans' right to vote?

Fast-forward to today, when ostensible anti-heroic *chutzpadiks* seem to be everywhere in government and public life—from Trump's daily blather to Elon Musk loudly inviting racists and anti-Semites to pour their bile onto X-the-platform-formerly-known-as-Twitter to obnoxious Florida Representative Matt Gaetz blocking his own Republican Party from choosing a House Speaker, in between his lascivious iPhone displays to horrified colleagues of his young sexual conquests. *Chutzpadiks*, no?

No.

To explain why not, let me provide a capsule view of history, as seen from the inside.

The forces that put me in Washington are the forces that have changed Washington—and America, and the world, and for that matter your school, your workplace, and your community. Those forces are the fragmentation and disintermediation of power in representative democracies.

In and of themselves, these forces are neither good nor bad; they just *are*. Without question, they contribute to social ills, notably the atomization of citizens' sense of the common good. Yet, as the nation's Founders understood, gatekeepers of various sorts—in the media, big business, and political parties—have a homogenizing effect on the nation that can be beneficial. Even when they engaged in more than their share of self-dealing, the gatekeepers played a role in restraining selfish factions from hijacking the public interest. The gatekeepers' diminution has made it easier than ever for cranks, liars, cheats, and sociopaths to make their loud mouths heard.

It's also true that their contraction also has made it easier to make good voices heard—and more essential than ever that we work, individually and collectively, to use our power to take ownership of the public debate and its outcomes.

To many people, *power* seems like a dirty word. It conjures up an image of dictators (or bad bosses) imposing their will on weak commoners (or defenseless cubicle-dwellers). That's a narrow, inaccurate interpretation. Sociologists describe power simply, and without a value judgment, as "an entity or individual's ability to control or direct others." But there's an even simpler definition, much closer to my own experience, offered up by the one of the world's best students of political power, the author Robert Caro: Power is the ability to "get things done."

In his masterful, Pulitzer Prize–winning biographies of President Lyndon Baines Johnson and New York power broker Robert Moses, Caro has drawn vivid portraits of men who could "harness political forces and bring something out of them, either for good or for ill." Whether it was building housing for the poor or guaranteeing Black Americans' right to vote (good) or tearing down those same Black Americans' neighborhoods, like Albina in NE Portland, or waging a futile, unwinnable war (bad), their power was premised on the ability to privately and often furtively manipulate people and processes to achieve goals.

"Power"—not science, knowledge, logic, or brilliance—"built highways and civil service systems," Caro has written, describing his subjects' philosophy. "Power was what dreams needed, not power in the hand of the dreamer himself necessarily but power put behind the dreamer's dream by the man who put it there."

What changed by the time I became an adult was that power was rapidly ebbing away from individuals and toward a new, radically restructured system of power dynamics—by which I mean a more complex, always morphing set of interactions among individuals, the organizations and institutions to which they belong, and the communications technologies by which they learn things and through which they interact with each other.

That change hadn't happened overnight. Protest movements had roiled America and yielded results going back to the earliest days of the Republic, and certainly had animated public life during my entire youth. From the Whiskey Rebellion to the Civil War draft riots through suffragism, pension armies, all the way up to the anti-war, environmental, and women's rights demonstrations of my high school and college years, the United States has been defined by our citizens' creditable *un*willingness to go along and get along.

But what made those protests necessary was the fact that the structures of power were hard and unyielding, embodied in potent individuals and gatekeepers who, more often than not, were so insulated and unapproachable that it took big, dramatic actions, amplified by the news media, to penetrate their consciousness and press them to act.

From the nation's Founders onward, political theorists have argued that an independent, active media were vital to the proper functioning of our republic. That the news media were not a benign conduit for information in society but rather had a formal, participatory role in governance was the gradually escalating view of one of the 20th century's most prominent public philosophers, Walter Lippmann. Crucially, though, Lippman believed the media's most important role was providing information and ideas to society's more educated and privileged insiders, the "elites," who would make the decisions that shape the way the indifferent masses would lead their lives. Outsiders would acquiesce to the decisions of insiders because the insiders understand best how to use the media to help shape the public's opinions and attitudes. "What you must lead in a country are the best of the country and they will carry it down," Lippmann once told an interviewer, in an accurate if chilling description of his era's power dynamics. "There's no use of the President trying to talk down to a fellow who can just about read and write."

By the time I was entering public life, however, a new political power structure was rising. The mighty elites in Government, business, organized religion, and the media were learning that they were not and never again could be insulated from the demos—the people. Fed by innovative new media channels and formats— from television's all-crime-all-the-time Eyewitness News programming to right-wing talk radio and ultimately to social media platforms—power in politics and life was becoming fragmented and bottom-up, not trickle-down.

To many, that disintermediated power structure has unsettled the foundations of democracy. The media's decline has let the loonies out of the booby hatch, and the country is no longer working like they want or expect.

Certainly, the 2016 nomination and election of Donald Trump as President, despite the feckless resistance of his own Republican Party and followed by Trump's wanton abandonment of economic logic, scientific guidance, diplomatic protocol, legal principles, national security, and common sense as he conducted his disastrous Presidency, underscored that something deep and seemingly permanent had altered American politics.

More ominously, the disorder has outlasted his single term. If anything, it appears worse. This year, the House Republicans showed themselves unable to lead even *with* a majority. A gang of eight ultra-right-wingers—a motley group of fanatics and fundamentalists—were able to oust an incumbent House Speaker, Kevin McCarthy, despite his overwhelming support from his caucus. They then proved incapable of agreeing on a new leader. Only after three weeks of wrangling did the Republican caucus barely elect Mike Johnson, a four-term Congressman from Louisiana, who is the least experienced Speaker of the House since 1883.

And who did the Republicans blame for their dissolution? Not themselves, of course; it was the media that made them do it. "The 24 hr news cycle has destroyed Congress," North Carolina Republican Representative Greg Murphy lamented on X-the-platform-formerly-known-as-Twitter.

It has not. But it has certainly changed Congress, along with the rest of the world.

It's a development that's rife with vicious ironies. Chief among them: When power did actually reside in a boss-driven "Deep State," people didn't fear it so much because they mostly knew who the bosses were and could count on their obvious motivations and self-interests. When Tammany Hall ruled New York and the Pendergast Machine controlled Kansas City, citizens knew whom to harangue to get their garbage picked up.

The reality, though, is that the "Deep State" doesn't exist. Now that any 14-year-old can create a global television network with the apps that come built into their mobile phone, politics, business, and public life generally are propelled by a more dispersed and enigmatic network of social, cultural, information, and political centers, and a far more complicated playbook for getting things done.

Today, the people *are* the media, with the power to foment vast, positive changes in societies and cultures.

How? By making a noise—productive noise.

Which is the first definition of chutzpah: Making productive noise. If you want to make change, you've got to make noise.

Chutzpah is a Yiddish word that describes a trait that many Jews consider inborn. Millennia of being chased from our homes

RON'S RULE OF CHUTZPAH

1

IF YOU WANT TO MAKE CHANGE, YOU'VE GOT TO MAKE NOISE

by Romans, Arabs, Inquisitors, Cossacks, Nazis, and Communists and then adapting to new environments does seem to have bred in us a kind of genetic fearlessness. But Jews are not unique. You saw chutzpah in the moral courage of Martin Luther King Jr. locked in the Birmingham jail, in the leap into the air and the unknown taken by the Wright Brothers at Kitty Hawk. Chutzpah is also global in its display and application. Lech Walesa, the

Polish anti-Communist leader; Malala Yousafzai, the young Pakistani education activist shot by the Taliban; and Ai Weiwei, the Chinese artist who used the power of film to expose injustices in his home country—all of them showed the international applicability of chutzpah for good.

"For good" is the vital phrase. When the notion of chutzpah was first heard by many in the United States, in a 1908 play about America by the British Zionist author Israel Zangwill (the title of which introduced another neologism to these shores, *The Melting Pot*), *chutzpah* meant "enterprise, audacity, brazen impudence and cheek."

Those personality characteristics have long incited rage among the powerful institutions, aristocracies, and dominant authorities toward those who would challenge them.

In one of his most malicious anti-Semitic screeds, Nazi Germany's chief propagandist, Joseph Goebbels, said chutzpah "means unlimited, impertinent, and unbelievable impudence and shamelessness…a system of public deception that, when applied long enough, lames a people both culturally and spiritually."

It's a plain fact that audacity and "brazen impudence" *can* be used to hurt people, to strip them of their rights and dignity. Donald Trump—a man who believed there were "good people" among the murderous anti-Semites who overtook the streets of Charlottesville, Virginia, in 2017 proclaiming, "Jews will not replace us!"—has been cited for his chutzpah so many times it'd make you…*plotz*. Trump's Rasputin, the convicted fraudster Steve Bannon, and his anarchic acolytes in the Republican House Freedom Caucus, hell-bent on destroying any capacity for Government to help improve people's lives, are engaging in a project that is "pure chutzpah," according to the online news journal *Politico*.

I'd argue that there's nothing *chutzpadik* about their behaviors, and that it is vitally important to claw back and reclaim the definition of chutzpah.

Jewish scholars do recognize that there is such a thing as "bad chutzpah." Rabbi Tzvi Freeman, a senior editor with Chabad, the 350-year-old international orthodox Jewish Lubavitch Hasidic movement, calls bad chutzpah "destructive and ugly," an application of insolence, impudence, gall, effrontery, presumption, and arrogance in pursuit of unscrupulous objectives.

Good chutzpah, by contrast, is "vital and fantastic," he says, and it is exalted in Jewish liturgy, which encourages Jews to be "fierce as a leopard" in pursuing the moral endeavors codified in Jewish law. "To be a good Jew," Rabbi Freeman says, "you need two opposites: A sense of shame that prevents you from acting with chutzpah to do the wrong thing, and a sense of chutzpah that prevents you from being ashamed to do the right thing."

To me, the dueling impulses Rabbi Freeman identifies require a new terminology.

First, let's call bad chutzpah by a different name, one that grasps its misuse by the immoral minority and their amoral enablers. It is not chutzpah to ridicule the disabled, undermine police and the courts, make racist attacks on other nations, deify murderous dictators like Vladimir Putin, or proclaim Hezbollah murderers "smart"—all of which Donald Trump has done, to his devotees' applause.

The best term for their arrogant contempt for beneficial social norms and actions is a purely American word, easily identifiable in both public and private life: bullsh*t. (Even though this curse and other profanities now grace the front pages of mainstream media, I'm refraining from using them because I want parents to feel free to give this book to their kids.)

Bullsh*t is not a lie, according to the moral philosopher Harry Frankfurt in his 2005 bestseller *On Bullsh*t*. Rather, bullsh*t is a knowing disregard for the truth, in furtherance solely of personal interests. To Frankfurt, bullsh*t is more dangerous than lying, and bullsh*tters are more treacherous than liars: "The liar asserts something which he himself believes to be false. He deliberately misrepresents what he takes to be the truth. The bullsh*tter, on the other hand, is not constrained by any consideration of what may or may not be true"—and doesn't care if society is damaged by such indifference.

Second, let's assert that chutzpah, by definition, *is* good. Per my introduction of this term at the beginning of the book, chutzpah's purpose is *tikkun olam*—literally, to "repair the world." Ancient Jewish literature describes *tikkun olam* as the commandment to maintain social order in ways that benefit all of society. The laws and customs that govern our formal and informal social relationships— relationships with spouses and children, with friends, with business colleagues—are temporal representations of God's desire for a continually improving world.

Here again, Chabad's Rabbi Freeman provides a useful footnote: The world (*olam*) isn't necessarily broken, and consequently *tikkun* doesn't specifically mean it has to be repaired, he says. A better definition, he offers, is "fixed up"—in the way that a perfectly fine home may be fixed up by the application of carpentry or craft. Everything in human existence, no matter how superficially perfect it might seem, can always use fixing up.

Or as I like to say: You always have to have a constructive purpose. Loudness, brashness, and boldness in and of themselves are meaningless, unless you're serving a greater good. Chutzpah—*making purposeful noise*—is both a fruitful craft and a high calling.

Today's Republican revolutionaries, who claim to be operating in the spirit of the nation's Founders, are doing anything but. The Founders were building lasting institutions to benefit we, the people. These Republicans, like Josh Hawley, are anarchically tearing down institutions, from the Justice Department to the military to the financial oversight system, with no notion of what will replace them, aside from the private militias they hope will protect their personal fiefs. They start with an utterly different value system. They are making *destructive noise.*

Franklin Roosevelt, despite being raised among great wealth, believed his responsibility was to serve people who did not have power and clout, and to put them in a position to secure their economic freedom. Senator Ted Cruz—who egged on the insurrectionists of January 6, only to flee from them and hide in a broom closet when they invaded the U.S. Capitol and threatened his own safety—starts with a different premise. Bred in comfort, educated at Princeton, untroubled by income inequality or corporate accountability, unbothered by school shootings or inaccessible health care, Cruz is carrying out an agenda for his wealthy supporters, his populism not a challenge to the powerful, but a craven symbol of Harry Frankfurt's bullsh*t.

〰

The meeting in Corvallis is over. It was the eighth stop on my "Oregon Bounty" tour. Thinking back on the verdant Medford fruit farms that had first entranced me 52 years earlier, I told the local business owners, county officials, and Oregon State University faculty who were taking part in the roundtable with me, "We do a lot of stuff well in Oregon, but what we do best is grow things, add value to them, and ship them all over the world." I figured I'd ask them for

28

ideas about innovations that could help Oregon growers and their food-manufacturing partners sell and export more successfully—innovations we might help support when the Senate takes up the big Farm Bill reauthorization. I was particularly charmed to discover that they make soy sauce in Benton County!

We've got half an hour before the next meeting. Just enough time to get to the Fred Meyer grocery store across town on NW Kings Boulevard.

Making productive noise isn't a one-way activity. Elected officials (I suspect it's true of many people in positions of authority) need to realize that they do too much talking and far too little listening. If you're going to build trust among people, you're not going to get anywhere unless you value the person who's in front of you enough to actually listen to them. As the great salesman Dale Carnegie said, "To be interesting, be interested."

It's not just the proverbial function of putting yourself in other people's shoes: You must actually go to the people and ask them, over and over, how their shoes are fitting. And then you have to sit back and listen and absorb what's on their minds—no matter where their minds might be focused, whether on their feet or on loftier topics. People won't consider your ideas if they don't think you're taking their ideas seriously.

With social media squeezing complex issues into 240 characters and encouraging people to hang out in filter bubbles populated only by like-minded peers, listening is even more of a prerequisite now. Business executives refer to this as MBWA, or "management by walking around." To me, it's more like LBLA: "leadership by listening around."

Here's what I've learned is the best way to listen: After introductions, let the other person talk without interruption for four or so minutes—or until they decide they're done. More politicians than you can imagine say they want to listen to a person, but then start interrupting within 30 seconds, usually with a mind-numbing avalanche of acronyms about bills and amendments.

That's the point of my "Oregon Bounty" tour, to listen and learn. I enjoy direct contact with Oregonians and other Americans who are as passionate as I am about fixing up the world. That's why I made a promise during my first campaign for Senate that I would do something no one else in Oregon government had ever even tried: convene open-to-all town hall meetings every year in each of Oregon's 36 counties. I beat that goal: I've had over 1,100 open town hall meetings over my 28 years in the Senate—and that doesn't include the thousands more meetings I've had on specific issues, with specific groups and individuals, inside and outside Oregon and Washington, DC.

Most of those meetings have not been in election years, and the vast majority have not been in Portland—Oregon's largest city, resilient and rambunctious, known for its music, farmers markets, soccer, beer, doughnuts, rain, roses, and running, now recalibrating, as are so many other cities, to furiously fight fentanyl, homelessness, and the plight of the mentally ill. Instead, I've trekked around every county, city, and town in Oregon, to absorb the concerns of people everywhere, unfiltered by staff and professional special pleaders.

Town halls aren't enough, though. Let's face it, they tend to draw heavily from people who have the time to devote themselves to public issues. It's hard to draw in the working mother with three kids at home under age 14, whose schedule is far more weighted toward soccer practices, dance rehearsals, her job, cooking dinner, and picking up prescriptions for her ailing dad.

So I go to them. At the citizenry's real town square: the grocery store.

The local supermarket is the best place to meet people and pick up ideas. It's the common denominator; everybody goes to the grocery store. So when I'm back in Oregon (which I do as often as the Senate schedule allows), my staff and I don't eat lunch at a desk, we go to Fred Meyer, the supermarket chain that was founded in Portland in 1922 and now has about 50 outlets across the state.

I've been to all the Fred Meyer stores, multiple times, and my routine never varies. I amble through the aisles and pick up a barbecued or baked chicken and tomatoes and oranges, and (my favorite) a Fred Meyer Private Selection cherry pie. Almost every Freddie's has a snacking area where you can grab a table. I'll introduce myself to people at the deli counter and the vegetable aisle; I'll say hi on the checkout line; and I'll often invite whomever I meet to join me and the team when we're chowing down.

Most of the time, though, I don't have to make these invitations. In Oregon we're pretty informal, and often folks just come up to me and say hello.

My attitude here—like my attitude about chutzpah and *tikkun olam*—also derives from my Jewish heritage. Judaism is about moral codes that have been arrived at through public deliberation, *which means you must expose yourself to discussion, debate, even argument.*

Consider that the Bible's first book, Genesis, is rooted in Abraham's disputing with God about protecting the innocents of Sodom. (Talk about chutzpah!) The great books of Jewish law and lore—the Mishnah, Gemara, and Midrash—are narrations of debates and arguments among many rabbis over many centuries about momentous temporal and theological issues. Perhaps our loveliest holiday, the celebration of freedom known as Passover, is not just the tale of Moses leading the Jews from slavery to liberty; the *Haggadah*, the holiday's main prayer book, is a book about Jewish families

31

and the transmission of Jewish values from generation to generation (represented by four quite different children, the Wise Son, the Rebellious Son, the Simple Son, and the Son Who Doesn't Even Know How to Ask a Question) debating the meaning of Exodus. Jewish morality is not determined on high and handed down to the flocks; we deliberate and decide it *together.*

The same is true in politics, now more than ever—even if pols don't fully grasp it.

Long gone are the days when party elders (or party hacks) could hand-select candidates, "the people" be damned. As access to the political power grid has become more and more democratized, it's become abundantly clear that, to succeed—not just in politics, but almost any human endeavor that requires the support of others—you have to be in the mix.

That reality has become harder for more and more of my colleagues. The rise of adversarial media, on Internet platforms as well as television, makes them warier of impromptu encounters, lest their opinions and words be grabbed and used against them. In many places public life is less spontaneous than ever. U.S. Senators, in particular, hold fewer town hall meetings than they once did—and when they do, the audience more frequently than not is pre-selected from among supporters. Compared with my early days in the Senate a quarter-century ago, fewer Senators take to the floor with extemporaneous remarks. In the chamber and in committee rooms, most of their commentary consists of prepared, pre-chewed, and pre-digested talking points vetted by staff, lobbyists, and consultants. The creativity necessary if we're going to fix up the world is now stripped from the public realm.

But it needn't be that way. The greatest joy in public life is not the recognition. It really is the representation…and you cannot represent without being present.

A case in point. A few weeks ago, after a grueling two weeks in DC, I landed in Portland International Airport, PDX for short, after a long, late, and bumpy flight. A guy with a hard hat and a name tag that read "George" came up to me and, with a touch of sarcasm in his voice, said, "Hey, Ron, great to see you just got in from your home *in New York*." Right-wing talk radio in Oregon has been trying for more than a decade to convince my neighbors that I live in New York City because my wife is the third-generation owner of the legendary Strand bookstore.

I suspect George thought I was going to duck him—you know, pull out my cell phone and mumble about an important call from the White House and then stride off. But I didn't (and I don't). I told him, "No, I'm going home now—right off Glenwood in Southeast Portland." (Giving away my home address isn't as surprising as it might seem; everyone knows where I live because I shoot baskets at the courts at Duniway Elementary School a few blocks from our house.)

George lit up and dropped the sarcasm. "Great!" he said. "I figured that stuff they were saying on the radio about you living in New York was a bunch of B.S." What he really wanted was to talk to me about all the construction he was working on at PDX. He wasn't complaining about anything; he mostly wanted to comment on the growth of the city, how much it had changed since his childhood, and the role he was playing in those changes. At the end, he said, "Ron, you guys take a lot of crap. I appreciate you taking the time to listen to me."

Although it's my job to represent George, his family, and every other Oregonian while doing my job in Washington, DC, I have no idea whether George will ever vote for me. But I am pretty sure he went home that night and told his family, "I met Ron Wyden at the airport, and he wasn't a jerk. He heard me, and asked me about this and that, and I think I taught him a thing or two."

In Washington, I'm "Mr. Chairman" and treated with deference. The minute I step on that plane for Portland, I am the employee of George and 4.2 million other Oregonians. Listening to them *and with them*, even if they're not going to vote for me, is a prerequisite at a time when adversarial media are driving people apart.

Which leads me to the last component of chutzpah. It's not only about boldness in the service of the good or making productive noise or exciting sustained attention to the objective you are trying to achieve. It's not only leadership by listening around. Chutzpah is also about humility wrapped within the outward display of confidence.

Most of us have to work at that. It was once said of me that I am not the textbook portrait of a Senator with rugged good looks in a fancy suit with an expensive haircut. And yet I have created public moments that have protected millions of people and moved the destinies of entire industries. You don't need to be born with this talent. You just need to embrace the ability of your brain, your ears, and your mouth to engage productively with the people and situations you encounter.

Or, as one of the greatest Jewish sages, Rabbi Hillel, says in the Mishnah: "If I am not for myself, who should be for me? And when I am for myself alone, what am I? And if not now, then when?"

TWO

THE LONG GAME, PART I

I t was early 1990, and I was still a young member in the U.S. House of Representatives and serving on the House Committee on Small Business. I represented the east side of Portland and a small part of a neighboring county, and both the state and the city had been experiencing a burst of business development, which made the committee's primary jurisdiction—overseeing Small Business Administration loans and activities—particularly relevant. But I yearned for more. I'd cut my teeth in public life in Oregon as the boy co-founder of the Gray Panthers, the first local senior citizens' rights organization. Just out of law school, I was fighting Medicare rip-offs, forcing Big Pharma to lower generic health-care prices, and ending dentists' extortionate pricing on dentures. I was hungering for that kind of action in Washington.

I went to my powerful Committee Chair, John J. LaFalce, a nine-term incumbent from Buffalo, New York, with a *chutzpadik* idea: He should create a Subcommittee on Regulation. John looked at me kind of stunned. First, the Small Business Committee had never really done anything in this arena. Second, Democrats like us hadn't particularly made their bones on business regulation, except, as the caricature goes, proposing more of them. Third, no one had ever suggested anything like this to him before…and in Washington, precedent mattered.

"What do you have in mind?" John asked me. I told him directly about my Oregon work on health care and science and consumer scams and made some connections (however tenuous) to our committee's jurisdiction. John, who'd won his seat as a "Watergate Baby" in the insurgent year of 1974, smiled slyly. Although he never said so, I'm fairly sure he liked the notion of subtly extending his committee's, and his own, power.

Shortly after my bold suggestion, he gave me the go-ahead, making me one of the first (if not *the* first) junior members of Congress to invent his own subcommittee. We even agreed to give it a bigger and more meaningful name: the Subcommittee on Regulation, Business Opportunity, and Energy.

There was a library behind our hearing room in the Rayburn House Office Building. As soon as I got LaFalce's assent, I went to it, found the section on business regulation, and started pulling down an armful of journals on health and science regulation.

Going to the library, conducting their own research, finding their own issues—those aren't things most members of Congress do themselves. They have lobbyists and constituents to give them the issues, legislative aides to do the legwork, and committee directors to reach the conclusions. But I'd had a different upbringing: My father was an award-winning journalist and author, and my mother a college librarian. My dad taught me to be nosy, and my mom showed me how to find the details.

That first day as the new chair of a new subcommittee, the details I discovered in those abstruse journals of science and health regulation constituted one of the greatest health-care stories never told: a global battle by scientists committed to women's health against religious fanatics who wanted to keep a life-changing medicine out of the United States.

At the time, the drug was called RU-486, after Roussel-Uclaf, the French pharmaceutical company that had developed it in 1980. It was the brainchild of a swashbuckling biochemist and endocrinologist, Dr. Étienne-Émile Baulieu, who had been a teenaged gunrunner for the French Resistance during World War II, a confrere of famous artists in the 1960s, and an ardent advocate for women his entire life. Conversations in 1961 with Dr. Gregory Pincus, the co-inventor of the oral contraceptive pill, led him to start research on the next stage of women's reproductive control, a concept he came to call the "unpregnancy pill."

He envisioned a new molecule, an "anti-hormone," as he termed it, that would instruct the body to abort a newly fertilized egg before it could implant in the woman's uterus. A drug built on such an anti-hormone might then replace the suction tubes and wire hangers that were the invasive—and, too frequently, destructive and deadly—tools of abortion's licit and illicit trade.

In 1980, the chief chemist at Roussel-Uclaf, where Dr. Baulieu had gone to work as a part-time consultant, synthesized the molecule he had conceived. Trials in France found that RU-486 (or, as it was later named, mifepristone) successfully aborted pregnancies in 97 percent of patients and removed nearly all the risks of surgery, including, notably, potential damage to a woman's cervix and uterus. Physicians speculated that the drug could be as revolutionary for women as The Pill had become, and be used as a once-a-month contraceptive, preventing pregnancy even before it started. That concept aligned entirely with U.S. scientific consensus and Government policy, which held that pregnancy does not begin until a fully fertilized egg is implanted in the uterus. A Harvard Medical School endocrinologist mused that mifepristone could be among the drugs, like penicillin, aspirin, and the polio vaccine, "that have changed the history of society."

"My intention was to give women a choice that, through a pill, respects their privacy and physical integrity and allows them to totally avoid the aggression of surgery," Dr. Baulieu told the *New Yorker*. "Paradoxically, the 'abortion pill' might even help eliminate abortion as an issue," he later wrote.

His work was prescient, but his hope naive. Almost as soon as the efficacy of the drug was established, opponents inside and outside the company tried to prevent it from ever reaching women in need—entirely for religious reasons. Through the 1980s, they mounted campaign after campaign to stop the drug from coming to market. They inundated the boards of directors of Roussel-Uclaf and its German parent conglomerate, Hoechst AG, with letters falsely calling mifepristone a "lethal drug," a "death drug," and a "human pesticide." They held protests at company events, comparing the life-preserving medicine to the Zyklon B gas used in Hitler's death camps—an analogy designed specifically to frighten the German Hoechst executives, and particularly galling to Dr. Baulieu, whose family, like mine, were Jewish refugees from Nazi Germany.

The religious opposition to the drug crossed the Atlantic. In 1987, the National Right to Life Committee convened a conference in New Orleans, at which it held workshops on political strategies to stop mifepristone and unveiled plans to lobby Congress and prevent any authorized trials in the United States. They followed up by threatening economic pressure on the French government, which was a minority shareholder in Roussel-Uclaf, and promised to mount international boycotts of all their and Hoechst's products.

Roussel-Uclaf's chairman was receiving dozens of threatening letters each day, some calling him and his colleagues "assassins," others explicitly threatening them with bloodshed because "your pills kill babies."

The anti-abortionists' strategy of threats and violence backfired, or so it appeared. In September 1988, the French government approved the sale and use of mifepristone, making safe, effective medical abortion available to that nation's women.

That inflamed the antagonists even more. A few weeks after the government's approval, religious extremists in France tear-gassed a Paris movie theater that was showing a historically based film about a French laundress who had been executed by the nation's pro-Nazi government during World War II for performing abortions. Roussel-Uclaf's chairman told Dr. Baulieu he feared similar violence against the company and its people. Only a month after they introduced mifepristone to market, the company's board voted 16–4 to withdraw it.

The about-face infuriated the French government. France's Minister of Health, Claude Évin, ordered Roussel-Uclaf's vice chair to his office, telling him, "From the moment government approval for the drug was granted, RU-486 became the moral property of women, not just the property of the drug company." Threatening to transfer the patent to another company, he ordered Roussel-Uclaf to restart distribution. The company complied.

French women were in their second year enjoying the freedom and security mifepristone was granting them to live their lives when I began the fight to secure that freedom for Americans. The medicine had still not found its way legally into the United States. With several years' head start in Europe, the religious right had managed to intimidate the submissive Administration of President George

H. W. Bush, and pressured the Food and Drug Administration to maintain a U.S. ban on mifepristone.

As I learned from University of Colorado breast cancer and hormone specialist Dr. Kathryn Horwitz, among other courageous whistleblowers my staff and I interviewed, on June 1, 1989, the FDA had issued an import alert against the medicine. This was an almost unheard-of regulatory mechanism that was impeding American researchers like her from exploring mifepristone's cancer-fighting capabilities. Such alerts historically have been used only when plainly dangerous drugs are being surreptitiously smuggled into the U.S., not when legitimate labs at accredited research institutions are doing essential medical research.

When I looked into Kathy Horwitz's account, I discovered that the FDA had acted without any evidence that mifepristone was dangerous (because there was no such evidence) or that it ever had been smuggled (because it had not). What I did find in the agency's files were letters from right-wingers like Senator Jesse Helms urging the FDA to ban it.

Before I was concerned, now I was furious. The tales I was hearing about government chicanery, of lobbyists squeezing politicians to push agencies to assure benefits to a favored few instead of the many, reminded me of past battles in Oregon. But there were additional elements that touched me personally, like the furious religious intolerance, which called up my family's efforts (some successful, others fatal) to escape Nazi Germany. And there were the decades when my younger brother, Jeff, struggled with crippling schizophrenia, as my family toiled through contradictory medical advice, hard-to-decipher research, insurance industry obstruction, and government inaction to get him the help he so desperately needed.

This I knew: Nothing is more personal than health care. How dare the Government and a coterie of favored insiders block it.

And this would be the first job of my House Small Business Committee Subcommittee on Regulation, Business Opportunity, and Energy. I would put my energy into invalidating a fraudulent regulation to protect the freedom of American women. It was long past time to make safe medical abortion legal in the United States.

⌐

The Rayburn House Office Building is often described as drafty, unsurprising for a million-square-foot, high-ceilinged, marble edifice opened in 1965.

It was anything but drafty on Monday morning, November 19, 1990, when I walked back into Room 2360, our hearing room. With months of study under our belt, I was about to chair the first-ever Congressional hearing about providing American women the ability to secure a legal, simple, non-surgical abortion. The fervor of women's health advocates like Kate Michelman, five years into her tenure as president of NARAL (and since has changed their name to Reproductive Freedom for All), and of researchers and academics inside and outside government, were fired with a zeal to reverse the wrongdoings of religious zealots—their fire made the room full and warm…even without the presence of my Congressional colleagues, none of whom showed their faces.

Even when you're a modestly tenured member of Congress, it's hard to be blasé about such settings. At least, it's that way for me. I always feel like I am looking at myself from the outside, almost as if I'm in a movie. As I gaveled the hearing to order, a jolt of positive electricity passed through me. I had sweat a fine shine onto my face; my hair was a bit unkempt. Quite explicitly, I was doing a mental pre-game pump-up. "Our work will bear fruit. The arc is bending our way," I kept telling myself. "The demand for safe, effective alternatives to surgery is growing. And so is the demand for privacy. We can go a long way to turn the lights out on the anti-abortion movement that had sentenced so many women to death."

Maybe I was bluffing myself. I had no idea how this movie would end.

My first hearing was on the FDA's June 1989 import alert that had blocked researchers from accessing mifepristone. I opened with what I already knew. Many scientists understood the drug could successfully treat debilitating and life-threatening illnesses such as breast cancer, brain cancer, and diabetes. But the FDA had banned its importation on the grounds that it was a health hazard.

"What proof does the agency have to back up its conclusions about RU-486?" I wanted to know.

We heard from a panoply of physicians, patient advocates, and patients themselves about how mifepristone had helped remediate ill-nesses that had resisted all other forms of treatment. Kathy Horwitz, my new whistleblower friend from Colorado, testified that she could no lon-ger obtain samples of mifepristone for cancer research because her work did not fit the FDA's criteria. Several witnesses from the National Insti-tutes of Health disclosed that they were abandoning research on mi-fepristone's ability to treat Cushing's disease, a rare and fatal hormonal disorder and cancer, because they no longer could obtain the drug.

Wanda Guesnier, a 57-year-old secretary and mother of three, had come in from Lubbock, Texas, to describe her four-year struggle with Cushing's disease, which had afflicted her with hypertension, muscle weakness, memory loss, and disorientation. "I felt the end was near," she told me from the witness stand. When tests showed that her levels of cortisol, a steroid hormone that regulates blood pressure and inflammation, were 100 times the normal level, doctors at the National Institutes of Health offered her mifepristone.

Within a week of taking it, she went into remission. "The feeling came back into my arms and legs, the swelling went down, my blood pressure returned to normal, and my mind was clear for the first time in months," Mrs. Guesnier said. Her 20-month use of mifepristone had produced no side effects and allowed her to return to her normal life.

The most moving testimony came from Helen Byrne, a grandmotherly executive from New York. She talked about her battle against breast cancer, then in its eighth year. She'd had a double mastectomy and went through punishing chemotherapy. When her hair fell out, she said, "I really at that point didn't want to live."

Treatment with mifepristone had enabled her to return to her work and her life. But what made her testimony particularly powerful were her moral underpinnings.

"I am a practicing Catholic who is unalterably opposed to abortion," Ms. Byrne said with strength. "The issue here is not abortion. The issue is the life or death of women with breast cancer. Without testing we will never know if RU-486 is the solution to breast cancer.

"I am not a theologian," she continued, "but I do know that in theology there is a theory of 'double effect' that states we must look to the greater good even if some evil happens. If RU-486 is tested and approved and saves the lives of women, many of whom have had and are raising children, then *that* is the greater good."

Two hours in, I put the FDA on the stand. Ronald Chesemore, the Associate Commissioner for Regulatory Affairs, had agreed to provide prepared remarks. Bearded, formally dressed, at age 47 a few years older than me, in tones marked both by restraint and a slight Tennessee drawl, he proceeded to circumnavigate a Möbius strip of tautological claptrap.

What had motivated the FDA to ban mifepristone, he told me,

wasn't knowledge about the safety or efficacy of the drug; the FDA had no evidence whatsoever that mifepristone was dangerous or ineffective. What had moved the agency to issue its import embargo, he offered up, was the prospect that people would learn about mifepristone.

"We...did become concerned that the publicity regarding the availability of these drugs overseas may create a demand in this country, which could in turn foster importation of these unapproved drugs, leading to unsupervised use and/or perhaps clandestine distribution," Mr. Chesemore said.

I mentioned earlier that Congressional hearings can feel like the movies, even to us participants. After all, they have the elements of theater—characters, conflict, catharsis. And like good films, even if we know the basic testimony in advance (as we know so many of the movies' conventional plot tropes), there are still moments that can be so revelatory, even shocking, that they take the story to new heights of drama.

This was one of those moments.

The "publicity" to which Mr. Chesemore was referring was not to, from, or about the public. The publicity they feared was political pressure, like the letter my staff had discovered in FDA files, transparently in response to an inquiry by Senator Jesse Helms, just a few months before the import block was imposed. The FDA "does not condone personal importation of RU-486," the agency's former Commissioner Frank Young had assured Helms, the fanatical avatar of religious ultra-conservatism, because "the FDA believes the drug to be unsafe or subject to abuse." He referenced "side effects" such as "nausea, vomiting, uterine bleeding."

I wanted to know from the witness what specific supportive evidence the agency had for the conclusions drawn in this letter?

"We certainly just felt like the personal importation of this drug was a very serious situation," Commissioner Chesemore told me.

"You're basically offering management by intuition to the American people," I retorted.

The hearing demonstrated what I and the pro-science, pro-health side was up against. Coerced by the Bush Administration and Jesse Helms, the FDA was executing a backdoor ban on medical abortion, a health procedure legalized by the U.S. Supreme Court 17 years earlier.

⤙

Let me tell you up front: I am not the hero in this battle. I am not even *a* hero in this battle. I'm just one of many fighting to uphold women's rights and freedoms in the face of a repressive onslaught. The real heroes are the 1.2 million American women who risked censure, prosecution, and death having back-alley abortions in the decades before Roe v. Wade legalized the procedure in 1973—and the tens of millions today who face these perils again, now that a religiously driven Supreme Court has rendered abortion increasingly inaccessible. The real heroes are the Planned Parenthoods and NARALs and their legions of volunteers who have fought for women's rights for a century and more. The real heroes are the doctors and nurses who've faced threats, office and home invasions, assaults, and murder for helping women take charge of their own health.

I'm just a warrior on their behalf—a warrior with a position in the U.S. Congress and a particular passion for assuring that the rights and freedoms of Americans aren't dismembered by ideologues, militants, fundamentalists, and their plutocrat patrons.

I decided to give the FDA and the Bush Administration the publicity of which they had been so wary.

I started by doing everything I could to make some productive noise that would turn mifepristone into a household word. I authored an op-ed piece in the *New York Times* about the Bush Administration "wielding the anti-abortion club" and "sacrificing science for politics." It was a theme we repeated over and over—echoes elevate chutzpah into a cause. I convened new hearings of my Subcommittee on Regulation and invited the Hollywood celebrity Cybill Shepherd (a Tennessee native, like the FDA apparatchik Ronald Chesemore), who garnered national headlines when she testified that "American women are being victimized in a war in which science is being held hostage to politics.

"America has become the leader of the industrialized world in unintended pregnancies, in teen pregnancies, in infant mortality and in its inability to provide safe, medical choices for women who terminate pregnancy," said Ms. Shepherd, who had famously become pregnant and given birth to twins while starring in the TV series *Moonlighting*.

The publicity the FDA had so feared grew more riotous when U.S. Customs agents at John F. Kennedy International Airport in New York seized a single dose of mifepristone from Leona Benten, a 29-year-old California social worker who was eight weeks pregnant, as she was returning from Paris to the U.S. She had deliberately brought the drug in to test the legality of the FDA's action. A week later, the U.S. Supreme Court, on a 7–2 vote in emergency session, upheld the FDA's right to exercise that authority.

The heightened exposure of the right-wing conspiracy to outlaw mifepristone turned into a national crusade to reverse the Government embargo. New York City Mayor David N. Dinkins led 33 other urban mayors in a letter-writing campaign to President George Bush and Roussel-Uclaf executives, affirming that "the rules of medicine, morality and the marketplace dictate that all women who choose to have abortions should have access to the safest, most effective and least expensive methods available." My colleague, the crusading progressive Congresswoman from Colorado, Pat Schroeder, joined me in introducing a bill to allow research on the drug.

The bill didn't pass, but it put the issue squarely in front of Bill Clinton, a women's rights advocate who defeated George Bush for the Presidency in late 1992 and who, a month before his inauguration, announced, "The FDA should treat these issues in a non-political manner and should aggressively move to evaluate RU-486 and determine whether it's safe for use under the ordinary standards that would apply to any other drug."

That was the boost we needed. Exactly nine days later, I received a letter from the Deputy Commissioner of External Affairs at the ever-politically-attuned FDA saying they were ready "to permit an adequate review" of mifepristone.

But there was a catch: The agency needed the manufacturer to apply for approval—and Roussel-Uclaf and its German owner, Hoechst, spooked by the anti-abortion terrorism to which they had been subjected in Europe and by the ferocious political opposition in the U.S., didn't want to do it. Executives and researchers at the companies privately told me and my subcommittee's staff director, Steve Jennings (one of many journalists I've hired over the years, because they know how to get to the beating heart of the story), that they dreaded having blood thrown on their lawns. They were afraid even to license the medication to a U.S. manufacturer—they said they couldn't find one.

We knew this was a lie. Over the course of our hearings (ultimately, we held 19 of them) we had built up a pretty good network in the women's health community, among FDA whistleblowers, and at advocacy groups. So I went public and accused Roussel-Uclaf of stalling, and released letters from three American manufacturers that had told us they would consider marketing the drug in the U.S.

The pressure worked. On April 20, 1993, Roussel-Uclaf announced that it had agreed to license the drug to the Population Council, the biomedical research and health NGO founded by John D. Rockefeller III in 1952, which vowed to find a manufacturer and market mifepristone in the United States.

A few days later, I got to disclose a coda: I announced that mifepristone's first clinical trials would take place in Oregon.

There were still years of foot-dragging, threats of boycotts from religious and conservative groups, and bureaucratic resistance deep inside the FDA, so mifepristone didn't actually receive full agency approval and make it to market (via a small manufacturer, Danco Laboratories) and to American women until 2000.

When it did, its impact was as extraordinary as Dr. Baulieu and his allies had predicted decades earlier. Today, more than half of all abortions in the U.S. are induced by pills women take at home, not by suction tubes in clinics or hangers in basements. Since mifepristone's full approval in 2000, only five deaths per million people have been associated with it, a death rate of 0.0005 percent, making it four times safer than penicillin.

RON'S RULE OF CHUTZPAH

2

IN A WORLD WHERE EVERYONE THINKS AND ACTS FOR THE SHORT TERM, ALWAYS PLAY THE LONG GAME

A victory for science and health!

Yeah…not quite. Sometimes, the long game is even longer than you'd ever anticipate.

THREE

CRYING WITH PURPOSE

The most important lesson in life is the one you learn the day you're born, even if you can't then articulate it: You have no power, but you have agency—you have the ability to act. However powerless you might feel in the face of neglect, institutional inertia, or outright opposition, outside forces can be moved in your direction. How? Exactly the way babies survive, even though they can't walk, talk, or feed themselves: They cry.

Maneuvering through or around the barriers that might block us requires us to learn to become martial artists with life itself. We have to play jujitsu with the various forces that come at us and learn to deflect or direct their strikes and blows to our advantage, even when we are inherently less mighty than the aggregate opposition. Learning those skills—especially that first, natural-born skill of crying with purpose—is how you transcend your position to become a powerful person.

How did I learn this? You might say I was to the manor—and the manner—born.

I am the grandchild and child of Jewish refugees from Nazi Germany. My parents, born Peter Weidenreich and Edith Rosenow, fled the Nazis with their parents in the 1930s, Peter after he was beaten up at school by Hitler's thugs for refusing to give the Nazi salute, Edith after giving vociferous scoldings to many of her Jewish acquaintances in Germany, whom she believed were making the tragic error of downplaying the Nazi threat.

The Weidenreich family was accomplished, and for a period was monied. Our name meant "willow rich." By the time my grandparents' generation emerged, the money had dissipated, but vestiges of prestige remained. My paternal great-grandfather, having failed as a haberdasher, had received an appointment by the local Jewish community to become superintendent of Europe's largest Jewish cemetery, in Weissensee, near Berlin. My grandfather Erich grew up in a cottage on the grounds of that cemetery. As a young adult, Erich went to work at a local textile company. Known as a comedian and entertainer, he evidently charmed the owner—and more importantly, his daughter Helen, known as Leni, whom he married in the early 1920s.

Peter Weidenreich, my father, was born in Berlin in late 1923. By that time, the family was firmly upper-middle-class. There were cooks, nannies, and housekeepers. They also were assimilated, as many well-off German Jews were. My dad did go to Hebrew school, and celebrated his bar mitzvah when he turned 13, but the family celebrated only major holidays, usually without my grandmother, because, as my father later wrote, "All religion struck her as too removed from reality, it offended her pragmatic self, her sense of now-is-now."

Dad, one of the few Jewish students in his Berlin public school, well remembered giving the Nazi salute and yelling "Heil, Hitler!" reflexively in the early years of the regime. As he related in his critically acclaimed 1992 autobiography *Stella*, one day, dwelling for the first time on the Nazis' ideology, he decided to abstain. At the end of the school day, he went outside to bicycle home, only to find his tires had been intentionally deflated. By 1935, he and other Jewish children were no longer allowed to attend public schools.

In 1937, my grandmother Leni, an indomitable force in the family, presciently determined that they had to leave Germany. My grandfather had a distant cousin in the Bronx, New York—a literal lifeline, in those days when the U.S. wasn't particularly welcoming to immigrants—and with the cousin's approval and the money from a cashed-in life insurance policy, my grandparents and my 14-year-old father sailed for America on the S.S. *Washington*.

My mother's family, the Rosenows, was better established— but equally prescient. Edith's grandfather Leopold Rosenow was a prominent business executive, civic leader, and politician in Berlin, where he thrived at the turn of the 20th century. A banker, he later owned a molding and frame factory, and served as the city's general fire chief. With a quarter-century on the Berlin City Council, and his 15 years in the Prussian House of Representatives, he established himself as a prominent left-progressive, advocating for activist social policies, and for the teaching of social medicine and newspaper studies at the nation's universities. Leopold was most renowned for the battles he waged against the public utilities, notably the new Berlin phone company, which he claimed was mistreating small business owners—a proud precursor to my battles a century later on behalf of sites and users on the nascent Internet.

Leopold's son George Rosenow, my grandfather, was a prominent hematologist, who studied in Heidelberg and Berlin, later becoming chief of the medical clinic in Königsberg. He published some of the earliest research about blood formation from stem cells, and with several mentors in 1925 founded the *International Journal of Hematology*, still today the most prominent scientific journal in the field. (When contemporary hematologists come into my office, as they do from time to time because of my work on health-care costs and access, and I tell them who my grandfather was, they treat me like I'm LeBron James.)

With Nazi pressure on Jews intensifying, my mother, her sister, and her parents found an opportunity to leave Germany in 1936 for Iraq, where my grandfather had secured an appointment as director of an important Jewish hospital in Baghdad. They emigrated to the United States in 1939, where my grandfather was able to continue working as a hematologist until his retirement 20 years later.

Many of my relatives didn't survive the Nazis. My father's Aunt Marie Weidenreich starved to death in the Theresienstadt concentration camp. My Great Uncle Max was one of the last prisoners to be gassed at Auschwitz. Even if our parents shielded us from the worst knowledge, the sense of apprehension and the need to be ever-attentive to the world around us was something they passed down from that personal history to me and my cohort, their baby boomer children.

That is also why Jews of my generation share a reverence for the United States and our institutions. This nation took in my parents, sheltered them, educated them, offered them paths to employment, and rapidly accepted them as Americans—full, unadulterated, complete Americans. This, too, they passed to us. We have inherited their utter American-ness...and their understanding that citizenship and its rights and responsibilities are never, ever to be taken lightly.

Both my parents assimilated with a vengeance. My mother earned a bachelor's degree in archaeology from the University of Rochester in 1941, and two years later earned a master's degree in what was then called Oriental Studies from Yale, one of the few women to achieve that honor. By then, my father, who had come to the U.S. knowing only eight words of English—he had worn green

German knickerbockers to his first day at DeWitt Clinton High School in the Bronx—was already publishing articles in English-language newspapers and magazines.

God could not create two more different people than my mother and my father. My dad was exuberant; he would bounce into a room and within minutes own it. My mom was very quiet. You couldn't pry personal information out of her under any circumstance.

Yet in foundational ways, they were very much alike. They were absolutely committed to their adopted country, the United States of America. My mother and my father both served in the U.S. Armed Forces during World War II. My dad was a member of the legendary Ritchie Boys, the World War II counter-intelligence unit, many of them German-speaking refugees like my dad, who interrogated captured German personnel and performed essential research and reconnaissance functions that propelled the Allied victory. My mom, fluent in three languages, was in the Women's Army Corps in England, France, and her native Germany, and served in the unit that planned for the postwar occupation of Germany. After meeting at a mixer, they married in 1947. By the time I became sentient a few years after my birth in 1949, they had, with determined effort, lost their German accents.

⤿

I am not a rabbi, nor am I a historian, and I am certainly not a psychoanalyst. So I can only beg forgiveness for blending all three disciplines into some autobiographical guesswork:

My parents, having been chased from their homeland, having become, in the famous phrase from Exodus, "strangers in a strange land," having experienced both the trauma of adolescent emigration and the exhilaration of survival, were in no mood to settle down.

My father, in particular, was afflicted with wanderlust. Bitten by the journalism bug, he launched into the life of an itinerant newspaperman. I was born in Kansas, where Peter Wyden (he'd changed his name as soon as he started getting bylines) had been hired as a reporter by the *Wichita Eagle*. A few years later, we went to St. Louis, where he'd gotten a job writing features for the *Post-Dispatch*. By the time I was ready to start elementary school, he'd landed a real plum—a correspondent's job in the Washington, DC, bureau of *Newsweek*.

"I'm a nosy guy," he would tell me. "I've got the best job around!"

I know that a good deal of my dad's innate inquisitiveness rubbed off on me. Peter Wyden wasn't a journalist because he was working for *Newsweek* or the *Wichita Eagle* or (later) writing for the *Saturday Evening Post* and editing the *Ladies' Home Journal*. Asking questions, finding out things—these were his calling. He was the kind of person who every day could leave his house, the same house he'd been living in for years, notice something he hadn't seen before, ask himself why it was there, and then go about finding the answer. His jobs in journalism were mostly a vehicle for his curiosity. If anything, he considered his jobs impediments: editors who couldn't understand the importance of something he absolutely *knew* was significant—feh!

I'm not sure, however, that our nomadic lifestyle was the best thing for my mom, who was more bookish and reserved than my gregarious father. Or for my brother, Jeff, who came along two years after me. We have a couple of pictures of Jeff and me in our shorts, on the steps of the U.S. Capitol. When I look at them now, I can see my brother was sad, frightened, and lonely, most likely already wrestling with the schizophrenia that would afflict him for the rest of his life. All that moving around—the journalism equivalent of being in the military—could not have helped.

To be sure, there was a spate of marvelous historical coincidences that came from our sojourn in Washington. One of our babysitters in the 1950s was Maurine Neuberger, who later was elected U.S. Senator from Oregon, succeeding her late husband, Dick Neuberger. (As strange as it seems, given the idiosyncrasies of the Jewish American experience, I am actually the fourth Jewish U.S. Senator from Oregon, following the two Neubergers and Joseph Simon, who served one term at the dawn of the 20th century.) And one of my classmates at the Radnor Elementary School in Bethesda, Maryland, was Gordon Smith—whom I later defeated in our first runs for the U.S. Senate, and who subsequently served beside me for two terms as a U.S. Senator from Oregon (and who has remained a good friend, despite our party and political differences).

But other than a few lasting friendships, memories of going to Gifford's for ice cream, and a vague recollection of my dad playing ping-pong with then Senator John F. Kennedy's speechwriter, Ted Sorensen, I can't claim that my Washington childhood had a lasting impact on me. Peter Wyden lit up any room he walked into. For me, the opposite: our family wanderings had made me a bit withdrawn.

My introversion only worsened when my parents (pressured by their personality differences, my brother's illness, and God knows what else) divorced in 1959, when I was 10 and Jeff was 8 and we were living in Chicago. My dad felt he had to go east to make a living. My mom took custody of Jeff and me and went west, settling in Palo Alto, California, where she had few connections, but thought the Golden State would extend opportunities to her and her sons. She worked at various defense contractors, before getting a research job at Stanford University.

I didn't feel abandoned by my dad; for years, every day without fail, he typed a single-spaced letter to Jeff and me offering us life lessons, observations from his work, and encouragements. But I did feel I'd been dealt a tough hand. Divorce wasn't common in the early 1960s; I knew that at school events and other family-oriented occasions, word would circulate that "Ron will be without his dad." My brother took the divorce much harder than me. I tried to be the man of the house, and whenever possible took Jeff wherever I went, leading him on our bicycles. I was clearly trying to drown some of the pain over the divorce by throwing myself into helping the family. It was the first time I thought about family and the fact that you often have no choice but to work your way through difficult times.

The entire United States was undergoing a postwar economic and demographic boom. Palo Alto's was boomier than most. With Government funds, particularly in defense, flowing freely, Stanford University and Dibble General Hospital, an Army institution in nearby Menlo Park, as well as the private high-tech industry that was establishing itself in Stanford Industrial Park and elsewhere in Santa Clara County, attracted more than their fair share of investment. Thousands of jobs materialized for decommissioned military personnel like my mom and others excited by what President Kennedy, in his inaugural address, was calling the New Frontier.

My latest home was at the hot edge of this frontier. Palo Alto's population more than doubled during the 1950s. Schools sprouted: Four new public elementary schools and two junior high schools were built between 1954 and 1957, as the student population swelled from about 8,000 to nearly 14,000 by 1960. Housing was cheap; two-bedroom, two-bath houses could be had for a down payment of about $5,000 in 1951 ($800 for veterans) and a monthly mortgage payment under $100. My mother was one of the beneficiaries. The only significant investment she ever made outside of Jeff's medical care was her small Palo Alto house, which became so valuable that its sale paid for her retirement residency at the Channing House adult community in town.

I was in the sixth grade when I arrived at Garland Elementary School. Every other child had friends; most had been together from grades one through five. I was just by myself most of the time when I was not helping my mom and brother.

The David Starr Jordan Junior High School was a block from our house. One day, walking across its playground, I saw a basketball lying on the grass of an empty field. I picked it up, and after watching other kids shooting around, I went to a basket without players, and took shot after shot.

This was a revelation. My bookish mom and dad may have been the least athletic people in history, but basketball was something I could *own*. I could dribble that ball all day long, get better and better, use it as an excuse to meet other kids in a town where I knew nobody.

In letters between them, which I found after they passed, my parents, both of them intellectuals with a passion for books and ideas, bemoaned my growing obsession with basketball, shooting hoops hour after hour. "Will Ron," they wondered, "ever do anything other than dribble through life?" (Solace, perhaps, for any parent worried at the moment about their kids Minecrafting through life.)

They realized something I couldn't articulate: Our rootlessness, my brother's challenges—I was coping with profound loneliness. Basketball was my diaspora—my place of escape and reinvention.

FOUR

LEADING IS COACHING

Basketball is different.

It's certainly not better than other sports. I wouldn't say it's harder (proficiency in any sport is difficult to gain). But it is different. Your team is small, you're all moving continuously; you're acting and reacting constantly, without pause, always planning ahead yet also understanding that every plan can be upended any second, forcing you to change strategies, tactics, and directions. With only four other players beside you, you're always exposed, playing offense and defense simultaneously. Players have to anticipate what their teammates will do under any circumstance and learn to adapt in the moment to myriad exigencies.

"Every time a basketball player takes a step, an entire new geometry of action is created around him," the writer John McPhee wrote in his classic 1965 *New Yorker* magazine profile of Bill Bradley, later my colleague in the U.S. Senate and still a dear friend. "In ten seconds, with or without the ball, a good player may see perhaps a hundred alternatives and, from them, make half a dozen choices as he goes along. A great player will see even more alternatives and will make more choices, and this multiradial way of looking at things can carry over into his life."

Of course, I understood none of this as a new-to-town 12-year-old sixth grader. I was a kid who'd moved cross-country, didn't have any sort of social network, and wrestled with the absence of a father I idolized. What I knew was that basketball was my ticket to finding my place and fitting in—my chance to get acquainted with the community, make friends, and pick up some stature.

My mother set up a hoop outside our house, and every day from the sixth grade through the ninth, I practiced. Before school, on lunch breaks, after school, I practiced. In the evening, as my mom kept one eye on me and Jeff and another on the stack of magazines she was reading, I practiced. On occasion, I borrowed her reading lamp and plugged it in outside, so I could practice until nine or ten at night.

By the ninth grade, I was getting pretty good—good enough to make the middle school team. I also was getting pretty tall, growing

about a foot, hitting six-foot-three around my junior year of high school, and adding another inch my senior year. All of which put me on the radar screen of a mensch (a person of integrity and kindness) named Clem Wiser.

History records that Jewish players and coaches were central to the development of basketball in the U.S., and several—like the two Reds, Red Holzman of the New York Knicks and Red Auerbach of the Boston Celtics—were still prominent during the 1960s. History also will now record, with my undying gratitude, that this Jew was accepted by his fellow jocks at Palo Alto Senior High School. Coach Wiser made sure of that.

Clem Marcus Wiser was my dad's age, born in 1924 in Pikeville, Kentucky. At age 18, he joined the Marines, and after boot camp at Parris Island, spent World War II in various domestic postings in the south and the west, along the way getting a Screaming Eagle tattoo on his forearm and a beloved wife, Livvie. After the war, he dedicated his life to coaching. With bachelor's and master's degrees in education from San Francisco State, he coached football, track, and basketball at several schools in the Bay Area, before coming to "Paly" in 1955 as basketball coach, a role he held for 28 years (10 of them winning seasons), after which he served another decade as athletic director. He was the most successful basketball coach in the school's history, ending his career with a record of 401 wins to 248 losses, and nine championship teams. A low-key man, he loved cigars, crossword puzzles, his four kids, Livvie, and inside his tough exterior, we were sure, us.

His friends called him Sandy. We, of course, called him Coach.

I'd gotten a reputation for scoring in junior high school. That, and my dedication in his suicide drills—where you'd run as fast you could 15 yards and back, then 30 yards and back, and so on, starting all over again if there was any sign of sloughing off—prompted

Coach to put me on the varsity team almost as soon as I stepped up to Paly in the fall of 1964. I was one of the first sophomores in memory to get a varsity berth.

I paid off Coach's faith in me. That first year, the Vikings won the South Peninsula Athletic League (SPAL)—the team's first league championship since 1961. Our yearbook, the *Madrono*, declared me a "sophomore star" and predicted I'd soon be an all-SPAL player.

The next season, my junior year, Coach put me at center. I was one of the smallest centers in the league, but as our school newspaper, the *Campanile*, reported, "Coach Clem Wiser says Ron should be able to make up more than the few inches by continually trying to get in a better position than his opponent for rebounding and shooting."

I indeed did both, under occasionally fraught circumstances. The South Peninsula Athletic League those years boasted two players who were so talented they would go on to careers in the National Basketball Association: Charlie Lowery, a point guard from our crosstown challengers, Ravenswood High School in East Palo Alto, who later played for the Milwaukee Bucks; and Charles Johnson, also a point guard, a six-foot fireball from our bitter rivals Sequoia High School in Redwood City, who later racked up 1,000 points during three starring years at Cal Berkeley before getting drafted by the Golden State Warriors, then ending his career playing for the NBA champion Washington Bullets.

Against these tough competitors, I more than held my own. In our league's opening game, I kept Johnson to 3 points in the second half, after he'd managed to pop 19 points in the first half. I began to dream of playing in the NBA myself.

My senior year persuaded me that my fantasy could come true. Coach put me back at forward. I was on my way to a Paly season record, averaging 25.5 points per game in league play. I made all-league and was even a contender for the SPAL scoring crown. Powered by some terrific teammates—notably my friend John Bennion, who set a school record with a 39-point game; and his brother Rich, a defensive standout—we went into the final game of the season with a chance to tie for the league championship.

All we had to do was beat Sequoia.

Charlie Johnson and I were trading baskets all night. But going into the fourth quarter, we were still down by eight points. Then Chris Greene, one of our shortest players, came off the bench and ignited a rally, pulling us within two. John Bennion got the ball outside the key, and with 0:00 seconds left on the clock, fired off a shot and tied the game 60–60 at the buzzer. With 13 seconds left in overtime, Sequoia fouled my friend Mark Daley, who sank both his free throw shots, securing our 70-68 victory (with help at the final buzzer from John Bennion, who blocked Charlie one last time). The crowd—we were told it was the largest in the 68-year history of the George Stewart Gym—streamed onto the court shouting with joy.

Thanks to Coach, in six short years, my entire outlook on life had changed. I went from a shy boy just trying to figure out how to find a place in a puzzling new town, to a kid abundant with friends, to something resembling a celebrity—my classmates, for our yearbook, voted me "Most Fun to Be With." The best new pals I made in Palo Alto were the Lerch family. They were role models for me. The Lerch children played all manner of sports at Paly. Their patriarch, Paul, became something of a father figure to me. He and one of my best friends, his son, John, knew my dad wasn't around on weekends, and they made it clear to me that I had a standing invitation to their Sunday night family steak and burger dinners. Nancy Noone, who lived across the street, and Neal Hoffacker (another terrific friend) usually dropped by around dessert time (Nancy and Neal later married); Ron Remmel also was close by and a frequent drop-in. I've been ribbed a lot during my public career for my seemingly paradoxical sunny attitude even in the midst of searing political battles. The fact is, my rosy outlook derives almost entirely from the kindnesses shown me by the Lerches and others during this tense inflection point in my young life, and my unshakeable belief ever since that Americans are inherently kind, their social media characterizations notwithstanding.

My mom never missed the Friday night basketball games, which were a big deal in Palo Alto. At 4 p.m., she'd make me a training-table supper of minute steaks, side salad, and sourdough bread. Post game, we'd always head out to Swensen's for ice cream with the other athletes and their families. My birthday dinner was almost always at Stickney's BBQ, a favorite jock hangout.

"Dear," my mom would say softly and repeatedly, "just make sure you're always hanging out with the right crowd." I was just thrilled that I had found a crowd. I had found my team.

Clem Wiser did more than help me transform into a happy kid. Playing under him, observing him, listening to the ways he cajoled, drove, and inspired us, I also began to notice things about his coaching methods. For example, my first year, when he wanted me to play power forward, to take advantage of my tenacity under the boards, he kept switching me with Chris Clark, a senior, a football player, and the winner of the school's scholar-athlete award. Despite having to split minutes with each other, Coach managed to keep both Chris, the dedicated senior, and me, the ambitious soph, happy, by showing us over and over how the team would benefit from our collaboration.

Although it took me many more years to articulate it, from Clem Wiser I learned one of my greatest lessons. Leading *is* coaching: Whether in legislation or in life, you've got to bring people and ideas together around a shared goal.

To coalesce our team, Coach modeled for us a term that was unknown then: diversity, equity, and inclusion—although the word he used was *respect*.

I'm not sure Kentuckian Clem Wiser had ever coached a Jewish player before me. But he was acutely aware of my "otherness." How could he not have been? When other adolescent boys were asking their would-be 15-year-old sweethearts if they'd wear their St. Christopher medals…I didn't have one to give. The Bennion brothers, for their part, were devout Mormons—a larger minority in Palo Alto than Jews, but a minority nonetheless. Coach made sure the concept of the team transcended everything else, and that we all would be judged based on one factor only: our willingness to work our tails off to contribute to Viking victories.

Coach's respect for our differences seeped deep into the team—no small feat, considering the anxieties of the era. Palo Alto's defense-industry-fueled growth of the 1950s (when the local papers were full of headlines like "Lockheed Tells Details of Stanford Site") was giving way to protests against the Vietnam War, which grew massive in the spring of 1966, my junior year of high school, when the Johnson Administration ended automatic draft deferments for students.

Even a preoccupied high school jock like me couldn't help but notice.

> **RON'S RULE OF CHUTZPAH**
>
> **3**
>
> LEADING IS COACHING: YOU'VE GOT TO BRING PEOPLE AND IDEAS TOGETHER AROUND A SHARED GOAL

A few miles away from Paly, at Cubberley High School, a more open-minded and experimental school where many of us had friends and family, a popular first-year teacher, a recent Stanford grad named Ron Jones, staged an experiment that showed how readily and unthinkingly otherwise normal people could fall prey to the impulses of totalitarianism and fascism.

Known to his students by his first name, he came in one day and declared that from then on, they would have to call him "Mr. Jones." He ordered them to internalize dictums he wrote on the blackboard, such as "strength through discipline" and "strength through action." He invented a special salute for his ersatz political movement, which he dubbed The Third Wave. Several days in, he secretly deputized three of his students as informers, who were to report to him any deviations from party discipline. Accused violators would be put on trial and, if convicted, exiled from class.

On the final day, he told his students that The Third Wave was not, as he'd originally hinted, an experiment. It was an actual political party. Its leader would be revealed to them at a school rally later that day.

The students arrived and settled into their seats in the Cubberley auditorium. A film soon played on a wall-sized screen: Hitler at one of the Nazi Party's giant Nuremberg Rallies during the 1930s.

"There is no such thing as a national youth movement called The Third Wave," Ron Jones told his students. "You have been used. Manipulated. Shoved by your own desires into the place you now find yourself. You are no better or worse than the German Nazis we have been studying."

The fervor that surrounded us peaked on April 15, 1967, weeks before my graduation, when 50,000 people crowded the streets of San Francisco 55 miles to the north, with hundreds of thousands of other demonstrators joining in other cities in the Spring Mobilization to End the War in Vietnam. Among the speakers was Coretta Scott King, the wife of the civil rights leader Dr. Martin Luther King Jr., who called LBJ "an uncertain President" torn by conflicting guidance from his advisors. "For God's sake," Mrs. King told the San Francisco crowd, "stop the bombing!"

Her presence highlighted the potent mix of issues that were roiling Palo Alto, the Bay Area, and the nation: the war...the environment...the women's movement...and race.

Race had long been a subtext in Palo Alto. My junior high school's namesake, David Starr Jordan, the founding president of Stanford University, had been an outspoken eugenicist at the turn of the century, a believer in "bionomics," a word he coined, which held that some races were inherently inferior to others and that "race degeneration" threatened the United States.

There were clear racial tensions in town. Menlo-Atherton High School broke down in a race riot in late 1967; more than 50 students were injured. The district's Director of Multiculturalism, Sidney Walton, quit shortly after he was hired. Palo Alto was a "racist town," he declared in his letter of resignation.

Palo Alto was segregated—and to a certain extent still is. An expansion of the 101 Freeway in the 1950s physically walled off Palo Alto from East Palo Alto. The latter became a largely Black locale, as whites fled to other towns in the area. East Palo Alto's high school, Ravenswood, which had opened in 1958 with some 600 students, more than doubled in size during the next six years and became largely Black, while the other high schools—including Paly, less than five miles away—were overwhelmingly white. Efforts to create better racial balances in the district either were thwarted by parents angrily decrying busing, or so tentative as to be meaningless. (One such stealth program brought about 200 Black kids from East Palo Alto to live with families in Palo Alto and Los Altos, so they could attend Paly and other majority white schools. The initiative was called Sneak-out.)

I wish I could say I was directly attentive to these racial currents. But I was almost completely unscathed by social awareness, even among the budding tumult of the 1960s. We had, I think, one Black basketball player my senior year, an outstanding multi-sport athlete named Greg Stell. For the most part, as my parents had correctly observed, I was dribbling through life.

Until the game at Ravenswood.

Normally in team sports, you travel to away games in street clothes and suit up in the visitors' locker room. This time, Coach Wiser let us know that the Paly administration had determined we would get into uniform in our own gym, and bus over to Ravenswood dressed to play. I felt strongly this wasn't Coach's choice—that he disagreed with the administrators' determination that Ravenswood might be "unsafe"—because he closed out his pre-game pep talk by demanding from us one thing, above and beyond the victory he wanted and knew would be hard-fought: "I expect you," Clem Wiser said, "to treat the Ravenswood Trojans and their fans with respect."

Given my parents' escape from the Holocaust and my own earlier feelings of lonely "otherness," it's shocking for me to recall that the Ravenswood game was the first time I could consciously articulate that *this* was what bigotry looked like and what discrimination felt like.

Certainly, Clem Wiser's moral authority had a profound impact on me. Without question, his emphasis on teaming, collaboration, and respect as the foundations necessary for victories of any kind affected every part of my life.

Equally important, I also learned some very specific things about coaching that have been central to everything I've done since.

First and foremost is the fact that teaching others is an essential condition of leadership.

Think about it: Coaches can't run down court. They can't score a single point. They don't touch the ball. Yet coaches' self-respect (not to mention their livelihoods) requires them to win games. There's only one way to do that: teach others how.

As in sports, so in life.

The University of Michigan management scholar Noel Tichy says the groups that succeed most predictably and continuously are those that become "teaching organizations," which he distinguishes from a more popular construct, the "learning organization."

"Self-absorbed learning is different from taking my learning and feeling a sense of responsibility to bring it to you," says Tichy, who led GE's Leadership Development Center during the giant conglomerate's most successful years. "If I learn something about a customer, do I run back and teach people? Then can I do that on a large scale? That's the trick."

Great coaches also involve the team and its members in their own progress. Too many average coaches—and far too many bosses—think it's all about them. Our society rewards such self-centeredness, plastering the faces of celebrity CEOs and title-winning coaches (and, let's face it, U.S. Senators, too) across magazine covers, bookstore windows, website home pages, and idol-worshiping television shows. Led by such masters of the first-person singular as Elon Musk and Donald Trump, we live more deeply than ever inside what the historian and social critic Christopher Lasch called a "culture of narcissism."

But to succeed, the coach, the Senator, and any leader—has to be able to, in effect, clone themselves. You have to teach people both the skills and the ways of applying those skills that you've learned, so your "pupils" can use them in new ways in different situations, ideally without requiring the coach's (or the boss's or the Senator's) ongoing intervention. Then you've got to get them to add their own special talents to the mix and embed that ethos deeply in the organization. The best teams are not micromanaged; they are partnerships of independent actors, all of them committed to improving themselves, each óther, and the enterprise.

This is actually easier to accomplish in sports than in other areas of life. Coach Wiser only needed to get 5 starters and a total squad of maybe 15 boys partnering together. In a company or volunteer organization, a leader may have to transform several dozen or several thousand people into teachers and teammates.

And for a U.S. Senator—well, in my case, I consider the entire voting population of Oregon my team.

The main reason I've been fixated on holding open town meetings every year in every county in my state is not because I want voters to see my presence, as important as that is. It's because they are teaching me and each other.

Nobody is sitting around waiting to hear the latest legislative report from the Committee on Acoustics and Ventilation—a comic construct of Speaker of the House Tom Foley, invented so he could explain to us the difference between the bureaucratic minutiae of our work and the real concerns of real human beings. The citizen who gets face time with a legislator wants that Government official to show that they, the citizen, are important enough to get their representative to lock in on them, on what they know, and on what they've experienced. They want to see that you, the legislator, are listening to them when they say, "My God, this summer was so hot I actually *could* fry an egg on my front porch." And you must understand that that's your opening to have a conversation (never a monologue!) about climate change, and to get their ideas for breaking the gridlock on it.

Of course, teaching organizations aren't like secondary schools or colleges; the teaching doesn't exist in a vacuum, and knowledge isn't created, valued, or transmitted for its own sake. Which is another of the subordinate principles of great coaching: It must lead somewhere.

"How do you teach people how to win?" muses Larry Bossidy, the former CEO of Honeywell and the co-author with Ram Charan of one of the best-selling management books of all time, *Execution: The Discipline of Getting Things Done*. "The day when you could yell and scream and beat people into good performance is over. Today, you have to appeal to them by helping them see how they can get from here to there, by establishing some credibility, and by giving them some reason and some help to get there. Do all those things, and they'll knock down doors. So you begin by creating values and putting an emphasis on goals."

Setting clear goals may seem self-evident, but all too frequently in business, and certainly in politics and government, process replaces results as the focus of people's attention and commitment. All public sector and private organizations can become dysfunctionally absorbed in strategies and tactics, often to their own detriment because they haven't been able to articulate clearly what those strategies and tactics are aiming to realize. "People have to know where they're going," says Larry Bossidy. "We want them to believe that the goals we're talking about are real, that we can do it."

After articulating clear goals, the third thing great coaches do is assess and assemble their talent—with the understanding that talent is fluid.

From Clem Wiser, I learned that human beings aren't machine parts, built to do one thing only and one thing well. To be sure, we each might have our own special skills, but we also are capable of learning new tricks and adapting to new situations.

My role on the Vikings changed every year I played at Paly. My first year, Coach wanted me at forward because of my hustle on rebounds. My second year, he had me at center—again, so I could grab rebounds and also use my spidery arms and legs to protect the post so the forwards and shooting guard had enough room to score. My last year, with John Bennion as floor manager setting up the plays and his brother Rich at power forward getting off the medium shots, Coach had me at small forward, scoring as much as I could from the outside and the inside, and grabbing offensive rebounds everywhere I could.

I appreciated the fluidity because Coach trained us to welcome it. He valued our flexibility and made us understand that our worth wasn't premised on our height alone or solely on our outside shooting percentage or some other single physical quality. He respected the fact that we had brains and instincts that enabled us to do different things at different times. As a consequence, playing for Coach Wiser was always stimulating, and he motivated us to improve across multiple dimensions.

For coaches to persuade players to test themselves continually, they require another quality: trust.

I'm writing these words shortly after right-wing Republicans ousted Speaker Kevin McCarthy. Democrats and Republicans alike used the same words to explain their votes to fire him.

"We don't trust him. Their members don't trust him. And you need a certain degree of trust to be the Speaker," said Representative Adam Schiff, a Democrat. Schiff lost faith in his fellow Californian when McCarthy first agreed to create a bipartisan committee to investigate President Trump's attempted coup to remain in power after his loss to Joe Biden, then backtracked, withdrew his appointees to the committee, and embraced Trump during a groveling visit to Mar-a-Lago.

At Paly, we trusted Clem Wiser completely. We knew he wouldn't set us up for failure; we also knew that if we failed despite our best efforts, we wouldn't get blamed or punished.

Equally important was the final sub-principle of great coaching I learned from Wiser: be rigorously honest, especially when it comes to identifying and diagnosing problems.

Coach was always willing to tell us things we did *not* want to hear. He never sugarcoated anything. When he felt, for example, the team was not rebounding well, he told us *and* he informed the press—a public signal that we were on call to fix the problem together.

Trust develops when your colleagues know that you will be open with them not just about their virtues, but about their deficiencies. A world of "attaboys" will only get you so far.

FIVE

TAKING HITS, BOUNCING BACK

M y high school yearbook summarized my dreams this way: "He would gladly sacrifice a career in law for a professional basketball contract."

They got that right! I paid careful attention to the full-court press I was getting from several top basketball schools. The legendary coach Bud Presley, revered in our neck of the woods for his time steering Palo Alto–area high school teams, later deemed one of the best basketball coaches in the nation, on a par with Bobby Knight, was then working at Gonzaga University, a Jesuit college in Spokane, Washington. He recruited me aggressively. Later on, John Bennion and I joked that if they had recruited him as well, they could have had a team of Jesuits, Jews, and Mormons—a kind of United Basketball Nations. John's son Daniel would later intern in my Senate Office. The Zag recruiters really impressed my mom, actively offering up details about the "Jewish community" in Spokane, to ease her concerns about me bouncing away to a Catholic school. She met their fervor politely, but ultimately there was no way Mrs. Wyden, who'd accepted a lot of her son's basketball *mishegoss* (that's Yiddish for "craziness") was going to let me spend four years in Spokane.

Which was perfectly okay by me, because the University of California, Santa Barbara, an NCAA Division I school, offered me a full basketball scholarship, and I grabbed it. The coaching staff was interested in me for the same reasons Clem Wiser had been: They saw me as both an offensive and defensive threat. Playing swing, I thought, would increase my chances of making it to the pros.

In my first game as a freshman, I scored 25 points. That night, I went to bed believing I really did have a shot at the NBA.

Until.

Every life has its "untils." Mine was heel, ankle, Achilles tendon, and back problems. A freshman leader, by sophomore year—even after a summer of stretching and therapy—I was riding the varsity bench. One of Coach Wiser's teachings kicked in: I had to be brutally honest with myself. I'd played 16 games at UCSB, and while my percentages were pretty good (50 percent from the field and 82 percent from the foul line) I'd eked out only 2.6 points and 1.5 rebounds per game. While in later years I could still hit 47 out of 50 free throws in the House of Representatives shooting contest, no amount of hard work on the court would ever get my injured feet to the pros.

In the middle of the year, with my mom's employment there improving my chances and keeping the price tag low, I transferred to Stanford University.

It was a very painful, even frightening, time for me. After nearly two years living independently four-and-a-half hours away, I was back in my old bedroom, commuting back and forth to Stanford with my mother, living with an ailing brother who was a constant source of worry. My mother hardly slept, and the whole house was on edge. Although John Lerch was nearby at Cal Berkeley, most of my friends and teammates had dispersed. Seemingly overnight, my weight dropped from 185 to 170 (where it's remained, for the most part, ever since). I'd lost something really important, my fantasy would never come true, and it hurt a lot.

I knew I was literally out of my academic league at Stanford, well aware that I hadn't done the preparation that my new classmates had. So I did what I'd done during those tough days a decade before, when we'd first moved to Palo Alto: I threw myself into an obsessive coping mechanism. Although this time, my tool wasn't a basketball. It was books.

Clearly, my parents' examples had rubbed off on me. My father had graduated from newspaper and magazine writing to books, and had already authored the first of several bestsellers about history and culture. Although he was back East, remarried, and making a living editing women's magazines, he continued to write letters to me and Jeff nearly every day and was always correcting our letters back to him with his legendary red pencil, then returning them to us. My mother was a scholar and librarian; while she'd been an avid supporter of my now-dashed sports career, she was even more visibly gratified by my new intellectual interests.

Something else had awakened in me, as well. Sports had taught me discipline and purpose. I learned that you have to show up every day prepared to play—to take whatever slings and arrows life might throw at you, deflect some, and catch and repurpose others. It also had exposed me to the risks of single-mindedness. Everyone takes hits. The test of a true *chutzpadik* is the ability to bounce back.

That meant studying. That meant becoming more aware of the world. A particular point of pride for both my parents: Toward the end of

> **RON'S RULE OF CHUTZPAH**
>
> **4**
>
> **SHOW UP EVERY DAY PREPARED TO PLAY**

my Stanford tenure, needing an elective to graduate, I took a course in reading German newspapers. Following my father's model, I'd often fall asleep surrounded by papers.

Like much of the rest of America, the Palo Alto to which I'd returned was ripped by politics. In 1968, a thousand demonstrators took to the city's streets to protest Richard Nixon's election, smashing windows and setting fires. Shortly after my return in 1969, anti-war protestors overran the Stanford Research Institute, injuring a police officer with a nail-studded bat. Ninety-three people were arrested.

Like most students then, I opposed the Vietnam War—it was a no-win debacle for my friends, my country, and me. Among the things I'd learned from my father's journalism was that the Federal Government was prone to avoidable fiascos. (In one among many memorable lines from his best-selling history, *Bay of Pigs: The Untold Story*, he deemed the hapless invasion of Cuba early in the Kennedy Administration "Waterloo staged by the Marx Brothers.")

But I also was somewhat insulated from the war. The foot and joint problems that had ended my basketball career also rendered me ineligible for the draft. I took the opportunities given me to work head-down to reinvent myself. By my senior year of college, that reinvention was pointing me in a direction that had been flagged in my high school yearbook: law school.

I had a girlfriend at Mills College in Oakland, a women's school that was a favorite road trip destination for Stanford men. It was spring of my senior year. She was going north to see her family in Medford, a town in southern Oregon, and asked if I wanted to drive up with her and hang out for a few days. Naturally, I said yes!

Seeing Oregon for the first time was the second inflection point in my young life, akin to my discovery of basketball a decade earlier. Southern Oregon was particularly gorgeous. We were only a few miles north of the California border, in an area dotted by small towns with historic, if worn, downtowns and breathtaking views of the mountains of the Cascade Range, surrounded by lush fruit farms. (The town of Medford has been the home of Harry & David, the nation's largest direct seller of fruit and food baskets, since 1910.)

Although I was unaware of it on that first visit, Medford's location in the Rogue Valley between the Cascades and Siskiyou Mountains protects it from the rain that drenches large swaths of western Oregon. Its warmer, drier weather enhanced its appeal. Walking the nearby trails with my girlfriend, I was transfixed. It seemed like the Real West—not the roiling Palo Alto West—independent and unburdened, a clear field. The place had it all: young people doing interesting work, a landscape of outdoor treasures. Most of all, it seemed less burdened by decades of old ways and institutions, a perfect place for a young guy to put his chips down, even if he had absolutely no idea what he might do with his life. Like the 19th century pioneers who trekked the Oregon Trail from Missouri, seduced by Oregon's "golden horn of plenty...suitable for growing or raising anything in abundance," I thought, here was a place where a fellow might actually chart his own path. Here was my manifest destiny.

I resolved to go to law school at the University of Oregon in Eugene.

As I gradually learned, Oregon wasn't so much open as it was ornery, rebellious, and by nature contradictory. It beckoned pioneers but was wary of strangers. Settled in some parts by taciturn Midwesterners and in others by reserved New Englanders, the state lacked the expansive worldview and tolerance for which our northern neighbors in Seattle, Washington (founded by the same open-minded Scandinavians who created Minnesota's Democratic–Farmer–Labor Party) were famous. Oregon attracted (indeed, it sought out) "pious and educated young men." One famous story, probably apocryphal, had it that at a far western branch of the Oregon Trail, there was a sign pointing south to California, with no words, just an illustration of gold quartz. The sign pointing north was for the literate: "To Oregon," it read.

"There was in the character of the people...a preference for isolation," wrote local historians Terence O'Donnell and Thomas Vaughan. "Oregonians liked the independence which isolation gave, and they still do. Here was a quality that was never to quite disappear, this feeling of isolation and specialness."

The insularity manifested itself in incongruous ways. Oregon entered the Union in 1859 as the only state whose Constitution had an exclusion clause banning free Black people and slaves alike. People of Chinese descent could not own property. Although the exclusion clause was rendered invalid by the 14th Amendment to the U.S. Constitution in 1868 ("no state shall make or enforce any law which shall abridge the privileges or immunities of citizens of the United States"), Oregon became the Pacific Northwest's center of Ku Klux Klan activity early in the 20th century. In a 1922 ballot initiative, the state's citizens, urged on by the Klan, voted to ban Catholic schools. Chinese and Black people were actively hounded out of towns and cities. Southern Oregon, the place where I first fell in love with Oregon, was where the Klan set up its initial outpost in the state. Medford became known as a sundown town; Blacks were not allowed to be within its borders after dark.

Yet the eponymous founders of Harry & David, the pride of Medford, were Jews, Harry and David Rosenberg. Oregon elected Joseph Simon, a Jew, as U.S. Senator in 1898, until then only the fourth Jewish Senator in American history. As if to prove his election wasn't a fluke, Portland elected Simon mayor in 1909. This was just a year after Reed College was founded. A hotbed of academic and cultural radicalism, the school banned fraternities and sports, considering them inimical to scholarship, and by the 1940s it had become a haven for the burgeoning Beat literary scene. The Beats evolved seamlessly into the freewheeling hippies exemplified by the Oregon writer Ken Kesey and his band of Merry Pranksters, whose cross-country ride in a psychedelically painted bus from which they dispensed LSD to willing acolytes was immortalized by Tom Wolfe in his epic *The Electric Kool-Aid Acid Test*. Years later, Oregon adopted a perfectly evocative state motto: "She flies with her own wings."

Economically, Oregon also was insular. Disdainful of both Eastern money and California wealth, it home-brewed most of its businesses. By the 1890s, four intermarried families controlled 21 corporations and partly owned 18 others, including most of the banks and insurance companies. Oregon's economy was heavily based on wood products, chemicals, and food. With some exceptions (such as Jantzen, the swimwear company), its brands were not widely known. It lacked the giant national and global firms that Seattle routinely birthed, like Boeing and UPS.

Yet the first seeds of a broader business outlook had already sprouted by the time I arrived for law school in 1971. Nike had been founded in Eugene seven years earlier, by the former University of Oregon runner Phil Knight and his college track coach, Bill Bowerman. Nike's first major advertisement, by the local ad executive John Brown, perfectly captured Oregon's complementary desires for isolation and freedom: a poster depicting a lone runner dressed in yellow, pacing along a road through a dense green forest, with the bold caption, "There is no finish line."

Oregon's ambiguities were in full flower politically by the time I arrived. Anti-war protests were peaking in the wake of President

Nixon's bombing of Cambodia, and the environmental movement was beginning to flourish. Ornery, independent Oregon embraced them, particularly the new environmental consciousness. The state had a groundbreaking electoral system of initiative, referendum, and recall that gave voters an almost unheard-of power over the political process. Its feisty liberal Republican Governor, Tom McCall, had used the ballot box to help drive through advanced, environmentally friendly land-use planning mechanisms, and—even more popular—made all of Oregon's beaches public. But the state's bear-hugging of contrarians didn't mean it wanted them present. Contrary to every tenet of civic boosterism, bumper stickers from the era discouraged visitors and transplants. "Don't Californicate Oregon," they read.

In my early 20s, I saw Oregon's freedom more than I perceived any aloofness. It looked like young people could break in there, without a lot of impediments that were passed from one generation to another. I loved the thought that in Oregon, I could be close to my mother and brother…but after years of living at home, not too close.

I also enjoyed the fact that outsiders never could figure out Oregon's secret sauce. In one of my first trips after starting law school, I visited my dad in Ridgefield, Connecticut, where he assessed that what I needed most in life was a classic, New York–style delicatessen sandwich. He took me to his favorite deli and introduced me to the gargantuan owner, who was standing behind a hunk of his treasured pastrami. "This is my son Ron!" Peter Wyden exclaimed. "He lives in Oregon!"

The owner took one look at me and shouted at the top of his voice, "Hey, kid, what do you do out there, run a whaling boat?!"

I didn't—but soon after arriving at University of Oregon as a 1L (first year law student) in 1971, I got a different piloting job that changed my life.

〜

There was a notice on a bulletin board at the law school. Former United States Senator Wayne Morse, who'd been defeated in his re-election bid three years earlier, was making a comeback. He intended to challenge Senator Mark Hatfield for his seat and was looking for volunteers.

I was a bit hesitant; the first year of law school is a boot camp where you're cramming your brain full of basics: criminal law, civil procedure, torts, contracts, property law, Constitutional law.

Yet the idea of working on Wayne Morse's campaign was tantalizing. He was a heroic figure, known to all of us who opposed the Vietnam War as one of only two Senators to vote against the Gulf of Tonkin Resolution that had authorized Lyndon Johnson to wage that godforsaken tragedy. I was already interested in putting down roots in Oregon; what better way to immerse myself and maybe get a connection or two than working for this icon? As for my studies, among the things I'd learned from high school and college sports was compartmentalization. I called Morse's campaign office to volunteer, and within a few weeks, he asked me to be his driver as he stumped the state.

If you read profiles of Wayne Lyman Morse, you'll find a recurring set of descriptions from his four terms in the United States Senate: "maverick," "iconoclast," "irascible."

They were all true.

He was born in 1900 in Verona, Wisconsin, and grew up on a farm, in a family that was always straining to make ends meet. Early in life, egged on by a socially conscious mother, he became entranced by the state's passionately progressive Republican Governor and Senator, Robert M. La Follette, whose scorching oratory and reformist policies supporting labor, farmers, and the working poor against corporate power was famously turning Wisconsin into a "laboratory of democracy."

Following the model of "Fighting Bob," Morse studied speech and economics at the University of Wisconsin, then taught "argumentation" and earned a law degree at the University of Minnesota. In 1931, he was appointed dean of the University of Oregon School of Law in Eugene, becoming the youngest law school leader in the country.

Morse rapidly became an expert in the new field of labor law, a negotiator so skilled he was valued and trusted by both unions and employers. That attracted the attention of the Roosevelt Administration, for which he helped settle a railroad strike. In 1942, President Roosevelt appointed Morse to the National War Labor Board, on which he became by far the most productive of the 12 commissioners.

Morse found Washington, DC, to his liking. Two years later, in his first election ever, he ran for the U.S. Senate from Oregon—in the La Follette style, as a progressive Republican—and won.

Morse was an unabashed liberal, a frequently strident proponent of FDR's New Deal, whose support for working folk, education, civil rights, women's rights, and health care was unflagging. Almost as soon as he was elected, he ran afoul of his Republican Party. In his first Senate term, he voted with the Democrats two-thirds of the time. Re-elected in 1950 with one of the largest margins Oregon had ever seen, he broke with the Republican majority again, signing with six other liberal Republican Senators an open "Declaration of Conscience" decrying the anti-Communist witch hunt of the right-wing Wisconsin Senator Joseph McCarthy.

His most sacrilegious heresy, however, came in 1952, when Morse refused to endorse the Republican Presidential ticket, largely because he abhorred the Red-baiting tactics of the Vice Presidential nominee, California Senator Richard M. Nixon. The Senate Republicans punished him by divesting Morse of his seniority and committee assignments. When he returned to the Senate for the opening of the 83rd Congress in January 1953, Morse brought with him a folding chair, which he placed in the center of the floor. "Since I haven't been given any seat in the new Senate," he declared puckishly, "I decided to bring my own."

Morse got his revenge against the Republican Party and the Eisenhower Administration in 1955 by declaring himself a Democrat, providing the party a one-vote majority in the Senate. Offered his choice of committee assignments by the new and thankful majority leader, Texas Senator Lyndon Baines Johnson, Morse chose two that would further his zeal for economic justice and peace: Banking and Foreign Relations.

Morse's new party, the Democrats, was no safer from his brickbats. "As long as I serve on this job," he once said, "I am going to serve my own master under obligation to no one."

In no arena was this more apparent and profound as in his opposition to the Vietnam War.

An unwavering anti-Communist, Morse championed a "one-world philosophy of permanent peace" safeguarded by multinational institutions such as the United Nations and the World Court and facilitated by American-led innovations such as the Marshall Plan and NATO. Although open-minded about a President's ability to wage war, he also staunchly advocated for Congress's oversight authority. The President, he said as early as 1952, cannot "exercise broad, undefined powers which the Congress thinks goes too far."

Two years later, increasingly dismayed by what he saw as creeping executive overreach, he specifically singled out the risks of entanglement in Southeast Asia. "The American people are in no mood to contemplate the killing of thousands of American boys in Indochina," he presciently warned his Senate colleagues.

Although many of his proposals went down to defeat in the Senate, Morse's opposition to unrestricted Presidential war authority remained unflagging through the Eisenhower and Kennedy Administrations. He pointed to the "rising tide of anti-Americanism throughout the world" that our nation's interventionism was generating; he disparaged our willingness to get involved in other nations' civil wars; he attacked the "unchecked executive power" of the Central Intelligence Agency; and he expressed "grave doubts as to the constitutionality" of JFK's intervention in South Vietnam.

As Kennedy's successor President Johnson ratcheted up American involvement in Asia, the Oregon Senator intensified his public opposition. He read into the Congressional Record hundreds of letters from Americans opposing the war. In August 1964, when LBJ used the occurrence of an attack on two American ships in Vietnam's Gulf of Tonkin to seek unlimited authority to retaliate against North Vietnam by air and sea without a formal declaration of war, Morse made the only speech in opposition before joining Alaska Senator Ernest Gruening in voting no.

"I believe that history will record this resolution as a historic mistake," Morse thundered against the "pre-dated declaration of war." "This kind of a program, in South Vietnam...in my judgment is going to kill needlessly untold numbers of American boys, and for nothing."

Democrats were as embittered by Senator Morse's independence as the Republicans were a decade before. President Johnson indignantly told a reporter, "You can lead a Morse to water, but you can't make him think." Morse's stridency was jarring even to younger

Democrats. Idaho's Frank Church, later an outspoken opponent of the war, at the time said the Oregonian was living in a "Never-Never-Land of radically ineffectual dissent."

But the fact is very clear that Morse, the seeming embodiment of establishment authority with his bushy eyebrows, avuncular mustache, and graying hair, was a leading driver—perhaps *the* driver—of the anti-war movement in the United States. "Morse didn't come early or late to the peace movement," one of his campaign workers said. "There was a time when he *was* the peace movement." His institutional credentials, his repeated invocations of universal ethics and Constitutional principles, his relentless barnstorming across college campuses and other public forums, and his counsel to his audiences that they had the ability to force the Government's hand, gave him extraordinary and growing influence, well beyond Oregon's boundaries.

That was the Wayne Morse I encountered when I first pulled up to his farm on 595 Crest Drive in Eugene in the fall of 1971. The Senator was *all* chutzpah—determined, self-confident, obsessed with making good things, giant things, happen. In his car, I was getting the opportunity to steer what was effectively a mobile political science classroom. (The Wayne Morse Family Farm in Eugene is now a 27-acre public park, with his preserved home a monument to his decades of service. In it, his office is set up exactly how he left it. On the bulletin board is a note reading, "Senator, Ron Wyden is going to be by at 12:30 to pick you up.")

His heresies had finally made him vulnerable. He'd backed Oregon's Republican Governor, Mark Hatfield, in the U.S. Senate race against Democratic Congressman Bob Duncan, because Hatfield opposed the war while Duncan supported it. ("If we don't fight the Communists in Vietnam, we'll end up fighting them on the banks of the Willamette," Duncan once declared.) When Hatfield won by a mere 24,000 votes, furious Democrats began to abandon Morse, and Duncan threatened to challenge him for his seat. The Democratic defections enabled an opportunistic Republican, Bob Packwood, to defeat Morse in 1968. Now Morse wanted back in—by challenging Hatfield, arguably one of his mentees!

Where Morse's history led me to expect a clamorous curmudgeon, what I discovered chauffeuring him from Portland to Ashland and from Coos Bay to Baker City was something more elemental: Above all, Wayne Morse was an instinctive educator. The first thing he'd do when he got in the car was take out that morning's edition of the *Oregonian*. "You know, Ron," he'd say, pointing to one story or another, "I gave a speech on this on the floor of the Senate in 1957. I'm glad I gave them hell. They eventually *did* wake up!"

It wasn't self-aggrandizement…not entirely. In town after town, knowing that many people perceived him as arrogant, he'd walk the main streets of the business districts on little listening tours. Nurses, lumberjacks, farmers, and all other sorts of working people, agog at seeing this Oregon legend in their midst, would flock to him and grab his hand. Several steps behind him, I'd hear them say, over and over, "You know, Wayne, I didn't vote for you the last time because I didn't agree with you on Vietnam, but damn, I agree with you now about Nixon and the war."

He loved these encounters. He took the long view of politics: People will come around if you keep giving them the facts. "You've got to educate them, Ron," he'd say as we returned to the car. "Everyone can be taught."

The Senator—I don't think I would've gotten in trouble if I called him Wayne as everyone else did, but I always called him Senator— was far from a Johnny One Note. Although Vietnam was the top issue, he repeatedly drew people into conversations on all manner of topics. The rights and needs of working people—especially mill workers—were another subject always on his mind. I often stood silently by as he engaged lumberjacks in complex conversations about antitrust law, the smaller sawmills, and sustainable logging practices.

I was aware—how could I not be?!—that Wayne Morse had many enemies. (Among his feuds was one with Dick and Maurine Neuberger, both of whom served alongside him as junior U.S. Senators from Oregon, and one of whom—a pre-Senatorial Maurine—had been my babysitter back in DC!) But I also learned from his yarns that you could oppose someone politically on an issue while remaining their friend personally and their ally on other issues. "Bill Fulbright can call the President a name and they are bitter enemies," *Time* magazine quoted one unnamed Republican musing during the height of the Vietnam War, talking about the anti-war Wisconsin Senator. "Wayne Morse can call the President a worse name and they are still friends. The difference is that Wayne smiles when he says it."

As Morse himself put it: "The real worthwhile abuse comes from your real friends."

I also came to understand quite clearly that you needed ideas and you needed depth to be a successful leader. You can't fake expertise. You can't know and don't have to know everything about everything—there's no shame in admitting technical ignorance— but there's no virtue in failing to explore. Morse was all about the power of ideas, and he wasn't shy in the least about criticizing less inquisitive colleagues. Countless times, I'd overhear him: "He's wrong about the war. He's wrong about antitrust. He's wrong about labor." These weren't the reflexive reproaches of an out-of-touch egotist. He'd studied the subjects, and he had found his way to answers.

He reminded me a lot of my father, the nosy journalist. "Ron, you gotta ask the hard questions," Dad would say. "Nobody's asking the hard questions."

I also saw how specifically fascinated the Senator was by science, medicine, and social trends. He'd be asked about them all the time, often randomly, and almost always, he'd have something cogent to say, because he spent much of his time devouring newspapers, magazines, journals, books, lectures, and conversations. One of the most important lessons from those hours, weeks, and months at his side was that if you can get to an issue early enough, before mistakes are made, you can shape outcomes far more effectively than a laggard.

The Senator understood something incredibly important. He always said that if given the choice between controlling the process that reaches a solution or controlling a foreordained conclusion, he would take the process. Far too many well-meaning people involved in government believe in trying to impose predetermined policies which, in retrospect, turn out to be badly flawed. Wayne Morse understood that you have to learn about a problem, involve people, bring ideas together, and reach the right conclusion—you can't just foist your ideas and expect them to work.

The ideas that animated Wayne Morse the most were fresh and still evolving. President Johnson had signed Medicare into law only a few years before. Like any Federal program, its implementation was filled with confusion and kinks. Morse believed at his core that politics had to be big—big enough that it could end an unconstitutional war abroad—but that it also had to be small enough to attend to the details that matter in citizens' day-to-day lives. So, for example, when an elderly woman would come up to him at a county fair or in a park or grocery store and start crying because she couldn't pay her hospital bill and was worried her home was going to be foreclosed on, that dual belief would provide him with the perspicacity and wherewithal to help her fix it.

On senior care, I was his chosen tool. When he was button-holed at campaign stops by elderly Oregonians—"Wayne, I'm having headaches with my Medicare benefits," he'd hear, "will you help me?"—Morse would smile at them, point at me, and say, "Happy to help. This young man here, Ron, is up from the law school in Eugene and he'll figure out Medicare for you and get you the help you need."

When I heard that the first time, I almost went into shock. I was 23, barely aware that a Social Security number had nine digits. After Senator Morse talked me up to the seniors several more times, we were walking back to the car and I started pleading with him: "Can we talk about this senior thing for a minute?"

Even before I could finish the sentence, he stopped me. "Ron, I know you are a young man and don't know anything about the elderly," he said. "But I need the help, and this could be a great future for you to get into. Take my word for it, this is going to be a really exciting field. The population's demographics are changing. Besides, seniors are always getting pushed around by the insurance companies, the utilities, and the business lobbies. Helping them will be good for Oregon, good for them, and good for you. Will you give it a try?"

It was not a natural calling. But as a newcomer to Oregon, there was no way I could say no to Wayne Morse.

Morse, expectedly, lost his 1972 election bid against Mark Hatfield, the popular incumbent. Oregon citizens had turned decisively against the war. Although Morse had been there first, Hatfield was more than good enough for them, and he was less cantankerous. But that race was just a dress rehearsal for a real comeback. Morse set off immediately planning a 1974 rematch against Republican

Bob Packwood, the fickle horse trader who'd defeated him six years earlier. Morse believed Packwood's political shiftiness made him vulnerable.

In my final year in law school, I signed up eagerly to help him again.

I'd already taken his advice, and between his first and second campaigns, while still in law school, had become something of a presence in Eugene on senior issues. A few years after President Johnson signed the 1965 Older Americans Act establishing Medicare, amendments to the legislation created grants to help local communities set up senior centers; offer job training and employment opportunities for older, low-income men and women; and provide nutrition assistance, health-care support, adult day care, legal services, and other aid to seniors. Knowing of these new requirements in the law, I determined to become something of a one-man senior support shop. I took out the phone book (yes, there once were such things) and called every attorney in Lane County to ask them to volunteer a few hours a month helping poor seniors who needed a will or were fighting scamsters or were attempting to get access to a program like disability insurance.

I got nearly every lawyer in town to agree—a heady experience for a 3L (third year law student), maybe even more exciting than working as the driver and aide to the once-and-future Senator from Oregon, Wayne Morse!

Morse won the Democratic primary in May.

He died of leukemia in July.

I'd just graduated from law school. I was devastated.

SIX

THE COURAGE TO
ENCOURAGE AND DISCOURAGE

N ot long after the shocking end to Wayne Morse's life and Senate campaign, I got a call from an energetic, 82-year-old, retired social worker from Portland named Ruth Haefner. My elder-advocacy had drawn attention. Would I, she asked, be willing to help her co-found an Oregon branch of the Gray Panthers?

Just for a moment, please take a step back in time with me. Since long before the Revolution, America has been home to interest groups and protest movements. The nation's Founders understood that pressure groups, which they called factions, were an unavoidable feature of life in a republic, and performed essential functions that kept governments in check. But factions could be dangerous in a democracy; they could get out of hand, take over governments, and become dictatorships, so they required their own checks and balances. Thus, our Founders' brilliance and our own history have bestowed on us a First Amendment that guarantees Americans' right to protest; and a tripartite government, consisting of the executive, the legislature, and the judiciary, which can register, assimilate, and, over time, turn many (but not all) of those protests into the law of the land.

By 1974, several protest movements had become important catalysts of groundbreaking Government activity. Under President Johnson, protesters, many of them courageous Black Americans who faced prison, beatings, and murder, had propelled the monumental Civil Rights Act of 1964 and Voting Rights Act, guaranteeing equal access to employment, education, housing, and political participation. Anti-war protests had led the Vietnam War to its negotiated close with the signing of the Paris Peace Accords in January 1973. Protests for women's rights hadn't yet gotten us (and still haven't) the Equal Rights Amendment to the Constitution, but they did provoke a spate of cultural and legal changes at the Federal and state level guaranteeing women increasing equality in the workplace, their homes, and in government.

But senior rights—that really hadn't crossed the threshold of public consciousness, not since 43,000 older, mostly poverty-stricken World War I veterans and their families had marched on Washington in 1932 to demand the benefits they'd been promised for their military service.

For most of American history since, senior citizens had been the invisible interest group, gratefully accepting benefits like Social Security and Medicare, but not organizing themselves to demand their rights.

That began to change in 1970, when a 65-year-old Buffalo, New York, native named Maggie Kuhn, in protest against a mandatory retirement law that required her to step down from a Presbyterian church job she adored, founded an organization with the unwieldy name Consultation of Older and Younger Adults for Social Change.

Four years later, during a guest appearance on *The Tonight Show*, Maggie and her protest group were likened by host Johnny Carson to the Black Panthers. He dubbed them the Gray Panthers.

Which was the name they had when Maggie's friend Ruth called me to ask if I'd start up a branch in Oregon.

Old enough to be my grandmother, Ruth Haefner had the spirit of a 20-something revolutionary. She shared Wayne Morse's congenital Midwestern progressive spirit. A 1918 University of Iowa graduate with a home economics degree who once had worked demonstrating canning techniques, she'd joined the NAACP in 1938—one of the first white women in their membership—and attended the 1940 Democratic National Convention as a delegate, voting to renominate Franklin Roosevelt for the Presidency.

By the time I met her, Ruth was referring to herself as a "wrinkled radical," whose zealotry was centered on older people—overlooked, exploited, and abused. She, Maggie Kuhn, and a handful of other aged crusaders aspired to transform their mistreatment with a five-point platform that was the essence of 20th century American social activism:

1. To generate positive awareness in our culture of the total lifespan of all persons as a continuing process in maturity, self-fulfillment, and social responsibility.
2. To strive for alternative lifestyles and opportunities for older and younger people which will challenge and help eliminate in our institutions and elsewhere all forms of paternalism, discrimination, segregation, and oppression based solely on age—which makes ageism, like racism and sexism, a socially destructive force.
3. To act as advocates for those who are powerless to throw off discrimination and oppression because of age.
4. To build a new power base in coalition with other movements to bring about needed change in order to achieve social justice, human dignity, and self-fulfillment for all people regardless of age, sex, race, or economic status.
5. To reinforce and support each other in our quest for liberation and to celebrate our shared humanity.

Was I willing to help the Gray Panthers realize their five principles of wrinkled radicalism? With several years' worth of Wayne Morse's demographic predictions ringing in my ears, I said yes. Besides, Ruth reminded me of an older version of my parents: Like my mom, she lived in a home surrounded by books and literature. Like my dad, she was gutsy as hell.

I took to the new role with gusto, stimulated by another Wayne Morse credo: Get there early and you can make sure the thing will work. Besides, "senior rights" was such a new concept—so new that if a town merely had a lunch program for older folks, that was considered a big deal—I was modestly confident we could make a difference.

From Senator Morse, I'd learned the famous Robert La Follette term from the early years of the progressive movement, that the states were "laboratories of democracy," and that's the way Ruth and I and our fellow Panthers treated our endeavor: Oregon was going to be a test center for improving seniors' lives.

Somewhat to my surprise, I discovered I enjoyed being a badass thorn in the side of the establishment. I was juggling three roles that, individually, didn't have a lot of clout attached but which, together, did offer an opportunity to exert influence over the state government, as well as over a culture that had rendered seniors invisible.

By day, I was working with a crackerjack administrator and office manager for Lane County named Jean Beachdel to build a Legal Aid Office to serve low-income seniors. Jean must have a size 9 halo above her head: more than a half-century on, she is still overseeing Lane County's Senior Law Service at the Oregon Law Center, "providing access to justice for people over 60." By night, with Ruth and the Gray Panthers, I'd sock it to out-of-touch politicians with the implied threat that I'd bring out their parents and grandparents en masse to protest the pols' misplaced priorities, which included putting the wishes of insurance companies before seniors. In between, I was teaching gerontology at the University of Oregon and at Portland State University, training more of my generation to advocate for the elderly.

Our threats to bring out older folks to campaign for their own rights wasn't idle. Oregon Governor Bob Straub, a Democrat of my parents' generation, early in his only term resolved to be an advocate for the elderly. When the state Senate, despite Straub's entreaties, refused to pass a bill that would lower the cost of dentures by allowing denturists to compete with dentists (the dentists, a powerful lobby, hated the bill), we brought busloads of older Oregonians down to Salem to excoriate them. We gathered enough citizens' signatures to get the bill onto the 1978 ballot, where it passed by a 3–1 margin.

Unsurprisingly, some state legislators took a dislike to our pressure, and to me personally, and even sought to investigate my Gray Panthers lobbying expenses, hoping to expose me as the only kind of lobbyist they'd ever known: a well-compensated one. They were disappointed to discover I had no big expenses. My lunches weren't at fancy steakhouses; they were takeout chicken from Fred Meyer supermarkets.

Ruth, Jean, and our merry band of seasoned citizens continued to notch up victories. We got a bill passed to appoint a gerontologist to the Oregon Mental Health Division. We fought the pharmaceutical industry and got a bill to lower prices on generic drugs. We were able to get the state to open an Office of Elderly Affairs in the Department of Human Resources.

Please, please, please understand that these bills—like all legislation—are not simply pieces of paper. I know it's easy to dismiss politicians when we wax on about "this act" or "that amendment" or "this statute" or "that rule." But all these acts, amendments, statutes, and rules that we were pushing through in Oregon then (and which I have continued to push in Washington in the decades since) mean help gets delivered to human beings in need.

With us, at that time, it meant that lawyers became available to help the elderly deal with door-to-door rip-off artists who peddled bogus home-repair swindles to lonely seniors. It meant that doctors were getting trained to understand and treat dementia in the elderly.

RON'S RULE OF CHUTZPAH

5

THERE ARE
TWO EQUALLY
IMPORTANT PATHS
TO PROGRESS:
START GOOD
THINGS AND STOP
BAD THINGS

It meant that banks couldn't cruelly foreclose on older people's homes without notice and intervention. It meant that nursing homes would be sanctioned and closed for cheating elderly patients out of their life savings. It meant that drug prices went down for people on fixed incomes.

With the Gray Panthers, I was learning a central principle of public life—and of leadership broadly—that no matter your profession or position, you have only two roles: Start good things or stop bad things.

The tools of this trade include incentives and disincentives. If you're starting or encouraging something, your leverage usually comes from funding—in the Government, that's the ability to allocate money, directly or through the Federal tax system. If your aim is to stop or discourage individuals or groups or companies from doing something harmful, aside from using the bully pulpit to jawbone the bad dudes into cleaning up their act, the Government can authorize penalties, through civil or criminal law or the tax code.

Doing good is hard, doing right is even harder. Stopping bad things is a necessary, constant, inescapable task, failing which, the good you do will be washed away.

⌢

Ruth liked to say, "Ron and I are perfect partners—I'm 82 and he's 28." The thing was, she treated 82 with the energy of a 28-year-old. And me, I learned that even a 28-year-old could make a real difference.

For sure, we didn't win everything, but I learned a ton about how making productive noise could make an enormous difference in the lives of real human beings. Oregon's senior citizens were my friends, my clients, and—my capable, committed volunteers.

After Wayne Morse's passing, the most exciting Democratic public figure in Oregon was a Portland activist and, later, state legislative leader named Vera Katz, who helped me take on Big Pharma at the legislature when we brought a large group of seniors to a hearing room and piled the witness table high with empty pill bottles of medicines they could not afford. I made another friend for life when I teamed up with a Legal Aid star, Steve Goldberg, to take on Big Insurance, which was then afflicting seniors with tons of private Medigap policies that claimed to plug holes in Medicare but didn't. To highlight both the uselessness and their impenetrability of these policies, we brought hundreds of seniors to Salem to demonstrate. Many carried magnifying glasses to showcase the murky fine print of these rip-off plans.

Talk about making productive noise!

Steve and I failed to pressure the legislature to take action then, so the scams continued with only modest progress against them. Insurance companies were happy to defraud seniors to beef up their next quarterly profit; most companies and too many individuals in this world focus exclusively on short-term gain. The insurance companies and their lobby kept the diddle going year after year while a colleague and I played the long game to outflank them. In 1990, U.S. Senator Tom Daschle and I pushed to passage a new Federal law forbidding insurers from selling Medigap policies to anyone who already owned one. The bill forced insurance companies to standardize their thousands of indecipherable, pathetic policies into 10 standard policies that could easily be compared with one another.

"The new law is a triumph," the *New York Times* wrote of our Medi-gap Fraud and Abuse Prevention Act. "For elderly Americans to spend meager incomes on redundant Medigap policies is an outrage about to disappear."

That's why you have to play the long game!

Win or lose, the more attention we got in Oregon, the more the powers-that-be chafed. In 1978, Governor Straub appointed me to the state Board of Examiners for Nursing Home Administrators—a selection that struck dread in the heart of a powerful industry that at the time had a firm grip on appointments to Government bodies that might hold them accountable. The nursing homes lobbied the state Senate, which rejected my appointment. The Governor told them to take a hike and swore me in—forcing an Oregon Supreme Court case on separation of powers that he (and I) won.

Through this period, I was learning that there's much more to chutzpah than making productive noise to do good in service to others. Like most of the tools in the tool chest in the basement of my house—like the hammers that have hard faces, cheeks, and ball peens or claws—chutzpah has several parts that make the complete tool much more functional than any of its parts.

To make productive noise, you first need to know it's not just creating shock value; any toddler dropping his diapers at a family gathering can do that. Productive noise, instead, is the ability to excite sustained attention to the objective you are trying to achieve.

As much as I wished that good, fix-up-the-world ideas could sustain attention on their merits alone, that's rarely the case in our culture. I was privileged to have been raised by Peter Wyden, a master storyteller, who'd long trained me in the power of a good yarn. He'd always repeat the same mantra to me: "Ron, tell them something they're interested in hearing about."

Voters, I learned quickly in public life, weren't interested in insurance regulations, but they sure as hell were interested in their grandparents' welfare. That was how I beat the system in Oregon. When the Gray Panthers started complaining about Medigap plan rip-offs, Insurance Commissioner Lester Rawls, a good man, but old school, retreated into closed rooms with industry lobbyists to cook up technical responses about why reform was impossible. That was no match for the story we kept pounding home every day, and the scenarios we drew to help people personalize that story: "These are your grandparents. We're not far past those years when older people who couldn't pay their bills went to poor farms. We built this safety net, particularly Medicare, to prevent that from ever happening again. But look at how much else we need to do."

The local media were an extraordinarily important factor in this equation. There was a wonderful reporter, Walli Schneider, with Portland's afternoon newspaper, the *Oregon Journal*, who had an almost inborn commitment to *tikkun olam*. Walli wrote about our crusade virtually every day in the mid to late 1970s. "A mélange of old and young whose furs get easily ruffled by social injustice," she called the Gray Panthers in a 1976 article.

Walli not only covered us as a social movement, she covered our issues, equally vividly. She gave extensive coverage to our 1976 "spring offensive" in which we asked Oregon residents to send their medical bills and written accounts of their medical experiences to Democratic Congressman Al Ullman, our "public target no. 1," because "he's the one who said there's no chance for a national health-care bill this year." She covered our assault against optometrists who illegally told the elderly that they had no choice but to buy their glasses from the doctors who performed their eye exams, without shopping around.

There's no question, Walli not only boosted our perceived power, she heightened our actual power. With her as our afternoon scribe and clarion, we Gray Panthers gradually perfected an essential element of chutzpah: how to command the narrative. Her coverage of our campaign to forcibly simplify supplemental insurance policies drew an unheard-of 300 senior citizens "jammed elbow to elbow in a hearing room," which was five times more than even we had anticipated.

We really weren't doing anything differently than what Walter Lippmann had described in his book *Public Opinion*, published in 1922. All people have mental models of the outside world and their own place in it, Lippmann wrote. "The pictures inside the heads of these human beings, the pictures of themselves, of others, of their needs, purposes, and relationships, are their public opinions," he said. "Those pictures which are acted upon by groups of people, or by individuals acting in the name of groups, are Public Opinion with capital letters." Getting things done (that's author Robert Caro's definition of power, as you may remember) meant adding to, reordering, redirecting, or otherwise influencing the pictures inside people's heads, to make, per Lippmann, "the unseen facts intelligible to those who have to make the decisions."

Gradually, I learned the craft of painting and rearranging the pictures inside people's heads. Playing off the examples of my senior mentors Maggie Kuhn and Ruth Haefner, older people would no longer be helpless and frail, but (in Walli Schneider's words) "plenty tough enough to growl, spit, and claw their way through bureaucratic red tape." Years later, in the U.S. Senate, the climate change portions of the Inflation Reduction Act of 2022 weren't about killing coal industry jobs in West Virginia—they were about adding many good, important, new jobs to West Virginia and across the United

States, in a transforming industry in which the U.S. Government would invest hundreds of billions of dollars, mimicking in modern times what FDR and LBJ had accomplished decades earlier with the Rural Electrification Authority and the Tennessee Valley Authority.

It's hard to convey how exciting this was to me in the late 1970s. I wasn't even 30. I wasn't making a lot of money. But my eldercare career was paying the rent and keeping me in cheeseburgers. I wasn't ambitious for anything else.

Then ambition knocked on my door.

One day in 1979, a group of my senior friends came to a meeting and said, "We never see our Congressman. He never talks about our issues. Tell us who we should support as a replacement!" Ever the dutiful son, I told them I'd check around. I didn't know the Congressman, Bob Duncan, except in passing, but I knew his popularity was shaky. A Democrat, he'd infuriated a lot of folks because he'd backed President Johnson on Vietnam, for which he'd lost one U.S. Senate race against the anti-war Republican Mark Hatfield, and subsequently two Democratic Senate primaries to my late mentor Wayne Morse.

I went to the library and collected names of the local politicians who might take on Duncan, and gave the list to the seniors. After a week or so, a delegation came back to me. "We know who we'd like to run!" they said.

"Who?" I asked.

"You know him," they responded. "Because it's you."

The idea was pure, old-school chutzpah. I, just 29, knew nothing about campaigning for Congress. I'd never run for anything before, not even student council. If I won, I would be one of the youngest representatives Oregon had ever sent to Washington. And such a big "if"! I was just a few years out of school. I'd been in Oregon for only seven years. Duncan, a World War II veteran, was nearing 60, had lived in Oregon for nearly three decades, was a powerful allocator of Federal transportation money, and had already run three statewide campaigns in addition to several successful state legislature and Congressional races.

Flattery has a way of overwhelming common sense. My gray-haired friends promised they'd make calls for me, put up campaign signs, and send letters to the editor on my behalf. But what won me over was when one of them looked me in the eye with a twinkle and, speaking both to me *and* of the voters, said: "Who can say no to their grandmother?"

She was right about me—I said yes—and hoped she was right about the voters.

The decision wasn't all casual, of course. I'd had a blast—professional and emotional satisfaction of the highest order—getting stuff done for the elderly in Eugene, Salem, and Portland. I'd learned I really could make a difference—that I could help vulnerable people. I had none of the advantages people associated with power in politics. I didn't have name recognition, a family that had been in elected office, a trust fund, or even minor celebrity-dom. But my senior patrons and I had managed to bust our way into public consciousness—and bust up the snug, antique relationships between state legislative leaders and their lobbyist buddies—and get terrific laws passed that shut down insurance scams that preyed on the elderly, ended nursing home abuses, and got good meals served to undernourished seniors in new senior citizens centers dotted across the state.

Moreover, the areas in which I was most interested, and where I knew the biggest differences could be made for seniors, were all Federal, such as Medicare. After years of study and toil, I felt I knew those issues better than anyone and believed I probably *could* make a difference in Washington.

Yes, the odds of unseating an incumbent in a party primary were more than long, but I had little to lose and a lot to gain on behalf of my activist friends and our issues. Besides, I persuaded myself that my recruiters were right—that the incumbent had lost touch with the district and its stakeholders, and he wouldn't pay me much attention. When asked about my challenge, Duncan pretty much shrugged his shoulders and dismissed me, saying, "My son likes him."

I announced in the fall, six months before the primary election. Two days later, all six-foot-four of me put on khaki slacks and a blue button-down shirt to meet my prospective bosses.

Those bosses were working class folk who lived primarily on Portland's east side. I was armed only with brochures and breath mints. I was more excited than nervous; I'd played ball in front of stadiums full of screaming fans and equally vocal opponents.

I began knocking on doors, and honestly, it was exhilarating. Everyone was cordial, a few folks were even engaged and asked me questions, mostly about classic Oregon concerns at the time like the parlous state of the timber industry, teacher pay, and gas prices (which, in those days of Arab oil embargoes and the Iranian hostage crisis, were skyrocketing). I kept eye contact with my would-be constituents. *Oh yeah, I got this!*

Everything was going swimmingly, until, at maybe my fifteenth house, my eyes registered two things about the prospective voter who had just answered the door.

First, he was munching on a Twinkie.

Second, he was wearing no clothes. Not a stitch.

I rapidly rifled through my mental copy of *Politics for Dummies*, only to realize there was no chapter on how to respond to a naked voter with a pastry. Utterly nonplussed, I handed over my brochure to the man—a photograph of me, a bunch of bullet points about my positions on seniors, economic development, environmental protection—and walked as calmly as possible back to the sidewalk, took a deep breath, and muttered to myself:

"Why am I here?"

Fortunately, there wasn't a lot of time for such existential dramas.

The campaign became a family affair. My mother would drop in from Palo Alto, my dad would travel in from Connecticut, even my grandmother Leni played a role. One night as the May primary was approaching, I returned to the home I shared with my then wife, Laurie, on Northeast Shaver Street in East Portland with my eyes itching like crazy from the springtime pollen. My grandmother said, "I've got the best eyedrops for allergies. You'll be better in five minutes!" I didn't even look, and just dropped them into my eyes.

About five minutes later, I lay prone on the floor, unable to open my eyes. My grandmother had given me her denture cream. Laurie came to the rescue: She practically threw me in the car and rushed me to the emergency room at Emanuel Hospital, where after two hours of flushing I was able to open my eyes again and continue the campaign. (Ron's Special Rule for Electoral Candidates: Read the labels!)

As Election Day neared, I got into a fight with the type of Big Media gatekeeper that had long aggravated my journalist father and my progressive grandfather.

Months earlier, I had chosen to put my very modest campaign budget into a paid television show I was creatively calling *Ask Ron Wyden*. We paid to run it multiple times on all four of the local TV stations, an advertising technique known as a roadblock. It was to be taped on May 18 at KATU, the ABC affiliate, and would begin airing the same day. The schedule was strategically timed so that multiple shows would be broadcast two days before the primary.

At 8:32 a.m. on Sunday, May 18, 1980, the Mount St. Helens volcano in southwest Washington State erupted, leaving Portland under a heavy coating of gray ash. Instead of spending a beautiful spring Sunday smelling the roses at Washington Park, every voter in the district was inside watching news about the volcano eruption on our four television stations.

When we arrived to tape, to our surprise one of the station managers, Skip Hinman, met us to say their rules did not allow us to purchase more than one airing, meaning they were going to deny us the original plan of multiple airings. My dad and I, recognizing the reach of those multiple shows, asked KATU management where the First Amendment limited our right to secure multiple broadcasts? The station management responded that there was no precedent for our buying multiple shows. That really got us riled up and we suggested that we would immediately sue them to advocate for our legal right to be heard (and figuring that, if nothing else, a lawsuit would provide additional exposure for our cause on the other stations and the local newspapers). The station backed down and the show was broadcast multiple times, as planned. But the incident left me with the sour taste for Big Media gatekeepers I have to this day.

Set up like a television telethon, it was a family affair: My mom, my grandmother, and Laurie answered the telephones, fielded live questions from voters, then ran the scrawled notecards down to my dad, the famous journalist and moderator, who grilled me. The campaign provided many more similarly sweet, rather than sour, experiences. As much as I hated asking people for money—and as much as I was perplexed by encounters like the one with the naked man and his Twinkie—I loved the town halls, the casual meetings, and just the plain chitchat with voters.

They appreciated me back. On May 20, 1980, I beat Bob Duncan—whom the seniors had complained was ignoring them, and who had certainly ignored me for most of the primary campaign—55,818 votes to 37,132.

In November, I crushed my Republican opponent by a 3–1 margin. I then prepared to return to Washington, a city I'd left as a lonely child of itinerant parents nearly a quarter-century before.

SEVEN

EMBRACING UNSCRIPTED MOMENTS

ongress is like high school or college in at least one respect: New friends materialize quickly to help you find your way. But not before they haze you.

In January 1981 in the U.S. House of Representatives, I couldn't even find my way to the cafeteria. Oklahoma Representative Mike Synar, a guy my age who'd been elected two years earlier, was one of the Democrats' orienteers, charged with getting us new kids acclimated. On the surface a gregarious good ol' boy, Mike was actually a fearless liberal intellectual at a time when his state still possessed a progressive populist streak left over from its Dust Bowl days. He was a great cook, loved visiting Oregon beaches, and was always surrounded by girlfriends. A literal Okie from Muskogee, he just wasn't oily enough for the Big Oil, Big Cattle, and Big Tobacco executives whose selfish interests he vigorously opposed.

It was hard not to love Mike Synar, who met an untimely death from cancer at age 45. I once went with him to a University of Oklahoma football game and donors' reception, where several fat cats who walked by us casually insulted him—"you're not one of us, go back to Berkeley"—which prompted me to explode: "Mike, if one more of these guys comes over and attacks you, I'm gonna stand up and start swinging."

Mike saw me early on the morning of Ronald Reagan's swearing-in to his first term as President. "You've got your top hat and tails, don't you?" he asked me.

"Uh, no," I replied. "Are we supposed to?"

"We're all wearing them," he said. He told me about a place in northern Virginia where I might be able to rent a last-minute set, so I drove furiously to the suburbs and found a tux whose sleeves and legs were too short. I looked like a drugstore Abe Lincoln, but what the hell. I hightailed back to the Capitol, donned the rental clothes in my office, and ran to the platform outside to take my place with the other Representatives and Senators.

Other than the new President, I was the only one dressed in a monkey suit.

I looked around and saw Mike Synar, doubled over in laughter. I squeezed by a group of colleagues and plaintively confronted him. "How could you do this to me?!" I asked.

"Man, you're in the big leagues now," Mike said between hysterical snorts. "Time to think for yourself."

Fortunately, this was in the days before our omnipresent iPhones, so I was able to jump out of the duds before anyone could take a picture of me. But I took in his advice, and my first thought to myself was the most basic: What exactly does Congress *do*?

The answer was as clear as the spring sky over eastern Oregon. My new job was exactly what I'd been doing with the Gray Panthers in Oregon, except on a grander stage: to use all the tools and levers of the Government to start good things and stop bad things from happening.

My second thought about my new position in Washington was

that I needed to widen my aperture of interests if I was going to be successful in accomplishing the things I cared about.

When I was running the Gray Panthers, I was blessed by the advantage of focus. We cared about one thing: aiding the elderly. Coming to Congress, I understood I could no longer be a single-issue guy. While a lone cause may propel your popularity, in the "big leagues" you no longer have the luxury of single-mindedness. When you get up in the morning, you have to juggle 10 different subjects. It's not that different than a CEO propelled into leadership after her success running sales, who now has to learn to care about an array of concerns—product, quality, supply chain resilience, costs, the talent pool…oh, and sales, too.

Several of those issues came up soon after the election when I had the good fortune to travel to Chicago with another newly elected Congressman, Sam Gejdenson of Connecticut. We were meeting with Linda Sher, the smart and feisty leader of the Joint Action Committee, a group of Jewish women who embodied chutzpah. They recognized that supporting Jewish causes meant supporting justice, including civil liberties, individual freedoms, and economic rights. Sam and I were there for their very first meeting with members where we discussed the ever-present and growing threat to the relatively new right to abortion. It was clear to me that this was an issue that required focus and determination.

And thus my third thought, very much obsessing me as I was shedding the infernal tailcoat that Mike Synar had duped me into renting: I had to get onto the right committees, and to land on those committees I needed patrons, senior members who might see me as a useful ally.

I thought I'd lost my most important patron before I'd even started. Almost immediately after winning my primary against veteran Democratic Representative Bob Duncan in May, I'd gotten a call from Toby Moffett, a young third-term Congressman from Connecticut who was cut from the same activist cloth as me. Toby had been an anti-war protester, a member of Nader's Raiders, and an environmental advocate before coming to Congress in 1975, and told me he was looking forward to welcoming me as a colleague if I could win the general election in November.

He then asked me: "Have you heard from Tip yet?"

"Uh, no. Was I supposed to?" I replied. It was becoming my mantra.

Toby's long pause told me all I needed to know.

Tip was Thomas P. "Tip" O'Neill Jr., then in the middle of his tenure as one of the longest-serving, most successful Speakers of the House in American history. It was a long tradition that the Speaker calls the winners of his party's primaries to give a preliminary welcome and pep talk to those who might be joining his caucus a few months hence. Tip, I learned, had been a close friend of Bob Duncan, the incumbent I'd vanquished. They'd both come up through the rough and tumble of local and state politics—unlike me, an utter neophyte. Tip's silence was ominous.

I fretted about how to turn things around.

The opportunity came several months later. The House offers a week-long orientation for new members after the general election but before their formal investiture. I came to Washington before the orientation started and asked the Speaker's office for an appointment. When it was granted, I put on my most serious dark suit (I only had one and was in the process of buying a second) and arrived at the Speaker's office in the Capitol. There I was met by Tip O'Neill himself. He was as big and broad-shouldered as his photographs would lead you to assume, with an impossibly full head of snow-white hair.

He looked at me gravely. The first thing he said was: "You beat a very, very good friend of mine."

RON'S RULE OF CHUTZPAH

6

EMBRACE THE UNSCRIPTED MOMENTS

I hadn't expected him to get right to it, but as I was learning quickly, a leader must embrace the unscripted moments. I took a deep breath, stood ramrod straight (giving me six inches on him), and delivered a monologue of earnest deference.

"Mr. Speaker," I said, "I greatly respect your long and close friendship with my predecessor, Congressman Bob Duncan. I want you to know I would very much appreciate your good counsel, Mr. Speaker, as I have never run for or been elected to public office. You may know my background is working with senior citizens, and I have long admired, Mr. Speaker, your strong advocacy for seniors in Massachusetts and here in Washington. I would consider it a great honor, Mr. Speaker, to pitch in with your staff and help in any way possible to tackle issues like the ones I've been addressing for seniors back home. I have read that you will try and work with the President wherever possible and that you said to the President, Mr. Speaker, that you and other longtime and loyal Democrats believe it is possible to keep our principles and help our great country."

At that point, I stopped, almost gasping, out of breath. Tip stared at me for a jowly moment. His grave expression then turned into a broad grin. "Look kid," he said, "you will do just fine around here."

I started breathing again. Chutzpah is most powerful when it's spontaneous. I had my first patron.

In formal settings, embracing unscripted moments can inject new life into an initiative or a campaign, and uncover the big "aha's" that no amount of preparation will ever surface. Fast-forward with me a few years, and consider the small but decisive role I played in my colleague Representative Henry Waxman's relentless 35-year campaign to get Big Tobacco to pay for killing millions of Americans with its deadly, addictive drug.

As Chair of the House Energy and Commerce Subcommittee on Health and the Environment, Henry had held the first Congressional hearings on smoking's risks in 1982. His tireless leadership had forced the tobacco companies to put more explicit health warnings on their products' packages, driven public awareness of the risks of second-hand smoke, and compelled the airlines to ban smoking. In 1994, he convened a hearing that featured for the first time the chiefs of what were then the seven major U.S. tobacco companies. He wanted them to respond to a new Food and Drug Administration report that affirmed the cigarette makers had deliberately manipulated their products to make them more addictive, even while hiding their actual levels of tar and nicotine.

For my Democratic colleagues and I, the goal was fact-finding, plain and simple. My Republican colleagues, especially those from the South, wanted none of it. The tobacco executives themselves sang from the same hymnal. No, they did not add nicotine to their products. No, "there is no justification for the FDA to regulate cigarettes as a drug."

This went on for seven hours! It was so predictable, repetitive, and scripted that I was ready to pack it up and leave.

But then I realized that no one had asked the most basic question of all.

So when my turn came, I pounced.

"Let me ask you first, and I'd like to just go down the row, whether each of you believes that nicotine is not addictive," I said. "I heard virtually all of you touch on it. Yes or no, do you believe nicotine is *not* addictive?"

One by one, they answered.

"I believe nicotine is not addictive, yes," said Philip Morris USA President and CEO, William Campbell.

"Mr. Congressman, cigarettes and nicotine clearly do not meet the classic definition of addiction. There is no intoxication," responded James W. Johnston, Chairman and CEO of the R. J. Reynolds Tobacco Company.

"I don't believe that nicotine or our products are addictive," followed U.S. Tobacco Co. President Joseph Taddeo.

"I believe that nicotine is not addictive," agreed Andrew H. Tisch, CEO and Chair of Lorillard Tobacco.

"I believe that nicotine is not addictive," repeated Edward A. Horrigan, CEO and Chair of the Liggett Group.

"I believe that nicotine is not addictive," Brown & Williamson Chair and CEO Thomas E. Sandefur said.

"And I, too, believe that nicotine is not addictive," said Donald S. Johnston, the Chair and CEO of American Tobacco Company.

They were under oath. And they lied.

Subsequent hearings uncovered internal company research and other industry documents proving the companies' prevarications. One of the companies, Brown & Williamson, sued Waxman and me personally, arguing that we were illegally using materials that had been stolen from them—an argument that got thrown out by the Federal courts. The companies' lies and the documentary evidence impelled whistleblowers to step forward with more damning testimony.

In 1998, four years after our hearing put the tobacco companies back on their heels, the attorneys general of 46 states, five U.S.

territories, and Washington, DC, forced them into a settlement. The companies agreed to pay $368.5 billion over 25 years to treat people with smoking-related ailments and to fund education campaigns to reduce smoking by young people. The Master Services Agreement, as it's called, also banned tobacco advertising aimed at kids, prohibited cartoons in cigarette ads, eliminated outdoor advertising for cigarettes, and put on permanent public display the millions of tobacco industry materials that documented the industry's legacy of lies.

Never let unprepped opportunities pass you by. A successful leader must welcome them as invitations to learn, and advance.

⌐

If House Speaker Tip O'Neill was my first older patron in Congress, my second certainly was Claude Pepper, the legendary former U.S. Senator from Florida, an outspoken liberal and Southern civil rights activist who had done something almost unheard of in American history—returned to Washington as a member of the Lower House more than a decade after concluding his tenure in the Senate, from which position he actually *grew* his influence. Claude was responsible for abolishing mandatory retirement ages for Federal employees; he also wrote the legislation creating the National Cancer Institute. When I met him, he was the 81-year-old Chair of the House Select Committee on Aging, which he was using as a bully pulpit both to advance new laws and services to aid the elderly, and as a bulwark against the Reagan Administration's proposals to eviscerate Social Security, Medicare, and Medicaid. Claude was a living, breathing model of chutzpah. He reinforced what I'd already observed in Wayne Morse: You've got to be audacious in taking on the powerful.

Claude invited me to serve on his Committee on Aging. He was like my earlier role models Ruth Haefner and Maggie Kuhn, a rich bundle of passionate energy who would not let age and its infirmities slow him down. Three months after I joined Congress and his Committee, we issued the report *Elder Abuse: An Examination of a Hidden Problem*, which concluded that "1 million Americans are physically, financially, and emotionally abused by their relatives or loved ones nationally." The report introduced the term "elder abuse" into the social policy lexicon, and led 21 states to join 16 existing states in enacting laws to provide reporting on elder abuse or to fund remedies for victims. Our 1985 follow-up study recommended Federal support for families to care for older relatives, buttressing the state activity. Claude's Select Committee became a platform for me to do at a national scale what I'd been doing in Oregon (learning the ropes means you can start climbing those ropes). I used my escalating seniority to introduce long-term-care insurance tax reform, Medicare improvements, insurance-scam penalties, and other innovations I couldn't have dreamed of in Eugene or Salem.

However elevated its stage, though, a Select Committee was not as meaningful or actionable as having a formal membership on a committee with jurisdictional authority. Committee assignments are everything in the House, literally the difference between consequence and obscurity. Because of my history with the Gray Panthers, I set my sights on the powerful House Energy and Commerce Committee, the oldest committee in the House of Representatives, and by far its broadest, with authority over the issues of greatest concern to Oregonians, including energy, climate, and environmental policy, and oversight of my professional passion, health care: Everything from Medicare and Medicaid to pharmaceutical regulation to biomedical research to supervision of the National Institutes of Health fell under the Energy Committee's control.

My new posse of more experienced young members—Mike Synar, Toby Moffett, the beloved progressive Ed Markey, who still serves with me in the Senate—and even the pals I was making in Tip O'Neill's office (his press secretary, Chris Matthews; Ari Weiss, the Speaker's legislative craftsman; and Jack Lew, his top economic aide and later Secretary of the Treasury) told me I was more likely to grow a second head than get onto Energy and Commerce as a first-termer from the Pacific Northwest.

I figured I had nothing to lose by making a bit of productive noise.

From Election Day through the first weeks of a new session of Congress, the Capitol's anterooms and the halls of the Rayburn, Longworth, and Cannon House Office Buildings pulse with gossip about who's going to get what and why. Leadership's job is intricate and tense. To take, maintain, or extend their majority, they want everyone in their party to win, so they want to do right by everybody. At the same time, there are only so many coveted positions, and leadership needs to make sure that the important committees, in particular, have the right balance of skills, geographies, discipline, and power arrangements to pass important legislation.

During these intervals between Congresses, paying attention to the hallway and anteroom chatter can be crucial. I knew that because I was Peter Wyden's son—the man who taught me, "You've got to listen. Most people don't listen enough."

I heard that House Majority Leader Jim Wright of Texas would personally be making the Energy Committee assignments, and that he potentially had three Democratic slots to fill. I further learned that he already had other freshman candidates locked into two of those seats: Ralph Hall of Texas and Billy Tauzin of Louisiana, both of them Big Oil enthusiasts from the South. I heard nothing about the third seat, leading me to believe it was still up for grabs. Before anyone else had time to weigh in, I asked to meet with the Majority Leader.

I didn't make the case I'm sure he was anticipating—that he needed a westerner from a hydropower state to balance out the interests of oil-producing states, or that he needed someone like me to appease the inevitable grumbling from the Democrats' environmental constituencies. A fearless old World War II bombardier and a masterful pol who'd worked his way up from small town mayor to Congressional powerhouse, Jim Wright was not easy to hornswoggle. Instead, I used a bit of homespun affability to hint that he might win me over to his constituents' point of view.

"If you sit me between Billy Tauzin and Ralph Hall," I offered, "you can tell all your energy allies that you got this northwestern environmentalist constantly marinating in oil."

Wright burst out laughing, volunteered that no one had ever made a "more creative" case for an assignment, put me on the powerful committee at age 31, and became my third patron. (Note to future Congressmembers and anyone looking for a promotion: Do not check your chutzpah at the door! At worst, the boss says no; at best, you get the assignment.)

My fourth patron was both one of my best teachers and my earliest and most terrifying competitor.

John D. Dingell Jr. of Michigan was among the most powerful members of Congress ever. He served for 59 straight years, a record, and followed his father, who'd held the seat for the preceding 22 years. Known in the halls of Congress as "Big John" (and, behind his back, as "The Truck") he was nearly my height but had 50 solid pounds on me. His life was as outsized as his physique. He loved to regale colleagues with tales of his hunts for big game; several heads, including an antelope and a whitetail he'd shot, were mounted on the walls of his Congressional office. He was so cultured that in one moment he could rapturously describe a ballet he'd attended, then with little segue "tell you how to gut an elk without getting any blood above the second knuckle," a former aide once recalled.

Big John was the Chair of the Energy and Commerce Committee when Jim Wright appointed me to it. Health care was a special priority of his; his father had introduced a universal health-care bill in 1943, and John Jr. reintroduced it every year from 1955 until his retirement, one of the 500 health-care bills he sponsored or co-sponsored during his career. Given my background, he was happy to have me on his back bench.

In addition to chairing the full Energy and Commerce Committee, John took on the Chairmanship of its Subcommittee on Oversight and Investigations, and hung in its chambers a photo of the Earth taken from space, to illustrate how sprawling its authority was. Legislative hearings—the kinds of things you read about in high school civics (if you grew up in the days when high schools required civics)—are among the more familiar activities of Congress. For instance, a member has written a bill and assembled co-sponsors. Should we reinstitute the Federal tax deduction for state and local taxes? Should we fund the building of a new type of aircraft carrier? The relevant subcommittee chair arranges a hearing. Witnesses march in to tell the subcommittee why they oppose or favor the legislation. Industry, labor, and NGO lobbyists weigh in with their opinions and proposed revisions. Staff huddles to pull it all together into a revised bill. If the subcommittee votes it out, the bill makes it to the parent committee, and if it succeeds there, it makes its way to the full House. If it passes that sluice and the Senate has done likewise, the bill is reconciled in a bicameral conference committee, and then makes its way to the President for his signature. Very pro forma.

Oversight and investigations are anything but. These can be the stuff of Hollywood drama. (And sometimes are: One fabulous example is *The Insider*, a movie about the lies told by tobacco companies, which even features the moment I caught industry executives in their big lie.) Congress can pretty much look into anything it wants, as long as it might have a bearing on future legislation. John Dingell's Subcommittee on Oversight and Investigations once held 42 hearings in 56 days, on such topics as the fraught state of the nation's blood supply, insurance industry insolvencies, insider trading, flaws in the U.S. Customs Service, benzene in sparkling water, and defense industry procurement abuses.

Two traits characterized John's approach to investigations. The first was his bipartisanship.

John was as philosophically partisan as they come, a New Deal Democrat to his bones. Working people and their labor unions were sacrosanct. Corporations oppressing average Americans must be punished. Health care is a right. With his muscle and his craftsmanship, he could have steamrolled over a lot of Republican opposition. Yet as an investigator, John, a former county prosecutor, was as impartial as they come. He strived to build coalitions, reduce inter-party disputes, and cut deals that would expose objective truths that could produce effective laws. Equally important and unusual, he made sure committee staff operated collegially and across party lines.

The second thing I learned by observing John was how to ask questions.

Yes, my father was a journalist who asked questions for a living. And yes, I'd been a citizen-advocate who'd been in dozens of hearing rooms since I'd graduated from law school. But I'd never been a reporter, or a prosecutor, or a trial lawyer. John showed me that inquiry, done right, is one of the most powerful tools of an enterprise.

As Presidential historian Richard E. Neustadt affirmed, a President's power derives in large part from his willingness to avidly seek information, even to the point of pitting aides against each other in his presence, to better expose new data and differing points of view that can lead him to the right decision and give him the raw material to persuade others to follow his lead. That's an essential principle for anyone who aspires to lead anything.

John had presence, and he knew how to use it in organizing and leading a hearing. He could be courteous to a fault, and he could use that civility to embarrass witnesses, if he felt they deserved it. Once, conducting a hearing on the illegal activities of Drexel Burnham Lambert, the disgraced junk bond investment firm, he was about to question a bank executive, when the witness's attorney haughtily offered to provide the Committee a lesson on securities laws. Chairman Dingell readily agreed, and told the attorney that he required all witnesses before his Subcommittee to testify under oath. The lawyer assented. But just as he was about to take the oath, the witness was informed by John, "If you are sworn, you do waive the attorney-client privilege." That meant anything he said could be used against him...and his client. Having thus been chastened in front of his own client, the attorney then declined to testify.

John Dingell also was a mass of purely American ambiguities. Perhaps most consequentially, he was both a powerful environmentalist, who had written much of the Endangered Species Act and played instrumental roles in passing the Clean Water Act, the National Environmental Policy Act, and much more; and he was an aggressive advocate for the auto industry and especially its labor unions, which accounted for and represented most of the employment in his hometown of Dearborn, Michigan. It wasn't inevitable that we would come into conflict, but because he'd taught me so much about playing in the Big Leagues, I didn't shy from it when the time came.

It happened at the exact moment I was joining the committee. The Clean Air Act, first passed in 1970, was a favorite scapegoat of Ronald Reagan. Its reauthorization was set to expire in September 1981, and the new Administration wanted to take the opportunity to gut it. Dingell figured he could partner with the Republican Administration and the new Republican Senate majority to eliminate some of the requirements the auto industry hated, while still holding the line on other environmental causes he deeply favored.

His longstanding opponent on the committee was Henry Waxman of Los Angeles. The two had serious differences of opinion on environmental issues, especially regarding automobiles. They had been skirmishing for years before I joined the Energy Committee. Almost as soon as the 1980 election results were in, Henry and his blue state environmental allies, and John, with auto, steel, and machine manufacturers and chamber of commerce folks in his corner, started assembling their respective teams. Each began recruiting. Although he never thought I'd get on the prestigious Energy and Commerce Committee, Henry called me shortly after I defeated Bob Duncan in the primary just to introduce himself. When, shockingly, I was appointed, he called me within hours to ask me to make the Health Subcommittee he chaired my first choice for a subcommittee. (Twist my arm—I wanted to be on his subcommittee almost as much as life itself!) John, always exquisitely prepared, knew almost as much about his members' states as we did ourselves. His Clean Air Act discussions with me involved few requests that weren't procedural. "Just give me a heads up" was his primary ask, should something important to him appear on the horizon.

My instincts and my district were far more aligned with Waxman than with Dingell. John felt the clean air rules that were written in the decade before I joined the Energy Committee put "hardships" on Michigan's industries. Among other things, he was taking aim at motor vehicle emission control durability requirements and the legal standards to protect agriculture and the general welfare, while thwarting the Government's ability to sue polluters. It would have diluted environmental protections for national parks and recreation areas, a program known as the Prevention of Significant Deterioration, or PSD, by allowing the states more leeway to raise pollution thresholds for those areas. At home in Oregon, though, our folks lived by the "polluter pays" doctrine, a simple legal concept by which the costs of cleaning up environmental pollution are allocated proportionally among the polluters.

From day one it looked like a bare knuckles fight. Oregonians certainly did not want to turn back the clock on air pollution; even if they didn't know what the PSD standard was, they wouldn't countenance the effects of its abandonment. Chairman Dingell's counter-argument could be summarized in the one word he repeated constantly when using his legendary persuasive powers to bring the rest of the committee's Democrats around to his point-of-view: "jobs." A potent word, especially as the 1982 midterm election grew closer.

Age 31 and green as Oregon ryegrass, unless I figured out a different political (and substantive) path, I would find myself right in the middle of a titanic battle between John Dingell's industries and Henry Waxman's national environmental groups that had backed my election.

I stayed up night after night trying unsuccessfully to come up with something that might allow me to navigate the perilous waters, struggling to find the right policy while not destroying my relationship with Dingell in my first few months on his committee.

Enter Danny Saltzman.

A native Portlander five years my junior, with environmental engineering degrees from Cornell and MIT, Danny was one of my first hires in my Washington office. Quiet and instinctively kind, Dan started brainstorming with me out-of-the-box ideas that might possibly change the Clean Air Act debate from a zero-sum contest between industry and environmentalists into a smart policy framework that could win support across the political spectrum.

The more we talked, the more we came to believe we had a generational advantage. As with the Internet and AI debates today, young people often are quicker to use an inherent technological savvy to resolve problems that have been gridlocked because older generations could not overcome their habituation to outdated methods.

Danny and I decided to intertwine two ideas in an attempt to transform a retreat into an advance: We could protect our parklands *and* help the auto industry. That is, instead of starting with the proposition that one side must lose—"jobs *versus* trees"—we'd develop a policy structure that was forward-looking for the automotive industry. We encapsulated our concept in the phrase "technological backsliding": If we disemboweled existing pollution controls and allowed nitrogen and carbon monoxides to spread in national parks and recreation areas, we argued, we'd be discouraging automakers from producing the very things Americans, in poll after poll, said they wanted: cleaner cars and less pollution in their communities. Any short-term victory would be a devastating long-term loss for Detroit, as U.S. consumers continued to flock to more technically advanced foreign vehicles whose makers were investing fervidly in innovation.

Danny and I had developed a lane to which few had given much thought—using new technologies to further innovation and development in old-line industrial sectors, while protecting the environment. This wasn't necessarily a comfortable place to be. Organizations fear change. Large, historically successful organizations fear it even more—but change happens regardless. Yet if America's Big Four automakers had not been forced to face the changes that were happening in the world, then all of them would have suffered the bankruptcy and dissolution that Chrysler and AMC already were heading toward, and America would be weaker for it.

John was sure he could win by melding industrial state Democrats and anti-regulation Republicans, and he had already signaled his discontent with our approach. Henry was busy courting our fellow majority Democrats, and he took no prisoners in his public comments, calling Dingell's efforts to negotiate a pro-industry outcome "an unholy alliance held together by greed."

We thought there was a third coalition that could be blended: environmentalist Democrats together with Republicans who were strong conservatives on most issues like taxes and defense, but who had local constituencies with strong environmental interests in parks and recreation. Other young members of the committee similarly saw that we might be able to rearrange the classic tradeoffs in new ways. Six months of grinding work in markup—the committee working sessions in which a bill is read, amended, and voted on, section by section, until the committee agrees to send the bill to the floor—looked like they might shape the new dynamic we were seeking.

And on April 28, the Committee voted 25–13 to stop the Dingell Express and approve my amendment to keep the Prevention of Significant Deterioration standard intact. Pundits and members alike were surprised that Republicans like Matt Rinaldo of New Jersey, New York's Norm Lent, and Dan Coats of Indiana voted with me (and their own constituents) to protect America's treasures.

With these losses, Chairman Dingell felt forced to adjourn the Committee for several weeks. But the damage to his cause had been done. Although his beloved auto industry and its unions favored the emergent legislation because it loosened some of their specific obligations, the bill fortified constraints on other industries. As a result, the coalition that the Chairman had painstakingly assembled fragmented, and the bill never made it to the floor of the House. The existing standards—the ones we wanted to protect, if we couldn't yet strengthen them—remained intact. We stopped a bad thing from happening—and at the same time, started propelling a very good thing: the retooling of the U.S. auto industry.

It was the rare major vote on the environment lost by heavy industry, and a big victory for those of us who believed that a clean Earth is a first priority. As important to me personally, I kept the respect of John Dingell Jr., and I have remained a dear friend to his widow and able successor, Debbie Dingell, to this day.

EIGHT

IDEAS MATTER

Mentors, patrons, allies, and colleagues are vital. So is the process of coaching them into a team or shaping them into a coalition. But of course, people and process are only two-thirds of the equation for getting things done. As Danny Saltzman and I showed during our successful effort to keep the air in America's national parks clean, you can't get anywhere without the third component: ideas. Ideas are "the what"—the core mechanism that starts a good thing or stops a bad thing. You don't need people, process, and ideas in equal measure to realize every goal you want to achieve, but you always need bits of each if you're going to try to change the world.

There's a library full of academic scholarship on what ideas are, where they come from, and how they work in policymaking. At a lofty level, I like this definition by the Dutch leadership expert Dr. Marij Swinkels of the Utrecht University School of Governance: Ideas can be sense-making frameworks that "guide people's actions," strategic tools "that actors use to craft political discourse," or "institutional frameworks that have an effect on their own and maintain some order throughout the actions of individuals, groups, and society."

But I can boil it down into simpler language: Ideas are the seeds of change; find them and plant them wherever and whenever you can, then let them grow until you can reap their bounty.

Ideas are distinct from an ideology or belief system, which is more comprehensive and structured. But ideas can derive from an ideology, contribute to the formation of an ideology, or both. Most importantly and most practically, you can't implement a belief system, at least not directly, but you can implement an idea. Ideas are your building blocks, the products and services and undertakings that realize your mission.

RON'S RULE OF CHUTZPAH

7

IDEAS ARE THE SEEDS OF CHANGE; FIND THEM AND PLANT THEM WHEREVER AND WHENEVER YOU CAN

An ideology without ideas is a form of mental masturbation: It might make you feel good, but it produces nothing of value. The current destruction of the Republican Party as an effective governing force rests on its abandonment of ideas, as represented in the fatuous (and thankfully unsuccessful) quest of the MAGA Ohio Congressman Jim Jordan to become Speaker of the House. The preamble to the U.S. Constitution charges the Congress with the development and implementation of ideas that "establish Justice, insure domestic Tranquility, provide for the common defense, promote the general Welfare, and secure the Blessings of Liberty to ourselves and our Posterity"—a summary of affirmative *actions* that literally constitute the practical functions of a nation. Yet here is an angry man who, over the course of 17 years in Congress, has never sponsored a bill that became law, but who claimed to have the skills and experience to lead the world's greatest law-making enterprise. Imagine the CEO of a consumer products company who never introduced a consumer product, or a basketball player who never touched a ball. You can't. From a Constitutional perspective, the Jim Jordan Republicans, wrapped in a smothering ideology devoid of ideas, are as corrosive as they come.

For political leaders especially, though, an ideology does serve a crucial purpose: It is the sieve that helps you filter a river of ideas into the relative handful of gold nuggets that might excite the enterprise. The biases that make this sifting process manageable (think of these as the cells in a sieve, or the little holes in a spaghetti colander) can come from many places: your parents' moral guidance, school teachers, the mentors who guide you at different stages of life, friends, bull sessions, books, hackathons. As in buffets, and so in life: You can't eat everything, so your tastes guide you. Ideology is a human being's moral, ethical, and political taste.

My ideology is the equivalent of a basketball team plus one reserve: People come before corporations. A clean Earth is a prerequisite for human survival. Freedom of communication is a basic human right. Liberty and security are not mutually exclusive. Health care is personal. Science transcends politics. I think of this ideology and the ideas I filter from it as practical progressivism. (A number of my colleagues give it a different label: "Oh, that's just Ron.")

An idea can be as grandiose as making electric vehicles a mainstream form of transportation in the United States. It can be as local as creating a farmers market for fresh vegetables in your hometown. An idea can be both idealistic and practical at the same time—like bringing Advanced Placement math or English to a school district that's never had AP courses before.

An idea also can be about visualizing a future and clearing the path toward it. Let me give you an example.

By 1995, near the end of my tenure in the House of

Representatives, I knew that Oregon needed to diversify its economy. Our forest products sector was and would always be vitally important, but I wanted to find new industries for Oregon, as well. One of my favorite conversation partners in that quest was Christopher Cox, a conservative, Republican Congressman from one of the strongholds of Republican conservatism, Orange County, California.

You non-Beltway readers (I hope that's most of you) may be surprised that one of my friends in Congress was a man whose political and cultural sensibilities were so different than mine. And they were: Chris had gone to an all-male, all-Catholic military school in Minnesota before getting both an MBA and a law degree from Harvard, then rising to a partnership at one of Washington's most powerful law firms, a position he left to join Ronald Reagan's second Administration. As President Reagan's Associate General Counsel, Chris shepherded three Supreme Court nominations, including that of Antonin Scalia, arguably the most conservative Justice of the 20th century. I was senior to Chris in Congress—he was elected eight years after me, in 1988—but his energy and Reaganite bona fides had rapidly made him a star in his party: In '95, he'd just been named Chair of the House Republican Policy Committee, the fifth-highest elected leadership position in their conference.

Despite those differences, Chris and I became true partners. He'd been a college jock like me (his game was soccer). He had an infectious curiosity and enthusiasm (Chris had once won $5,400 competing on the television game show *Password*). We were both amateur tech geeks (Chris built his own computer). We both looked up to each other professionally, and personally we had chemistry.

Chris and I had a weekly lunch in a small space near the official House dining room where members could grab a quick bite from a buffet and find a seat mate to visit or a quiet place to read. Occasionally, we'd get others to join us, specifically targeting a couple of the other young guys and women who cared about technology, innovation, and "fresh thinking"—which was our young-Congressperson code for breaking through the fustiness and crustiness of the seniority system to (how can I put this politely…I know, I'll use asterisks again!) get s*** done.

That day in 1995, Chris's and my shared appetite for technology, innovation, and action landed squarely on a newfangled invention called the Internet.

It's hard to overemphasize how strange the Internet was in 1995. Only about 20 million people in the U.S. had access to it. The Netscape Navigator browser, which enabled the seamless delivery of visual web pages over dial-up phone lines, was less than two years old. There were only some 100,000 websites (today, there are more than 2 billion) and most of today's most trafficked and popular Internet destinations did not exist, including Facebook, Twitter, Google, and TikTok.

Yet there was something transformative about the Internet. The Yahoo search engine (search engines were still being compiled by hand!) could direct you to multiple sites devoted to old comic books or new sports teams. A Seattle Internet company, Amazon, was giving readers access to almost any book that was then in print. Another little Seattle startup named Progressive Networks (later changed to RealNetworks), where one of my best Senate friends, the tech-savvy and low-income-housing champion Maria Cantwell once worked, had just streamed the first live baseball game over the Internet. About a quarter of American adults were writing to each other using "email." The Internet was still esoteric for the majority of Americans, but among techies, it was exciting and very promising, "one of the hottest new markets to develop in years," according to Morgan Stanley, the investment bank. It was exactly the kind of acclaim to hasten the heartbeats of two Congressmen in their 40s whose biggest interests included creating tons of good jobs in their districts.

Chris Cox needed those jobs: The Los Angeles area had been a center of the aerospace industry for decades, but the end of the Cold War had battered the sector. What's more, because of financial mismanagement by local officials, Orange County had gone bankrupt less than two years earlier. Chris's district needed some good economic news.

My story was a bit different. In '95, the Oregon economy was booming—"help wanted" signs were everywhere, and Oregon was experiencing one of the largest net in-migrations in its history from job seekers. That represented a notable shift in the state's economy, which through most of our history had been relatively insular, and hadn't birthed a lot of companies that exported goods and services to the rest of the world. But Intel had moved major chip-making operations to Washington County, Oregon, near my Congressional district, in 1974. A completely different kind of homegrown, tech-forward Oregon company, Nike, had prospered astronomically since its founding in 1964. I believed that sort of technology-centered business development would guarantee jobs and growth for my constituents in the decades ahead.

But there were two problems with our vision for the burgeoning Internet economy, and that was what consumed Chris and me that day as we consumed our burgers: Congress, and the courts.

Congress was in the midst of a major, much-needed repair of one of the most important pieces of economic and cultural legislation of the 20th century, the Communications Act of 1934. That bill had established the Federal Government's authority to regulate the telephone industry and the broadcast spectrum; created the Federal Communications Commission to oversee the regulation; effectively recognized and created legal boundaries limiting AT&T's monopoly over telephone service; and gave the Government the power to license the publicly owned spectrum to radio (and later, television) stations. It was the foundation of the telecommunications era.

Sixty-one years later, that legislation was badly in need of an overhaul. Primarily, the Government needed to remove the heavy hand of regulation and spur competition within an industry that was rapidly decentralizing and disintermediating. Not at all incidentally, the Telecommunications Act update that was winding its way across Capitol Hill was getting its paws into the Internet, mostly for the beneficial purpose of, as the Brookings Institution put it, "accelerat[ing] the deployment of an advanced capability that will enable subscribers in all parts of the United States to send and receive information in all its forms—voice, data, graphics, and video—over a high-speed switched, interactive, broadband, transmission capability."

That wasn't good enough for some members of Congress. Where legislators like Chris Cox and I saw jobs and economic growth in the Internet and its newest subdivision, the World Wide Web, they saw something else: pornography.

As the Telecommunications Act revision was being debated in 1995, a censorious senior member of the U.S. Senate, James Exon from Nebraska, read a prayer into the Congressional Record that asked "Almighty God" for "the wisdom to create regulations" aimed at "controlling the pollution of computer communications." Fine sentiments, but attacks on the First Amendment are often cloaked in such high language—disguising the existential threat they pose to the foundations of our freedoms and our Republic. Even in the mature democracies of Europe and Asia there are greater controls on the freedom of speech—controls that serve to protect the wealthy, the powerful, and the crooked—sometimes one in the same. With the great share of human communication moving onto the Internet, Senator Exon and his cohort were threatening to bring those controls to the American marketplace of ideas.

A conservative Democrat and the founder of a Nebraska office supply company that bore his name, Jim Exon hadn't had a particularly distinguished career in the Senate. He was more famous for forcing Esso, the oil company, to pay him off when it wanted to change its name to Exxon. But now he planned to introduce a bill to ban "obscene, indecent, and destructive" content from the Internet. He had earlier failed to get his proposal inserted into the new Telecommunications Act, so now he was opting to introduce his own bill, the Communications Decency Act, as an amendment to the other bill—an amendment that would be hard for members to vote against. It was explicitly intended to prevent anyone under the age of 18 from encountering "any comment, request, suggestion, proposal, image or other communication that, in context, depicts or describes, in terms patently offensive as measured by contemporary community standards, sexual or excretory activities or organs."

Not only would the writers and producers and posters of said indecencies face fines or jail, so would the websites on which they were posting. Even the Internet service providers that enabled access to these sites could be criminally liable. Such liability would have strangled the Internet in its cradle.

Senator Exon's proposal was unscathed by an understanding of networks, the First Amendment, or any aspect of the dawning Internet Age. The original Communications Act was grounded on the assumption of "natural" monopolies in telephony and broadcasting—on the belief that only giant companies like AT&T,

RCA, and NBC could muster the resources to build, run, and maintain enormous technology networks with wires, cables, and towers connecting thousands of stations and millions of homes. Based on political concepts pioneered by a diverse array of leaders from both parties, including Teddy Roosevelt *and* Franklin Roosevelt *and* Woodrow Wilson *and* Herbert Hoover, there was a further assumption that these giant private entities needed a similarly enormous counterparty, the U.S. Government, to regulate them.

Fast-forward to Jim Exon, who figured if the Government had been able to regulate broadcast speech for so many decades (through mechanisms like the FCC's licensing procedures and its so-called fairness doctrine), then it could justifiably and realistically regulate Internet speech.

Only it wasn't realistic in the least. Whereas there were some 15,000 radio stations and 1,700 TV stations in the U.S. at the time, and only a handful of national networks, "on this new medium," as Chris wrote in a later retrospective, "the number of content creators—each a 'broadcaster,' as it were—was the same as the number of users. It would soon expand from hundreds of millions to billions." Chris knew where this was going.

And Chris and I both understood that it was physically impossible for the Government, the service providers, or the platforms to review in advance the avalanche of Internet content that was already being created to screen out anything that might be "indecent." Exon's proposal was a recipe for vast, new, intrusive, and ultimately ineffective Government bureaucracies, rivaling the worst of the Soviet Union's oppressive regime. You can see this happening today in Florida, where MAGA Governor Ron DeSantis's offensive and unconstitutional "Don't Say 'Gay'" law is generating large new state and local government bureaucracies whose role is to authorize whether school libraries may carry Merriam-Webster dictionaries, and whether boys require parental permission slips to be called by their nicknames in class. Exon's own proposals to overcome the pre-screening problem were even more frighteningly Big Brother-ish, including empowering the telephone companies to snoop on their users' communications to find and eliminate any indecencies. This snooping, as Chris later wrote, "would have to destroy the real-time feature of the technology that made it so useful."

Not that that was going to stop the U.S. Senate! Fewer than half the Senators then had email. (Our colleagues in "the people's body" weren't much better—barely a quarter of House members had email.) Exon's bill passed 84–16, and we were pretty sure the House was going to follow suit. Who wanted to appear weak on porn?

The court system didn't look like it was going to offer the Internet much hope. As early as 1991, in a case involving CompuServe, one of the first popular online services, a Federal district court had held that CompuServe could not be considered a publisher, and thus liable for any civil or criminal content posted on the site by users, because it didn't engage in any form whatsoever of content screening, editing, or control. It was, the court said, more akin to a warehouse for user content.

But then the New York State Supreme Court issued a contradictory decision that online service providers *could* be held liable for postings made by their users—even if those service providers played no active role in generating that content.

The case, Stratton Oakmont, Inc. v. Prodigy Services Co., involved a forum devoted to financial discussions on the now-defunct Prodigy network. On it, an anonymous user had posted a claim that Stratton Oakmont, a Long Island investment banking firm (and the subject of the film *The Wolf of Wall Street*), had committed fraud in an IPO. The bank sued both the unidentified user and Prodigy for defamation, arguing that Prodigy was a publisher—just like Random House in the book industry or Steve Forrester's East Oregonian Publishing Company in the newspaper biz—and was responsible for those postings, just as any other publisher would be. Because Prodigy posted content guidelines and deployed software to screen posts for foul language, the Court agreed.

The case struck at the very heart of the Internet's novelty and value, which was its ability to allow users to communicate not just one-to-one with each other (as the phone system had enabled for more than a century) but one-to-many, in myriad configurations, in a super-customizable form of broadcasting. CompuServe, Prodigy, and other early online services had grown because they allowed users to set up many different types of forums to exchange information and opinions with each other about their interests. Their successors, who were building all sorts of novel sites and services on the World Wide Web, were growing even more dramatically, because they were providing simple tools and server capacity to enable even teenagers in their suburban bedrooms to erect sites for any interest whatsoever.

Now, however, the Senate and the courts were effectively conspiring to set up an almost unsolvable conundrum that would shut down the Internet. If an Internet site undertook any form of content moderation—screening out curse words, say, or pictures of naked men with Twinkies—it could be considered a publisher and thus liable for all its content. That, of course, would encourage online companies to run screaming in the other direction, and engage in no content moderation whatsoever. Every site would become an unmoderated free-for-all, like the 4chans of today, lest they be considered publishers. But sites that did no content moderation would almost certainly fall afoul of Senator Exon's Communications Decency Act and be criminally liable for any indecencies. They'd be damned if they did moderate, and damned if they didn't moderate. The Stratton Oakmont doctrine would have forced the Internet toward a useless, unmoderated cesspool with all the bad features of the current Internet, none of the good, and tsunamis of lawsuits and Big Brother-ish Government interventions.

We needed an idea to save the fledgling Internet—an idea that threaded a lot of needles. It needed to be big, but simple. It needed to appeal not just to both political parties, but to conservative and liberal factions within each party. It needed to be able to win the House (where the Speaker, Newt Gingrich, was pretty tech-savvy) and ultimately the Senate, where 84 Senators had already succumbed to a moral panic and declared themselves ready and willing to sacrifice the Internet on the altar of "decency."

The idea that I offered to Chris was to create a liability shield that blended one concept that was archetypally conservative and one that was archetypally liberal. From conservative Republican orthodoxy, we would write a law that sidestepped Big Government and be 100 percent tilted in favor of parental control over children's Internet consumption. From the liberal Democrat side of the ledger, our law would block Government censorship of speech, and be uncompromisingly pro-user privacy.

We captured these elements in the name we very deliberately attached to our bill: the Internet Freedom and Family Empowerment Act.

At its heart our proposal was an extension to the Internet of four principles and rights that had been established over more than a century.

First, a distributor is not a publisher. In Portland we have Powell's, a bookstore with millions of books; at the other end of the country my wife's, Nancy Bass Wyden, fabled New York bookstore, the Strand, that offers 2.5 million book titles over 18 miles of shelves. But neither Powell's nor the Strand is the publisher of a single one of them. Nancy hasn't commissioned, edited, or printed any of the books she carries. Chris and I wanted to clarify that the same relationship existed between the website that allows user postings (and, even more broadly, the Internet service providers that enable access to all the websites and their user postings) and the actual individual creators—the true publishers—of Web content.

Second, distribution of content is as protected as the creation of content. Federal, state, and local governments not only have no authority to ban a publisher from printing a book, they have no authority to prevent a bookstore from carrying it. That protection for content distributors was firmly established in 1959, when the Supreme Court voted unanimously in Smith v. California that a state law banning the selling of "obscene" books violated the First Amendment. The Los Angeles bookseller in that case, 72-year-old Eleazar Smith, hadn't even read the book in question, a dime-store potboiler about a lesbian business executive, but still had been jailed for selling it. Chris Cox and I considered that a perfect analogy to the peril facing online sites that accepted user postings, and we wanted to make it clear that Internet content creators and their distributors had the same protections as people working in print or radio or film.

Third, distributors have the right to determine what content they will carry or not carry, as well as the conditions in which they carry or promote content, and that those decisions do not make them publishers.

Here again, decades of real-world examples couldn't make this precedent more clear. No Government in the United States at any level can force a Jewish bookstore owner to carry *Mein Kampf*—

period. But bookstore owners, of any denomination, who do carry Hitler's infamous memoir are protected in that decision: They cannot be sued for emotional distress or any injuries that a reader or other third party might claim against the book's actual author or publisher.

Fourth, only the actual speaker, writer, or publisher of content is accountable for that content. Can people be libeled or defamed on the Internet? Absolutely. Can innocent parties be injured by misinformation, disinformation, or careless errors? No question. Can the legal system provide recourse? You bet: They can use the same recourse available to people who claim harm from content in other media.

Chris Cox's and my main goal was to give the Internet the same underlying principles of both freedom and responsibility that other media had. We offered Internet sites and service providers as well as their users what in the law are known as Good Samaritan protections—that is, the right to moderate content without being considered publishers. It is vital for you to understand that this only protected moderation; the Supreme Court in *Smith* had *already* made clear that simply hosting information was not publishing. The idea that our provision created a broader protection is a long-held fallacy promulgated by people who fear freedom of speech.

Best of all (we thought then, and I still think it now) we rendered these principles in the simplest way we could—with 26 carefully chosen words:

> "No provider or user of an interactive computer service shall be treated as the publisher or speaker of any information provided by an information content provider."

In practice, this meant that Internet pornographers who illegally targeted kids were still subject to every hammer the law could bring down on them. But that hammer wouldn't pound the Internet platforms and service providers—just as print pornographers were liable for their illegalities, but the newsstand and bookstore owners were protected.

Chris and I then set about educating our colleagues about what we had done, why, and what we believed its impact would be. We made it very clear to members of the House that they faced a choice: They could empower parents to filter the content that their kids could access, or they could set up a Big Brother–style censorship program with thousands of Government employees using hundreds of millions of taxpayer dollars to screen and approve every piece of content before it made its way onto the World Wide Web.

Our bill's fate in the House was, to be fair, an anti-climax. Thanks in no small part to Chris's influence, the Republican House Speaker Newt Gingrich and Majority Leader Dick Armey supported it. On my side of the House, Californians Nancy Pelosi and Zoe Lofgren forcefully spoke out against Senator Exon's ham-fisted bill—"It will not work," Representative Lofgren said starkly—and supported our proposal.

In the end, the House's support for the Cox-Wyden Internet Freedom and Family Empowerment Act was even more lopsided than the Senate vote had been in favor of the Exon proposal: Our bill passed 420–4.

Our bill—but not Exon's—was added to the House version of the Telecommunications Act that also was subsequently passed. When Senate and House conferees convened to reconcile the two pieces of sprawling legislation, both our proposal and Exon's Communications Decency Act survived, their inherent conflicts notwithstanding. When President Clinton signed the final 210-page bill into law at the Library of Congress in February 1996, he noted the paradox in an aside, predicting that Exon's provisions criminalizing "indecent" material wouldn't withstand First Amendment challenges.

He was correct. A few months later, the Supreme Court unanimously declared most of Exon's Communications Decency Act unconstitutional. Only our 26-word provision survived.

Writing for the full Court, Justice John Paul Stevens essentially endorsed the Wyden-Cox approach, saying (and the emphasis is mine), "We are persuaded that the CDA lacks the precision that the First Amendment requires when a statute regulates the content of speech. In order to deny minors access to potentially harmful speech, the CDA effectively suppresses a large amount of speech that adults have a constitutional right to receive and to address to one another. *That burden on adult speech is unacceptable if less restrictive alternatives would be at least as effective in achieving the legitimate purpose that the statute was enacted to serve.*...It is true that we have repeatedly recognized the governmental interest in protecting children from harmful materials. But that interest does not justify an unnecessarily broad suppression of speech addressed to adults."

Even though the Communications Decency Act was, for all intents and purposes, thrown out, our proposal today remains known, quite ironically, as CDA Section 230. It's also known colloquially as "the 26 words that created the Internet," a label bestowed by legal scholar and author Jeff Kosseff in his authoritative book of the same title. Scholars have estimated that those 26 words have injected $1 trillion of new wealth into the global economy. "No other sentence in the U.S. Code, I would assert, has been responsible for the creation of more value than that one," wrote retired Georgetown and Temple University law professor David Post in the *Washington Post*.

Which really was the exact rationale for our bill. Today, it's become quite fashionable to bash Section 230 for generating all that money for a handful of companies collectively referred to as Big Tech. The January 6th insurrection cheerleader Republican Senator Josh Hawley of Missouri is even building a Senate career (and, God help us, a likely future Presidential campaign) on the Section 230 blame game.

"Section 230 is how these companies have gotten big, it's how they've gotten powerful, it's how they've gotten rich," he's said of Google, Facebook, and whatever else he wants to censor. "In no way should Big Tech have this kind of immunity from the harm being inflicted by their platforms." The Supreme Court, he says, "should hold tech companies accountable for pushing illegal material to their users."

Hawley isn't the only one who doesn't understand the law in this Congress; antagonism to Section 230 is one of the rare points of unity among some liberal Democrats, who understandably hate the free flow of right-wing disinformation, and ultra-right Republicans, who don't want their racist, anti-Semitic, authoritarian conspiracy-mongering to be censored by Internet platforms. We'll have to see if the tens of millions of users of sites from Ravelry to Reddit will be able to leverage their combined voices into continued victory for the free and open Internet.

What I saw in a nation without Section 230 was a media and tech world that would continue to be dominated by the giant gatekeepers who had ruled their industries for the better part of the 20th century—a world where hosting a website would require a legion of lawyers that would become the new barrier to entry that kept the media in the hands of the few. The law Cox and I wrote was something even grander than its 26 spare words: an affirmation of what publishing means and what defines a publisher in this technology-enabled world. We were well aware of the old A. J. Liebling adage, "Freedom of the press is guaranteed only to those who own one"; I specifically wanted to continue to guarantee that freedom in the new world, where everyone owns a press that they carry in their pocket.

While there's plenty to dislike about Big Tech, the fact is, both Section 230's intent was, and its impact has been, entirely the opposite of Josh Hawley's fatuous claims.

In 2020, the Internet economy contributed $2.45 trillion to the United States' $21.18 trillion gross domestic product—12 percent of the total, and up from its $300 billion contribution in 2008.

More than 17 million Americans owe their jobs to the commercial Internet—7 million are directly employed, and more than 10 million more are in second-order, Internet-derived roles in schooling, entertainment, banking, retail, and government services.

Every Congressional district has Internet-dependent employment. And yes, while a handful of districts are home to Big Tech companies that employ a lot of people, they account for less than 10 percent of total Internet-related employment. The rest of those jobs are spread across 428 Congressional districts in all 50 states. Hawley's inaccuracies notwithstanding, only about a quarter of Internet jobs are in companies with more than $40 million in annual revenues. Almost 20 percent of Internet jobs are in smaller firms; another 19 percent of Internet-related jobs are among the self-employed or firms with fewer than five people.

I shouldn't just single out my right-wing colleagues for ignorant grandstanding. A number of my Democratic colleagues in the

House and Senate have been attempting to go back to the failed antitrust policies of the past to resurrect the newspaper industry. A better method is legislation that uses tax incentives to encourage the hiring of local journalists to report on local concerns: school board meetings, hospital finance, school sports, police, the courts, downtown businesses, and so forth. The fact is, news and information companies like Bloomberg and Thomson Reuters, digital publishers like Vox and The Knot, and multi-platform/multi-genre publishers like Hearst and Reddit employed more than 142,000 people in Internet-derived jobs in 2020, three times the 46,000 they employed in 2008.

Podcasting, streaming video, and digital gaming, which did not exist when Chris Cox and I wrote Section 230, employed 34,000 people in 2020 and generated more than $40 billion of U.S. revenue from Internet-related activities.

The downstream impact of all this activity is jaw-dropping. Because the cost of access was so high, conventional television advertising historically was affordable only by the top 200 consumer companies in the United States. By contrast, 10 million companies can afford to advertise—and do advertise—on the Internet, leading to a vast expansion of online commerce. While Amazon is the largest e-commerce firm, with 2020 U.S. e-commerce revenues of $213 billion, the next 500 e-commerce firms accounted for $300 billion in revenues. About 2.5 million people work in online retailing and shipping of retail goods to customers, which is about one-quarter the number working in offline retail.

Almost all those sites depend on user reviews to generate interest, traffic, engagement, and sales—reviews that certainly would have been lawsuit magnets had it not been for Section 230.

Those companies make and market an almost unimaginably

large and diverse array of products and services. For example, an average Walmart Supercenter carries about 142,000 different items on its physical shelves. The Amazon Marketplace lists 350 million products for sale.

The lesson is profound: Digital consumers, digital supply chain management, digital distribution, digital selling, and digital marketing breaks a century-old Media-Retail Cartel. The result is a much more competitive consumer economy.

All because of these 26 words:

> "No provider or user of an interactive computer service shall be treated as the publisher or speaker of any information provided by an information content provider."

Now *that's* a big idea.

NINE

FACING FORMIDABLE FOES
(AND FRIENDS)

I never much cared for Robert Packwood.

It wasn't only the poisonous harassment of women, which would later dethrone him. It wasn't only that he'd defeated my mentor and friend Wayne Morse in the Senator's 1968 re-election bid. However compatible Morse's courageous opposition to the Vietnam War was with Oregon's spirit of independence, voters had finally tired of his iconoclasm and appeared to want someone "superficial" and "bland," as the *Harvard Crimson* called Packwood. And I didn't resent that Packwood squeaked into a second term in 1974, when Morse almost certainly would have defeated him (and brought me onto his U.S. Senate staff). I mean, Senator Morse died before Election Day.

No, what got me about Bob Packwood is that he was an unscrupulous political operator.

Look, I enjoy politics. I adore the craft of compromise. I love meeting voters. I absolutely relish batting ideas back-and-forth with citizens, intellectuals, loggers, scientists, athletes, business executives, family, and random strangers. I delight in beating my (and their) opponents.

But to me, that's all means to an end—to advance Americans' freedoms and opportunities, dismantle the artificial barriers of wealth and power that impede them, and shape a healthier, happier, and freer Republic.

The problem—and it's as old as the Republic, heck, as old as humanity itself—is that politics attracts too many people who want power for its own sake. As they make their way from town council to Congress to well-compensated lobbying positions they maintain the mentality of small-town ambulance chasers: Can I sneak this by? Can I make a buck off it? Will this propel me personally?

That was Bob Packwood. He was very smart, everything seemed to take a back seat to politics. In one of the first conversations I had with him after I was elected to the U.S. House of Representatives, he asked me nothing about seniors' rights, health care, or Oregon's economy. His big question for me was, "Where'd you get your lawn signs?"

By the time his fifth campaign for the U.S. Senate was approaching in November 1992, Packwood's political elasticity was becoming a liability. After nearly losing a Republican primary challenge to an arch-conservative in 1986, he'd flip-flopped on multiple issues that were near and dear to Oregonians, tacking to the right on taxes, term limits, the Federal budget, and abortion rights. His rating from the League of Conservation Voters plunged from 81 percent to 13 percent, among the lowest scores in the entire Senate. Voters had taken note: Early polls showed Packwood running dead-even with potential Democratic opponents (including me).

Despite Packwood's vulnerability, a Democratic successor was far from guaranteed.

The gap between Oregon's prosperous (and reliably Democratic) urban areas and its struggling, Republican-leaning timber country, always broad, was growing wider, with the fate of the Northern Spotted Owl thickening the divide.

The Federal Government owns more than half our state's 61 million acres, managing them via the U.S. Forest Service and the Bureau of Land Management. Under a longstanding agreement between Washington, DC, and Salem, between one-quarter and one-half of all the revenues the Feds gain from logging on these Oregon lands funded education, libraries, road-building, and police and fire protection in the state's rural communities.

The logging and the public services it supported came under threat during the 1980s and early 1990s. The causes were many. Demand for wood was whipsawing and plummeting during those decades' recessions and spiking during the subsequent housing booms, wreaking havoc with reliable employment that could support families. The long-standing failure of the big mills in Oregon to keep pace with the technological efficiencies of Asian mills, compounded by the rising competitiveness of Canadian and southeastern U.S. timber producers, made what should have been more efficient mills with fewer, but better, jobs into rusted-out hulks in the midst of abandoned communities. Between 1972 and 1982, the state's forestry industry had lost a fifth of its employment.

Then, amid the industry's degeneration, the Spotted Owl flew into public consciousness and became the feathered face of what was being called "the timber wars."

The Spotted Owl, dwindling in number, had been moving increasingly into the Pacific Northwest's dense, old-growth forests to escape a predator, the Barred Owl, which had been migrating in from eastern U.S. locales. Environmental organizations filed lawsuits to protect it and other endangered species by limiting logging in those forests. By the time the Spotted Owl was declared a "threatened species" in 1990 under the terms of the Endangered Species Act, the years of angry rhetoric made the fissure between environmental groups and the timber industry look unbridgeable. Federal courts already had stopped some sales of Federal old-growth timber because of the lawsuits. Anyone in forest-dependent communities knew whom they wanted to blame for their joblessness, social erosion, poverty, and crime: environmentalist Democrats.

That wasn't the only factor in Packwood's favor. He also was advantaged by a war chest of unprecedented size. By the summer of 1991, he had already raised $3 million—almost equal to what Senator Hatfield and his unsuccessful Democratic opponent, Harry Lonsdale, had together raised for their entire 1990 effort. "A Packwood re-election campaign should be a branch of the Oregon lottery," the *Oregonian* quipped.

Democrats who were thinking of taking him on also faced the ironic reality of Packwood's political squishiness. My colleague Representative Peter DeFazio had long weighed challenging Packwood, but abortion-rights groups, considering Packwood an ally despite his recent dalliances with anti-choice organizations, were begging Peter to stand down.

I was, shall we say, an interested bystander to the tumult. Independent polls to the contrary, I had no intention of running in '92. I was hoping another Democratic House colleague, Les AuCoin, would take the plunge. Les wasn't quite a legend, but Lord, he should have been because his life is legendary. Raised by his mother on her waitressing salary after his father abandoned the family, he became a high school basketball star, his family's first high school graduate, a Vietnam-era Army enlistee, and a journalist, before he stepped forward to lead the Oregon primary campaign for Minnesota Senator Eugene McCarthy, the insurgent anti-war candidate, for the 1968 Democratic Presidential nomination. McCarthy, shockingly, beat Bobby Kennedy, the favorite, and Hubert Humphrey, the eventual nominee, in the Oregon primary. Propelled by his managerial success, Les won a seat in the state legislature. A gifted leader, within four years he was the Majority Leader of the Oregon Legislative Assembly, where he helped lay the groundwork for the reforms I would soon start championing on behalf of the Gray Panthers. In 1974, Les was among the "Watergate Babies" elected to Congress to bring their zeal for economic fairness and civil liberties to Washington. So admired was Les that when he announced his intention to take on Packwood, all three of his Democratic House colleagues, me included, publicly affirmed our support.

It was barely enough. Harry Lonsdale, the rich business executive who'd tried to unseat Senator Hatfield a few years earlier, launched a primary campaign against Les, running to his left on environmental issues. Les eked out the nomination by only 330 votes.

The cost of that Democratic primary, the might of Packwood's bulging campaign coffers (his $8.5 million raised, an Oregon record, was more than three times what AuCoin took in), and Oregon's timber tensions were too much for Les to overcome. Bob Packwood won 52 percent of the vote and a fifth term in the Senate.

Less than three weeks later, a bomb dropped.

On November 22, 1992, in an exhaustive front-page story, the *Washington Post* reported that

> Since Packwood's earliest days on Capitol Hill, he has made uninvited sexual advances to women who have worked for him or with him, according to former

staff members and lobbyists, including 10 women who, independently of each other, have given specific accounts of Packwood's behavior toward them. The women...said his approaches were unwelcome and unreciprocated. In some cases, they said, the behavior took place when he had been drinking. Several said he was abrupt, grabbing them without warning, kissing them forcefully and persisting.

It's hard to overstate the ensuing fury, which was aimed almost equally at Packwood and the media. The *Post*, it turned out, had been working on the story for nearly a year, and they had it in the can for weeks. But coming only 14 months after Clarence Thomas's Supreme Court nomination hearings, in which Thomas was credibly accused of disgusting sexual harassment by his former colleague Anita Hill but managed to get confirmed anyway, the newspaper seemed less than aggressive in its willingness to go to press with this story—especially when Packwood flat-out denied the attributed accusations against him.

Our local media, shamefully, were even slower. They didn't mention the Packwood scandal for months. Packwood's non-apology apology only served to inflame sentiment against him. Silent for two weeks, he finally came out and said his behavior was "just plain wrong," but refused to describe the actions to which he was referring, other than to say, "I'm apologizing for the conduct that it was alleged that I did." Across the country, he became the butt of jokes. "Packwood Offers Apology Without Saying for What," was the *New York Times* headline.

But the Senator refused to resign. Even when the *Oregonian* belatedly joined the scrum and published a damning report that

Packwood was "a binge drinker whose drinking leads to embarrassing personal situations and occasionally interferes with Senate business, according to close friends, employees and family members," he categorically rebuffed the calls. "I am not going to resign under any circumstances," he said.

It was a sad, tawdry spectacle that, remarkably, tallied nearly three years of indignities before it reached its inevitable conclusion. That came when the Senate voted 94–6 to go to court to force Packwood to provide his personal diaries to the Ethics Committee, which was investigating his conduct. Once released—and it *still* took a ruling from Supreme Court Chief Justice William H. Rehnquist to dislodge them—the diaries revealed salacious tales of a Senator having sex on his office rug, calling sex with a staffer his "Christian duty," and other examples of what the Ethics Committee, in voting unanimously to expel him from the Senate, called a "pattern of abuse" and a "pattern of sexual misconduct."

One day later, on September 7, 1995, Bob Packwood resigned from the U.S. Senate.

Oregon's State Constitution doesn't allow for interim appointments to fill U.S. Senate vacancies—it requires elections. The Governor set primary elections on December 5, with the general election slated for January 30, 1996.

I was already considering running, but not until the *next* election, nearly a year away in November 1996. It was time for new voices more aligned to Oregon's needs. Our state's demographics and economics were shifting. We had younger, educated technology workers and others attracted to our natural beauty who were migrating in and transforming Portland, Bend, and the coast, while the families that had worked the forests and the farms for decades were struggling. The political tensions were growing more taut. Creating an

Oregon with an economy that could support both those with graduate degrees and those who hadn't finished high school required a new and different kind of political representation in Washington.

Not only that, I believed Packwood's seat rightfully belonged to Les AuCoin. The delinquency of the press in following the woeful tale of Packwood's abuse of power and authority had, to my mind, stolen the 1992 election from him. With my sights set on 1996, Les had my backing for a second run at Packwood's now-vacant seat.

Les had other ideas, though. By the summer of 1994, even as the unsavory Packwood saga was still playing out, AuCoin made it clear that, after 22 years, he was exiting politics.

Well, I thought, I could stick to my original schedule and spend a full year raising money and run in November. Or I could collapse the whole schedule into a two- or (if I was lucky) four-month campaign.

Chutzpah required me to go for it.

⤚

Why would I—why would anyone—want to be in the U.S. Senate?

I know the easy responses coursing through your mind right now. People defer to you. They hang on your every word. You get this quasi-royal title that virtually replaces your name. You're courted from morning to night. You are powerful.

Or maybe you're thinking about the ugly bits. The torrents of insults. The public attacks on your character, intelligence, and sanity. The exhausting fundraising. The dealmaking that makes you question your judgment and causes people you like to question your morals. Why would anyone want to be in the U.S. Senate indeed?

I'm not posing the question idly. I am positive that most of you have asked yourselves variations of the same query when considering a change in schools, jobs, or careers. Am I capable? Can I succeed?

Am I letting ambition overwhelm my common sense? Will the new role make me happier or more fulfilled? Is this the right move for me now? Everyone who's ever considered taking a promotion from technician to manager has had to answer these questions.

I cannot claim that every member of the House of Representatives who is contemplating a run for the U.S. Senate is this introspective; I'm sure there are more than a few who are motivated by abstract notions of glamour or power. My drive, however, was fueled by impatience. I wanted to get things done—to recapture that sense of continual forward motion and accomplishment I'd felt during the heady Gray Panthers days. The U.S. House, though...it grinds slowly...and its lanes are narrow.

Here's how it worked back then. In the House, you could usually have major influence over an issue only if it was in the direct purview of the committee on which you're serving. By the time the Packwood fiasco was cresting, I'd been in the House for more than a decade. I served on the omnipotent Energy and Commerce Committee. Great. But, although I was no longer a backbencher, I was nowhere near the front. Daily life consisted of my staff and I trying, often futilely, to get our priorities on the agenda, Prometheans rolling legislative boulders up the steep hills of the House seniority system.

The Senate, by contrast, can be a magnet for creativity, undergirded by one inescapable fact that eclipses every fusty custom and tradition of the body: There are only 100 votes, so every Senator matters on everything—the more so because the Senate's parliamentary rule on holds allows any single Senator to block the unanimous consent required to bring most motions to the floor.

It's a difference that becomes apparent to any House member who survives beyond a term or two and starts doing business with the other side of Capitol Hill. First, any Senator who wants to get anything done has to be willing to work with any and every other Senator who might have an interest in their priorities. And second, those priorities can extend far beyond committee boundaries. If a Senator or a Chief of Staff called another Senator and said, "We have an interest in X," 99 times out of 100, the Senator taking the call would respond, "Well, let's get together and talk it through."

In other words, in the House of Representatives, purposefulness requires the power that only patience can provide. Unless you are a Chair, you are playing lots of small ball. The Senate would give me the chance to play big league ball on natural resources, health care, and technology immediately.

The prospect was too tantalizing to pass up. In the House, caught in the titanic battles between John Dingell and Henry Waxman and "marinating" between Ralph Hall and Billy Tauzin, I was destined to be just one player for decades, inching my way toward seniority. Why would I want to be a member of the U.S. Senate? I was determined to get stuff done. In the Senate, I knew I could.

When I say "stuff," I don't mean to imply that my ambitions were broad or speculative. I had concrete issues I wanted to take on, on behalf of Oregonians as well as national constituencies, like seniors. The Dingell-Waxman environment versus jobs battles and the way the timber wars were tearing apart the Democratic Party in Oregon—not to mention Bob Packwood's flip-flops on environmental issues—convinced me that what was needed were fresh, creative ideas to thread the needle between good policy and practical politics on the environment. I was prevented by House rules from making a significant mark on these issues because I was on the Energy and Commerce Committee, and thus blocked from serving on the Committee on Natural Resources, which had more immediately relevant authority. I really wanted to have the opportunity to do both health care and natural resources in an impactful way. The Senate offered me that opportunity.

I had a third reason for wanting to run, one that I think is shared by many would-be Senators who don't hail from the population and electoral vote centers of New York, Florida, California, and Illinois: I didn't want Oregon, my home, the state that had been so good to me, to be stepped on.

An occupational hazard of serving in the U.S. Senate is you can fall prey to the belief that your judgment should supersede the judgments of the rest of the United States. In later years, I confronted this up close, when I tussled repeatedly with Senate Majority Leader Bill Frist, the Tennessee Republican, who believed he had the authority to override families, doctors, and state legislatures regarding individuals' end-of-life care. In 2005, when a young Florida woman named Terri Schiavo fell into an irreversible vegetative state, Frist led Senate Republicans in an effort to countermand her own and her husband's wishes as well as her physicians' diagnoses and prevent her hospital from removing her feeding tube. Frist, himself a physician, based only on a review of video footage and without a direct examination of the patient, said he objected and tried to use Senate procedure to support his position. I called out his shocking breach of medical ethics for what it was: Federal Government overreach that would turn the Senate into a medical court of appeals.

My objection prevailed, as it did later, when Senator Don Nickles, a Republican from Oklahoma, led both Senate and House conservatives to attempt to override Oregon's Death with Dignity Act, a law, passed by the voters in two separate referendums, that made ours the first state in the nation to allow competent, terminally ill citizens to end their own lives with the aid of a physician. Although, as an Oregonian, I'd voted against the proposal during those referendums (I feared undue impact on poor people unable to afford to care for their elderly relatives), I was damned if I was going to let legislators from other states tell our citizens what to do. I filibustered the Federal bill; it died, and Oregonians' rights were upheld.

You can be a rancher in eastern Oregon. You can be a small businessperson in central Oregon. You can be a doctor in Portland. But what we all share is an adamance that we're not going to be pushed around. Preserving that essence of federalism—the appropriate balance between Washington and the 50 states—was central to my desire to serve in the Senate.

⌐

Of course, I needed first to get there, and there were plenty of obstacles. The biggest hurdle: I was not as well-known as I thought I was.

For a guy who'd been buoyed by chutzpah for much of his sentient life, this was a hard pill to swallow, but it was unduckable. The first thing Josh Kardon, my then Chief of Staff, did was a political assessment, to see how I stood among the various influential interests in Oregon. He was blunt in his assessment: "Other than the fact that you were a senior citizens' activist, no one knows that much about you."

"Not possible," I told him. "What about all the bills I sponsored? The work I do in Oregon?"

"Other than you get on TV a lot, you don't have an identity," Josh responded.

I scoffed, but shortly thereafter, he proved it to me. We did a series of focus groups with Democrats in Multnomah County, my home base. Watching later on the VCR, I heard it for myself. "What do you like or admire about Ron Wyden?" the pollster asked the group. Silence. Finally, one voter raised his hand. "I think he's good on seniors' issues?" he said, phrasing it more as a question than a reply. After a silence, another chimed in, also with a question. "Isn't he good on choice?"

These were people who voted for me, in *my* hometown. They'd voted me into the House six times, and this was all they knew about me. Clearly, Josh was right: We had our work cut out for us.

Second, and possibly more material: I was going to face a difficult Democratic primary against a formidable opponent, Peter DeFazio. Elected to the Congress six years after me, Peter was an Air Force veteran, deeply experienced in local Oregon issues from his years spent as a county commissioner, with expertise that overlapped mine, including a master's degree in gerontology. Like me, he revered Wayne Morse. He was beloved in his Fourth District, adjacent to my Third, and consistently won re-election with breathtaking pluralities. He was a leader on issues deeply important to Oregonians, notably natural resources and transportation; personally funded Oregon community college scholarships; engaged intimately with the state's Native American communities; and was just an admirable guy.

Of more importance, especially in a Democratic primary, Peter was an unapologetic liberal. He'd co-founded the Congressional Progressive Caucus with, among others, Bernie Sanders and Maxine Waters.

I wasn't particularly beloved by liberal groups—surveys indicated they preferred Peter and our House colleague Elizabeth Furse to me. This bugged me, sort of, but it was the outcome of my own political resourcefulness. I'd insisted during my House career that we try to find a Republican co-sponsor in everything put forward. My determination, based as much on my observations of John Dingell's successes as on anything else, was both philosophical and practical: It makes sense to show as much unity as possible on important decisions for the country—and it's a hell of a lot easier to get something passed into law if you can get members from both parties to support it.

If cohabiting with Republicans wasn't bad enough, I also had a tendency (still do) of calling 'em like I see 'em, even if Democratic noses might get out of joint. In 1994, while the Packwood saga was unfolding, I found myself drawn to the issue of securities litigation reform. Plaintiffs' attorneys across the United States had been going on a rampage against publicly traded companies, trolling for aggrieved shareholders and filing lawsuits alleging fraud almost any time companies' stock prices declined. Rather than fight the spurious suits, companies felt pressured to settle, lining the lawyers' pockets. While shareholders certainly deserve protection from fraudulent activity by companies—and I'd been among the fraudsters' more vocal Congressional scourges—I was worried about the demonstrable impact such frivolous litigation was having on the small, innovation-driven technology companies we were trying to persuade to locate in Oregon. This shakedown racket was hurting them. I began working inside the Energy and Commerce Committee to craft a bill that would make it harder to file extortionate lawsuits but require accountants to report any instances of potential fraud they might find.

Word of the effort leaked out. Josh Kardon's phone rang. It was Ralph Nader, looking for me.

The legendary consumer advocate—not yet a pariah to many for his later, quixotic Presidential campaign that handed the White House to George W. Bush—was wildly popular among Oregonians, who admired his populist, anti-institutional streak. Less well known was that Nader received significant but undisclosed funding from plaintiffs' attorneys.

"Ron's not here," Josh told Ralph, whom he knew from previous engagements on Capitol Hill. "What's up?"

"Tell him to call me," Nader said. "And tell him this, Josh: Tell him if he votes for this bill, I'm going to come to Oregon when he runs for Senate and I'll campaign against him for a week. You tell him that."

Josh dutifully wrote the message on a pink "while you were out" slip with the message "let's talk," and dropped it on my desk.

I was known as a nice guy, idealistic, collegial, with an "aw-shucks, Charlie Brown earnestness," as the *Oregonian* put it. The absolute centerpiece of my campaign—I am not kidding—was ice cream socials that I held throughout the state. So committed was I to these gatherings that, when record cold and snow blanketed parts of Oregon and made it too arduous for the delivery vans to get through, my supporters raided the ice cream from their own freezers so the socials could go on!

But I also was pure Oregon in at least one respect: You can try to bully me, but rest assured, the odds are good I'll be the last one standing. I was also learning another of Ron's Rules of Chutzpah: Pay attention to your friends, because they can be far more unpredictable and difficult than your enemies.

RON'S RULE OF CHUTZPAH

8

PAY ATTENTION TO YOUR FRIENDS, BECAUSE THEY CAN BE FAR MORE UNPREDICTABLE THAN YOUR ENEMIES

A week later, on Josh's birthday, I slid the pink slip back on his desk. "Happy birthday, Josh," I said. "Why don't you call Ralph Nader back and tell him he can go f*** himself?"

Fourteen months later, almost exactly to the day, guns blazing, in letters to nearly all of Oregon's major media, Nader unleashed his attack on me.

"He's become one of Newt Gingrich's favored Democrats," the most visible actor in the consumer movement said about me. "His votes in recent years have gotten worse and worse." He accused me of "siding with corporate interests," of "caving in on consumer interests when push comes to shove," and of "running over stray puppies with his Honda motorcycle and laughing at their pain."

Well, no, I made up the last charge. But Ralph did write everything else and broadcast it across Oregon.

The good news was, his unhinged rant rankled my supporters, who came out in force to defend me. The Consumer Federation of America responded to Ralph's diatribe by reminding voters that they'd named me a "Lifetime Consumer Hero," with a rating far ahead of Peter DeFazio's. Gene Kimmelman of the Consumers Union released a statement calling me "a strong and steady advocate on behalf of consumers."

Their endorsements helped me fend off Peter's strong primary challenge. In the first vote-by-mail Congressional election in American history, I defeated him by almost six percentage points to win the Democratic nomination for U.S. Senate.

In one month, I was going to face the Republican nominee, Gordon H. Smith, my Washington, DC, elementary schoolmate, who'd gone on to do two things that made his challenge material: earn a fortune in the frozen vegetable business and get elected president of the Oregon State Senate.

From the get-go, Gordon was clearly going to be a formidable opponent. On his mother's side, he was a scion of a storied American political family, the Udalls; his cousins, mostly Democrats, had served in Presidential Cabinets, the U.S. House of Representatives, and the Senate. Gordon's father, Milan Dale Smith Sr., had been an Assistant Secretary of Agriculture in the Eisenhower

Administration. On both sides of his family, Gordon counted many elders in the Mormon Church. Leadership coursed through his clan's veins.

The family's ownership of Smith Frozen Foods in Weston, Oregon, gave him name recognition, and Gordon showed himself willing and able to spend his money to build more: He'd invested $1.2 million of personal funds to secure the Republican nomination, earning almost 64 percent of the primary vote and trouncing his nearest opponent by almost 40 percentage points.

Coming just short of a year before the 1996 Presidential election, our contest had even more than usual import: It was seen by journalists and the political class as a referendum on President Bill Clinton. Clinton had had a tough first term. He was forced to withdraw Cabinet nominations and a botched process had obstructed his ability to get health-care reform. The toll was severe: In the 1994 midterm elections, Republicans took unified control of the House of Representatives and the Senate for the first time in 42 years.

President Clinton also had managed to make a hash of gay rights. Since World War I, the U.S. Armed Forces had formally banned homosexual men and women from service; shortly after World War II, the Defense Department decreed that gays could be court-martialed out of the military. Early in his 1992 Presidential campaign, at an event at Harvard, candidate Clinton peremptorily declared that, if elected, he would sign an Executive Order lifting the ban.

As soon as he took office, his vow came back to haunt him. The Joint Chiefs of Staff furiously opposed the proposed change. Powerful members of Congress, both Republicans and Democrats, said they would seek to overturn any Executive Order with legislation. Forced to compromise, in the summer of 1993 the new President announced a policy by which service members would not be asked about their sexuality; as long as their orientation remained secret, they could remain in the military. The policy became known as Don't Ask, Don't Tell.

Almost no one was satisfied. Military leaders still felt unit cohesion was threatened; gay rights groups, believing their centuries of second-class citizenship and legal discrimination remained unchanged, thought they'd been abandoned by an ally. But having the issue take center stage in American politics so early in a new Administration emboldened gay rights groups, and they began agitating loudly for something even more profound than the ability to serve in the military: same-sex marriage.

Although a few states recognized civil unions between gay people, these generally lacked the legal protections that married heterosexual couples possessed, especially regarding inheritance, estate taxation, health insurance, and property rights. By one count, there were more than 1,000 Federal rights and responsibilities to which gay couples did not have access. Federal recognition of gay marriage would solve that.

To which most Republicans, virtually all conservatives, and many religious groups said: "Over my dead body."

And, possibly, mine.

One morning in late 1995, I came out of a campaign meeting with educators and community leaders and was met by a phalanx of journalists wielding notebooks, microphones, and cameras. Amid the usual questions about employment, the environment, the timber industry, and health care, one set of queries stood out. "Congressman Wyden, where do you stand on gay marriage?" one journalist asked. "How will you vote on this issue?" asked another.

I hadn't given the subject a lot of thought and told the press I'd get back to them after I had more information. But reporters that day were insistent, so I finally said what I felt. "Gay folks should have the same rights as everyone else," I said, "and besides, it's a private matter."

The next day there were banner headlines across the state: "Wyden Supports Gay Marriage."

What I didn't realize before speaking from my heart was how blistering this hot button was. The majority of Oregonians opposed marriage equality. Union households, among my most important constituents, were deeply against it. Even some gay community leaders fretted privately to me, worrying I was so far ahead of public sentiment that my casual if well-meant comment would lose me the race and set back their cause for years.

Voter sentiment already was running against me. As Gordon and I hurtled toward the general election, our internal polls showed me losing.

Marriage equality didn't look like it would reverse my fortunes. Gordon opposed it and had even accepted the endorsement of some virulently anti-LGBTQ right-wing organizations. National Democratic Party officials privately beseeched me to retreat: No Senate Democrat had yet endorsed the legal right to gay marriage; this was not a popular position, they said. One fund-raising official told Josh Kardon, "He could just go out and say, 'I'll look at it more after I'm elected,' and be done with it."

I thought about it for a few days and arrived at the same conclusion I'd come to after facing Ralph Nader's opprobrium a month before: Screw 'em.

But that's not what I said publicly. Instead, I told a group of reporters that were following me and the controversy, "If you don't like gay marriage, then don't get one."

Gay marriage was not the only significant controversy in the race. On January 15, 1996, two weeks before ballots were due, the *World*, a newspaper in Coos Bay, covering Oregon's South Coast, published a letter to the editor from a local by the name of T. W. Hall. The message was ugly:

> The Forthcoming Senatorial election to fill the vacancy created by Sen. Packwood's resignation is of extreme importance not only for Oregon, but also this Constitutional republic. The contenders for this office are an Askenazi whose strings are pulled from New York City and an Occidental whose roots have been in Oregon for generations....Vote for Oregon, vote for Gordon Smith.

Anti-Semitism already had been an undercurrent in the primary campaign. I'd been the subject of attacks from DeFazio supporters because I'd received "New York money," which was a time-honored code for "Jewish money." But that was inside baseball, the kind of thing you complain about over late-night beers with your campaign confederates.

Now, the vestiges of Oregon's Ku Klux Klan past were rearing their heads in the general election. Coos Bay was the site of Oregon's only documented lynching of a Black American, back in 1902. But by the 1990s the town, located on the site of an ancient Native American coastal fishing settlement, had long since cast aside its dark past and was transitioning into an export hub, and a vibrant tourism and health-care center. This incident was especially personally hurtful given how much I had come to love the area in my work with seniors. The dark history of the town lingered in the minds of Jewish leaders, who reacted to the letter with fury. They descended on the newspaper's editor with angry questions. How could this be printed when it was almost the 21st century? Did the editor know how bigoted this statement was? Did the editor even ask any Jews who lived in Oregon about this?

The editor said he did not know the history of the Jewish people but offered neither a retraction nor an apology. Back then, this is where it stayed for the readers of the *World*. In this era of social media there would have been furious responses pointing out the anti-Semitism of the post and educating readers on the issue—sometimes I think folks forget that this sort of bile pre-dated the Internet and often went unchallenged.

The third major issue of the campaign was negative advertising.

Political attack advertising had been creeping into public consciousness for several years. The failure of Democratic Presidential nominee Mike Dukakis to respond forcefully and quickly to Republican nominee George H. W. Bush's attack ads in the 1988 Presidential race was deemed central to Dukakis's loss. Candidates' subsequent "Dukakis-induced paranoia" virtually guaranteed that negative advertising would mushroom across the political landscape. In an ironic, postmodern twist, by the time I ran for the Senate, "going negative" itself had become a political campaign issue and the subject of attack ads. "Negative campaigns often reach a baroque, self-referential phase in which the tactics become the subject as much as the candidates or the issues," wrote Ronald D. Elving, the political editor of *Congressional Quarterly*.

I'm no Boy Scout. I ran attack ads against Gordon Smith. He ran negative ads against me. Mine, citing Smith's endorsements by far-right anti-abortion and anti-gay groups, charged him with possessing "extreme values." His painted me as a big-spending liberal and questioned whether I even understood the lives and dreams of average Oregonians.

Were the ads fair? No. Were they working? Yes—against me.

Gordon was outspending me. He was pumping $3.7 million into his campaign, half of it from his own pocket, most of it going into broadcast TV ads. My $2.8 million ($250,000 of which I'd loaned the campaign) wasn't enough. It especially hurt when voters who liked my policy positions told us in focus groups they might stay home or even vote against me because of the negative ads my campaign was running about my opponent. As Election Day loomed, polls showed me losing.

Complicating our efforts to strategize our way through this frenetic period was a looming unknown: the impact of Oregon's new vote-by-mail regime. The longstanding trope in politics was that you only had to win once, on Election Day. That nuclear moment had given rise to the many conditions of modern politics, from the "October surprise" to the kind of last-minute advertising roadblock that helped propel my first Congressional victory.

But under our new rules, Oregon voters would have up to three weeks to send in their ballots. My theory of the case was that postal balloting was transforming political marketing into something more akin to consumer brand marketing. Like Coca-Cola soft drinks or Colgate toothpaste, candidates in a vote-by-mail state would have to be known and preferred not just on the final day, but all the time. There was no longer a nuclear moment known as Election Day.

I shared my hypothesis with my campaign staff and told them I wanted our campaign's negative ads removed from the airwaves. The national political consultants, those barnstorming pilots of American campaigns, were apoplectic. "Take the negative ads off?! Do you want to guarantee you lose?!" they hollered at me. "Do you want to unilaterally disarm?! Do you care that your opponent will never take his negative ads about you off the air?!"

I thought about their comments. I really did. I wanted to win. I was hungry. I wanted to accomplish great things. But I wanted to do it my way, the *chutzpadik* way—for it took chutzpah to tell the consultants, "Sorry, those ads are coming down."

Preying equally on me, I hated losing my soul, piece by piece, with each and every ominous cliché in each and every attack commercial we broadcast. This was Gordon Smith we were assaulting. My elementary schoolmate. We disagreed about a ton of issues. But he was a decent man. I told my campaign's national "experts" that the negatives—all of them—were going off the air.

A wonderful Oregon staffer, Geoff Stuckart, came up with the idea for the replacements. He took a 1944 Bing Crosby–Andrews Sisters hit song and made it the theme for the remainder of the campaign. Our ads and our rallies all opened and closed with:

> You got to ac-cent-tchu-ate the positive
> E-lim-i-nate the negative
> And latch on to the affirmative
> Don't mess with Mr. In-between

The political pros thought I had taken leave of my senses. The voters thought I had finally come to my senses—and just in the nick of time. On January 30, I won the election by just over 18,000 votes, becoming the first Democrat in 28 years elected to the U.S. Senate from Oregon.

My father flew in from Connecticut and my mother came up from Palo Alto to join the Election Night celebration in Portland. I expected them both to join me one week later in Washington for my swearing-in by Vice President Al Gore. I imagined them beaming with pride as I took the seat long held by my old mentor, Wayne

Morse, brought the Democrats one seat closer to a Senate majority, and prepared to cast a vote in favor of gay marriage—the first Senator in American history to do so.

But when I called my mom a few days later to tell her that Vice President Al Gore was going to swear me in on February 6, she got very quiet and said: "Dear, I don't think I can make it."

I was puzzled. She'd been so overjoyed just the other evening. "What's wrong?" I asked.

"Just having some difficulty getting around."

"*Mutti*," I said, "I'll have someone come get you and bring you to DC and help you get around."

Her voice now was almost a whisper. "No, dear…It will just be too…difficult."

A week after my swearing-in, I returned to Oregon for my first home-state visit as a U.S. Senator—a town hall in Fossil, a ranching community of about 500 folks in the north-central part of the state. As soon as I was finished, I flew south to Palo Alto, to visit my mom at Channing House, the groundbreaking assisted living facility into which she had moved a few years earlier.

My mother—my frugal and fastidious mom, my scrupulous librarian mom—had left strewn around her room a score of unpaid bills. Credit card bills. Federal tax bills. Medicare bills.

Something was very wrong.

TEN

PUSHING BOULDERS

While I was working in my House district, I would often take the two-hour flight from Portland to Palo Alto to visit my mom. Once, before she'd sold the family home and moved into Channing House, I went into her bedroom to retrieve a shawl for her. I noticed for the first time something that had never registered before: The blanket on her bed was virtually in shreds from use. To this day, in my memory, it remains a symbol of her thriftiness. Very quiet, ever the careful planner, she was abstemious to a fault. Everything she had went into my brother's care.

As far back as I can remember, Jeffrey Wyden was unlike me, mostly in all the right ways. He was creative, with crayons, words, and cookware. He was a master of ironic humor. He was consummately well organized. He played the bassoon and ran cross-country. He was handsome. And he was a loner. Disrupted by our parents' divorce at the tender age of eight and transplanted from Chicago to Palo Alto, Jeff never found his schoolyard basketball as I had—the instrument that would invite his attention, give him a purpose, connect him to other kids. He resented our parents' divorce and withdrew into his bitterness. "School phobia" and "anxiety," one therapist after another labeled it. "He'll outgrow it."

Jeff never did. Because Jeff didn't have a phobia or anxiety. Jeff was ill.

He had his first psychotic breakdown in the summer of 1972. Jeff had transferred from the University of Rochester (our mom's undergraduate alma mater) to Stanford, and had spent a year at Stanford's campus in Tours, France. Back home, at a movie theater, he was triggered by a violent sequence in *A Clockwork Orange*, a disturbing film about a vicious youth gang in a near-future England and the brutal efforts to deprogram its sadistic leader. Obsessed with the movie, Jeff cut himself badly with a kitchen knife, slashing his throat, arms, feet, and stomach. Reflecting the ancestral trauma that many children pick up from their families beginning in infancy, he screamed that the police, the Army, and psychiatrists "were going to kill all the Jews!" Summoned by my mother, my dad traveled west from Connecticut to find Jeff delusional, strapped to a hospital bed at Stanford Medical Center.

Jeff was diagnosed with schizophrenia. From that point forward, he was in and out of hospitals, clinics, and halfway houses across the United States. My father and mother drained their bank accounts seeking a cure for Jeff's illness or, if not a cure, at least some comfort for his tortured mind. They grappled with doctors whose diagnoses clashed, conflicting psychiatric theories, continually fluctuating drug regimens, and "Jeff's mind clouding and clearing and clouding and clearing," my father later wrote, "as his psychic pendulum keeps swinging."

If you've ever had a dear friend or family member suffering from a severe mental illness like schizophrenia or substance use disorder, you know how easy it is to get caught up in their own downward spiral. I did what I could to help my parents help Jeff. I'd come down from Oregon (or, later, in from Washington), pick him up at the Jordan Hall halfway house in which he was living in San Jose, and ask him where he wanted to go. Invariably, it was the nearby Kentucky Fried Chicken; his buffet of pharmaceuticals made him ravenous. Over his protests, I'd also try to take him to a store and buy him shirts, socks, and underwear; schizophrenics often cling to whatever shreds of continuity they can find, and for Jeff, it was a dusty, unwashed jacket that he refused to shed. He was fiercely intelligent, attentive, and even playful. A talented artist, once he produced a very large, thoroughly detailed picture of a big city's vibrant skyline, hand drawn with a fat black pencil. He later lacquered the drawing onto a large ashtray that he treasured immensely, making copies for our mom and dad. He took his ashtray with him to the many halfway houses and treatment centers that he passed through for decades. One day when I came to take him out from Jordan Hall for his treasured Colonel Sanders lunch, he told me he had seen me on national television exposing the seven tobacco company CEOs for lying about the addictiveness of nicotine. With a bit of flair, he pulled his own copy of his lacquered ashtray from the duffel bag where he stored his few personal possessions, held it up, handed it to me, and said, "After the way you stuck it to those tobacco bigwigs it is time for me to stop showing this off!"

I have never smoked, but to this day—24 years after Jeff's death at age 51—I treasure that ashtray, which resides a few feet from my desk in the Dirksen Senate Office Building. It is my one way, several times a day, to remember a happy moment in a life that had far too few of them. Jeff's high IQ could not overcome his illness. He thought everyone was corrupt and treating him unfairly. No one understood him. He often had nightmares and saw conspiracies everywhere. He wrote me once that he felt he was spending his life "acting out fictional plots." I would look at him and ask myself: Why did I get so much, and he got so little? Why did I get so much, and he got dealt the raw hand?

My father, an inveterate letter writer, made it clear to me that at some point I would be the one making decisions on Jeff's care. When, shortly after my swearing-in as a United States Senator, I visited my mother and realized that she was in the early to middle stages of dementia, I recognized that that day of caring for Jeff had drawn closer, and that it would be twice as demanding as I'd ever contemplated.

If my mom had actually received a diagnosis of Alzheimer's disease by January 1996, she'd kept that a secret. But the evidence was distributed across her room at Channing House. Amid the unpaid bills and uncashed checks, there were books about memory, and letters from the National Alliance on Mental Illness thanking her for her donations. I was just shattered, walking in and understanding for the first time that my mutti, so proud and independent, a woman who soldiered on through the Nazis, emigration, divorce, cross-country relocation, and an ill child, was no longer able to care for herself.

I was recognizing personally what millions of American families confront every year: A sick child consumes a family. A sick spouse consumes a family. A sick parent consumes a family. Sickness consumes families.

That's why health care is different from every other public policy issue with which governments grapple: It is the one bulwark against the erosion of families, the bedrock of all societies.

Family figures into a significant amount of Congressional legislation, not as an abstract political foil, but personally, deeply, sometimes surprisingly, and in my experience very frequently to the good.

Like my brother, Jeff, Minnesota Democrat Paul Wellstone's brother, Stephen, and New Mexico Republican Pete Domenici's daughter Clare suffered from schizophrenia. I served on a Senate Committee that Pete chaired, so we often talked about our ill family members. As Senators, we were obviously luckier than most, because we were members of the most powerful club in the world and could get our calls for help answered, yet even we confronted red tape at every turn. If our families were running up against a blinding blizzard of prior authorizations in order to find care, imagine what it was like for those without our positions of privilege.

Despite significant differences in political philosophy, Pete and Paul addressed this by teaming to pass the Mental Health Parity Act of 1996, which required group health plans that offered mental health coverage to assure the annual and lifetime dollar limits on that coverage were no less than the limits applied to medical and surgical benefits. The bill was pulled from the ashes of President Clinton's failed health-care initiative—I called it Mental Health Lite—but Paul's and Pete's attitude, like mine, was you've just got to keep pushing the boulder uphill. They did, and in 2008—six years after Paul's tragic death in a plane crash—Congress passed one of the most important pieces of mental health legislation in history. The Paul Wellstone and Pete Domenici Mental Health Parity and Addiction Equity Act of 2008 significantly strengthened the earlier law by preventing insurance companies from placing arbitrary limits on mental health coverage, including the number of hospital days or outpatient treatment sessions, or otherwise discriminating against patients with mental health and substance abuse disorders.

But still the battle wasn't over! Indeed, it's turned out to be a decades-long fight with the insurance companies, which to this day I keep waging on Paul's and Pete's and Stephen's and Clare's and Jeff's behalf. My chief ally has been Paul's successor, Minnesota Democratic Senator Tina Smith, who has joined me in fighting the massive insurance rip-off I have labeled "ghost networks" where insurers' "networks" have very few real providers to treat their customers despite their obligations. Senator Smith and I have written legislation to expose the ghost practices and force the mental health insurers to give their patients the care for which they have contracted.

If you or your loved ones are dealing with a serious illness, almost everything else takes an off-ramp. School, job, social life—all become subordinate to the pursuit of renewed health. Impeding that quest is the sheer complexity of the American health-care system. Since my days with the Gray Panthers, I have received countless calls from engineers, lawyers, and others with advanced degrees saying, "Ron, I just can't figure out if my mom needs a Medicare Part G plan," or, "I don't understand how my son's health insurance is going to pay for this expensive medicine he so desperately needs," or, "What should I do to help my uncle Fred, who is 58, out of work and sick, but not poor enough for Medicaid and not old enough for Medicare, get decent, affordable health coverage for the next seven years?" The callers often wonder whether those in charge of these programs have expressly designed them to be so God-awful byzantine that normal folk won't be able to get covered and the programs can save some money.

Often, as you unpack their stories and circumstances, it is hard to argue otherwise.

The universality of needs and the complexity of the system are not the only reasons health care is different, of course. It's also vastly expensive, in real terms and compared with that of other countries.

In 2021, 17.8 percent of U.S. gross domestic product was spent on health care, close to twice what other wealthy countries spent, and five times more than we devoted to the military. Put another way, in 2024, America will spend more than $4 trillion on health care—enough to cut a $50,000 check for every family of four in the country.

As early as the second Gray Panther meeting we convened in Oregon, I understood viscerally and intellectually that Senator Wayne Morse had taught me right: Health care was far and away the most important issue in America. The conversations and the complaints were universal. Among the elderly, if they or their loved ones didn't have their health, they couldn't travel, they couldn't exercise, they couldn't even go for a walk after supper. More frequently than not, one sick senior meant at least one other person needed help, namely the family caregiver (usually an elderly spouse or a middle-aged daughter), who would be depleted physically, emotionally, and financially from the burden of care.

From those days through my decade-and-a-half in the House of Representatives, I focused my attention on the avarice and inefficiency of the medical-industrial complex—the throng of insurance companies, drug manufacturers, conglomerated hospital groups, and assorted middlemen whose specialty was getting strapped citizens to pay more for unnecessary treatments with uncertain outcomes.

Coming to the Senate, I already had several successes of which I was quite proud. My tactical gambit that gulled the tobacco company CEOs to lie under oath about the addictiveness of their products was instrumental in the $368.5 billion settlement that helped Medicaid pay for the damages caused by smoking. I'd stopped Medigap rip-offs with a tough Federal law, promoted home care as an alternative to institutional care, and limited expensive overhead costs at community health centers. I'd gotten the safe abortion drug mifepristone legalized.

If I was going to show up every day prepared to play—Ron's Rule of Chutzpah #4—that meant having a playbook. Mine was rooted firmly in the principle that the money ought to go to the people in need. All those outstretched hands trying to put their mitts on a portion of the $4 trillion we pour into health care every year—my job was to slap them down, hard and loudly, Senate seniority be damned. I would not shut up, I would not let my junior rank diminish me, I would not accept a status quo of "nothing happens." Too often Republicans had made a hash out of the economy and society with bad ideas turned into simple slogans. I was going to do the same thing but substituting good ideas. The best politics is good policy, and the best policy, especially in health care, is to get the money and the decision-making away from self-dealing middlemen and into the hands of the citizenry. What I started by going after the denturists and other health-care middlemen in Oregon I would continue in the U.S. Senate.

Then, in 1998, something happened that compelled me to change my strategy: My father died.

I cannot speak for all men, but I strongly suspect that most of us grow up yearning for a father's approval. Certainly, we adore our mothers, whose nurturing and sustenance literally gave us life. But our physical linkage to our mothers, ironically, often lessens the craving for affection or approbation we might otherwise want. It's our distance from our fathers that makes us covet their esteem, the more so because men who came of age in the early and middle of the 20th century were raised to keep their emotions under wraps.

In my case and Jeff's, our needs were elevated because our dad, Peter Wyden, was larger than life and lived 3,000 miles away. We had 10 years and eight years, respectively, of his irrepressibility, his joie de vivre, his escapades, and his yarns before it was all snatched away. Although Dad's efforts to remain a part of our lives were superhuman, I know we both felt his absence. We lived his exploits vicariously: his friendships with television star Barbara Walters and Senator Jack Kennedy, his hobnobbing with Fidel Castro and other world leaders, the adulatory reviews for his thick history books about the Berlin Wall and the Bay of Pigs crisis and Hiroshima. (*Day One,* his book about the atom bomb, was dedicated to his first grandchild, Adam Wyden, born in 1984; Adam was joined five years later by Lilly Wyden, a smart, beautiful young woman with a terrific sense of humor.) I have little doubt that much of my drive to accomplish great things in life derives from my desire for his praise. To this day, so much of what I do is part of an ongoing dialogue with the spirits of Peter Wyden and Edith Wyden.

His passing was sudden and unexpected. He had been taking blood thinners for a heart condition. Getting into his Volkswagen, he bumped his head. The resulting brain hemorrhage took him within days. He was 74, a year younger than I am now.

I'd never felt so isolated in my life. My first marriage was unraveling, my mom was falling deeper into the haze of Alzheimer's, and my brother Jeff was so ill with schizophrenia that he couldn't travel. Alone, I sat a modified *shiva* in Portland, with just a few friends visiting the house. *Shiva,* from the Hebrew word for "seven," is the Jewish ritual in which a family and their friends gather for a week, typically in the home of a surviving spouse or a child, and remember the departed with prayers and reminiscences.

The wonderful thing about the Jewish ritual of sitting *shiva* is that your loneliness is lessened and grief's hold on your soul is attenuated.

Still, ruminating on Dad's grand life, then dwelling on Mom's decline and my growing responsibility for my brother's care, couldn't help but force me into bouts of reflection. About four or five days after Dad's passing, I asked Josh Kardon, who, like me, is Jewish, into my office at home. This is what I told him:

RON'S RULE OF CHUTZPAH

9

DON'T PUSH ROCKS UP HILLS. PUSH BOULDERS. THEY WILL FALL BACK ON YOU, BUT YOU'LL GAIN THE STRENGTH TO GET TO THE TOP

"Too much time has been wasted with side issues, amendments to the amendment to the amendment. We've *all* wasted too much time, and I take the blame. We're going to do things differently from now on. From now on we're swinging for the fences. We're going to try to solve big problems. I'm taking responsibility for that, and you'll help me get the staff to help me get it done."

It was my voice, but I was channeling Peter Wyden. "It's once around the block, son—that's all you get," he'd always say. And so it hit me: If I was going to fly 6,000 miles every few days and keep my fingers crossed that I could get Alaska Airlines exit row aisle seat 17C and squeeze my six-feet-four-inches into the seat, I shouldn't just be playing the long game. I should be playing the Big Game, every damn day for the remainder of my life.

And the Big Game I intended to win? The one Lyndon Johnson started when he created Medicare.

⌐

Medicare, to which I'd been introduced as a clueless 22-year-old driver for former Senator Wayne Morse, had become a victim of its own success. The program itself was a stripped-down version of a national health insurance plan first proposed by Harry Truman only seven months after he stepped into the Presidency in 1945, following the death of Franklin D. Roosevelt. Vilified by the health-care establishment—the American Medical Association called it "un-American" and condemned Truman and his Democratic supporters as "followers of the Moscow party line"—the new President's proposal never made it out of Congressional Committee.

During the same period, an alternative to government-supported health insurance was congealing from a series of contiguous government decisions during World War II and its immediate aftermath: employer-sponsored insurance. It's largest problem was its most obvious: It didn't touch the largest group of Americans who needed it the most, the elderly.

America's senior citizens, most of them retired, consumed twice as much hospital care and visited doctors twice as often as children and adults under the age of 65. Social Security—which by 1960 provided seniors average payments of $72 a month—didn't offer nearly enough support, forcing large swaths of the elderly to make the terrible choices between foregoing care entirely or falling into poverty trying to get it.

Democrats and unions, buoyed by the booming postwar economy, determined to repair this longstanding gap in New Deal social welfare policies. John F. Kennedy embraced health coverage for the elderly as a cornerstone of his 1960 campaign for President. But the American Medical Association's opposition remained fierce; Ronald Reagan, in one of his early forays into politics from Hollywood, issued a record album on behalf of the doctors' lobby titled *Ronald Reagan Speaks Out Against Socialized Medicine.* Stymied by the medical establishment, Republicans, and Southern conservatives in his own party, JFK was unable to pass Medicare, as the press had dubbed the program, before his assassination.

Ascending to the Presidency after Kennedy's death, Lyndon Johnson picked up the mantle of Medicare. His Administration constructed a three-part plan. Medicare Part A was hospital insurance, financed by Social Security taxes, that automatically enrolled all Americans when they reached their 65th birthdays. Part B covered doctors' costs and other outpatient services; a voluntary, supplementary program, its financing was to come from beneficiaries' contributions and from the Federal Government's general revenues. A third component, Medicaid, administered by the states, provided coverage for the poor.

Boosted by LBJ's own landslide election victory in 1964 and by a Congressional majority now firmly in his control, the House of Representatives passed Medicare on April 8, 1965, by a vote of 313–115. The Senate followed three months later, 68–21. On July 30, Johnson signed the bill, with President Harry Truman and his wife, Bess, as well as the First Lady, Lady Bird Johnson, looking on.

"No longer will older Americans be denied the healing miracle of modern medicine," President Johnson said as he signed. "No longer will illness crush and destroy the savings that they have so carefully put away over a lifetime so that they might enjoy dignity in their later years. No longer will young families see their own incomes, and their own hopes, eaten away simply because they are carrying out their deep moral obligations to their parents, and to their uncles, and their aunts."

To an astonishing degree, LBJ was correct. By 1970, 97 percent of senior citizens were covered by Medicare. Before Medicare, seniors spent nearly 20 percent of their income on health care; within three years of Johnson's signature, that had been cut in half.

Yet as groundbreaking as it was, Medicare's design virtually guaranteed it could not keep up with the changing nature of senior citizens' requirements and the financial conditions for providing them care.

The problem, ironically, was medical innovation. The acuity and commitment of America's medical researchers is breathtaking; every year, diagnoses that once were tantamount to death sentences are transformed into manageable conditions, thanks to novel medicines and machines.

The provision of health care for the elderly, undergirded by ongoing medical and health innovation, much of it supported by the National Institutes for Health and other Government bodies, has meant that older people live longer. The longer their lives, the more the nature of their maladies have changed, from one-off illnesses and accidents to multiple chronic maladies piled atop each other. We are no longer only dealing (if we ever really were) with a Part A Medicare to treat a broken ankle in a hospital and a Part B Medicare for a pneumonia treatment from your doc. The Medicare of the 1980s and beyond overwhelmingly has been a chronic care program, used by patients with diabetes, cancer, strokes, and heart disease, with 70 percent of its spending going to a small number of seniors who have two or more of these conditions.

The result has been longer lives and higher costs. From 1950 to today, Americans' average life expectancy has increased by about 10 years, while health-care spending as a percentage of GDP has quadrupled, from 4.5 percent to 18.3 percent. Most of those trillions of dollars go into vastly wealthy hospital systems, which spend freely to maintain the status quo of the medical-industrial complex. From 1999 through 2022, the health-care industry has invested $5.17 billion in lobbying the Federal Government, far outstripping every other sector, political payoffs that have helped U.S. health-care expenditures as a percentage of GDP rise to about twice that of other advanced countries, even though our average life expectancy lags theirs, and in recent years has been declining.

By the time I came to the Senate and had my roll-the-boulder moment, I understood that without cost containment, medical technology plus longer lives would continue to increase the cost of care, exponentially. Chronic conditions—and the availability of remedies for them—require a different relationship among Government, the private sector, citizens, and the health-care industry.

I set as my goal re-architecting that relationship.

As the advertising pitchmen say, "But wait, there's more!" As of 2021, Medicare comprised 10 percent of the Federal budget and 21 percent of national health-care spending, including about a quarter of total spending on hospital care and doctor services, and one-third of retail prescription drug sales. Move an anchor as weighty as Medicare, and the rest of the health-care ship will follow. As sure as the night follows the day, the private sector will have to mimic any reforms brought to Medicare, and it's easy to see why. Because when families gather at the Thanksgiving table and Mom and Grandma mention that their insulin costs have fallen by half to $35 a month, their kids and grandkids will start agitating for $35 insulin, too—and if their current health insurance won't offer it, then they'll shift to another private plan that does.

If I could update the Medicare guarantee, I understood that I'd effectively be redesigning the entire American health-care system.

That would definitely be big enough for my mutti and my papa.

ELEVEN

PRINCIPLED BIPARTISANSHIP

M y top priority was a seat on the Senate Finance Committee, whose purview extends over Medicare. I knew there was going to be a wait. When I joined the United States Senate, I was number 100 in seniority. The lowest of the low. My seat was directly next to the fabled candy dish, hidden in a drawer in the back of the Senate chamber, full of mini Milky Way bars, M&M's, and butterscotches. It was heaven for Senators with a sweet tooth and a great way for a Senate newcomer to meet colleagues. But it was a symbol of—I'm going to invent a word—my "juniority."

When Senate Majority Leader Tom Daschle called me in January 2001, I thought that wait was finally going to be over. Tom, a long-time friend from our days together in the House of Representatives, had always supported my pursuit of a seat on this mega-important Senate Committee. But his news wasn't what I was expecting. Committee assignments for the next two years were being decided and it would not be possible for him to place me on Finance. He'd looked at the demographics and realized that if I got the next slot, there would be no women on this powerful committee. Tom said he felt badly about the circumstances and renewed his pledge to get me a seat as soon as possible. But with history as my guide, oy, that could mean quite some time. Tom seemed almost as down in the dumps telling me the news as I did hearing it.

A few hours later, Tom called me again. Would I like to be appointed to an open seat on the Senate Select Committee on Intelligence?

I was initially flabbergasted by the question. I had never previously considered Intel, and the idea seemed strewn with pitfalls. I had not been in the Senate long and all the advice I was getting was: Go home to Oregon *a lot* and focus on the bread-and-butter issues that animate Oregonians. I also learned that the work of Intel was classified, so I basically wouldn't be able to talk to Oregonians about what went on behind those closed doors. I admit I was intrigued when Tom told me that two of the other openings were going to Senate heavyweights Jay Rockefeller of West Virginia and Dianne Feinstein of California—what did they know that I didn't, I wondered? Still, initially, I demurred.

But that night, relaxing at home, I started thinking about the Nazis.

It wasn't a particularly linear bout of introspection. It kind of went like this: Short term, yeah, dealing with classified materials about foreign threats and domestic terrorism in a closed committee whose work I couldn't share carried political risks. But I conjured Peter Wyden's voice haranguing me, "Ron, you gotta ask questions!" And I thought about his work as a journalist exposing the intelligence agencies' failures in the Bay of Pigs fiasco—a terrible foreign policy embarrassment that would have been less likely had there been a functioning Senate Intelligence Committee out there asking questions.

And finally, I thought about the Nazi surveillance state that had chased the Wyden and Rosenow families out of Germany to the

United States. "What Jews feared most," Peter Wyden had written, "was the knock on the door in the middle of the night." I have always believed that surveillance is the foundation of tyranny. The U.S., too, could become an unconstrained surveillance state if we didn't subject the CIA, the NSA, and the rest of the Government's intelligence infrastructure—not to mention this newfangled data-gathering Internet industry that Chris Cox and I had helped unleash—to the deepest scrutiny possible.

I called Tom Daschle back the next day and said yes.

Less than eight months after my appointment the Committee was consumed by the terrorist attacks of September 11, 2001—our greatest intelligence failure since the 1960s. I'd made the right choice. I saw I could make a difference both domestically and internationally by focusing on the surveillance state on the Intel Committee; serve Oregon's timber and public lands priorities from a spot on the Energy and Natural Resources Committee; and devote myself to my passion for health care as a basic right even without a coveted perch on the Finance Committee.

The Senate's structure allowed such "off-premises" work. Where the structurally constrained House encourages biding your time and finding small projects to pick off, the tinier Senate allows dabbling but promotes digging. Many Senators don't actually choose a "major"—a specific subject area to which they will devote the lion's share of their study, time, and energy. Instead, they might specialize in visibility, kibbitzing (giving unsolicited advice) publicly on any and every issue that crosses their path, secure (if not necessarily safe) in the assumption that a steady diet of news coverage will smooth their path to re-election. Some specialize in obstruction—the way freshman Republican Tommy Tuberville of Alabama determined in 2023 to gum up the entire, previously routine system of military promotions in an inhumane quest to reduce the health-care coverage of women soldiers in the Armed Forces. Senate rules make it easy (and, honestly, somewhat mindless) to turn "no" into a career. (By the way, notwithstanding Tuberville's success at Auburn, anyone whose own Senate team rebels against both his style and substance, as the Republicans did in joining the Democrats to oppose his lunatic blockade against military promotions, obviously isn't much of a coach.)

Becoming an expert, in several areas no less, though, while more strenuous, offers immense satisfactions. Because in the Senate, ideas drawn from the many corners of the nation's and world's expertise can translate into hugely constructive changes in the ways Americans pursue life, liberty, and happiness.

By the late 1990s, health care had been left open for my digging by a wave of retirements and deaths. Moderate Republican Jack Heinz of Pennsylvania, an ardent advocate for the elderly with whom I'd partnered on Medigap reform during my House tenure, had died in a 1991 airplane accident. Another moderate Republican health-care expert, John Chafee of Rhode Island, was planning to retire, before his untimely death in office in 1999.

Among Democrats, many with a zeal for health-care reform were being drawn by other needs. Kent Conrad of North Dakota was our budget specialist; New Mexico's Jeff Bingaman was devoting himself to energy; John Kerry of Massachusetts, his eyes on a Presidential run, was increasingly interested in climate change and international relations. Jay Rockefeller was passionate about medical care (his family's Rockefeller Foundation had invested billions of dollars in health innovation and reform, going back decades), but his legislative emphasis increasingly was commerce, along with intelligence.

That left me and Teddy Kennedy.

You probably know a good deal about Senator Edward M. Kennedy of Massachusetts. That he was universally regarded as "the lion of the Senate." That he was a fierce advocate for America's have-nots. That his storied family's devotion to public service was marked by tragedies that only reaffirmed their commitment to soldier on, doing good. That he was Mr. Health Care, crusading year after year to try to assure that all Americans, regardless of their circumstances, had access to decent, affordable medical coverage as a basic human right.

Coming into the Senate, I knew one other thing about Senator Kennedy: Like a flower to bees, he attracted talent—outside experts, legislative allies, and a staff of true policy all-stars. I soon learned something else: No one was more generous with his time, his connections, and his decades of accumulated wisdom than Ted Kennedy.

As a new member of the Senate, I could easily have been stiff-armed by Massachusetts' senior Senator, then in his sixth full term. But it was quite the opposite. At our caucus lunches on Tuesdays, on the floor of the Senate chamber, or in impromptu phone calls, he was kind and open with me about our mutual desire to build a new American health-care system.

Just as important, he laid a foundation for others, like me, to build on his work. In the U.S. Senate, information is the coin of the realm, in both its core meanings: as ideas about *what* to do, and as guidance about *how and with whom* to do it. Ted was a storehouse, a veritable Fort Knox, of such information, and he offered his bullion freely to me.

One of the most useful nuggets of wisdom he gave me came in 1998, when I told him I was thinking of partnering with Olympia Snowe—a Maine Republican I'd befriended in the House and who had preceded me in the Senate by a year—and Republican House

Ways and Means Chairman Bill Thomas to repair Medicare's most egregious defect. We were going to try to get the Government to offer prescription drug coverage for the elderly, a foundational change that would revolutionize their health care.

"Any time you can get a Republican as a teammate," Ted said, "go for it." His own collaboration with Utah Senator Orrin Hatch to design the groundbreaking Children's Health Insurance Program (CHIP) that gave health coverage to 6 million previously uninsured kids illustrated one of the Senate's open secrets: Republicans loved to work with Kennedy. Yeah, come election time they'd turn him into their bogeyman, roaring about Democrats-and-their-Ted-Kennedy-socialism like barflies bellowing "Margaritaville." But come the first Wednesday in November, those same Republicans (if they were lucky enough to win) would line up outside his door to partner with him, because Ted got stuff done that they could take back to their constituents and declare as their own.

Although I'd lived and breathed this credo in the House, working across the aisle with Republican highfliers like Chris Cox, Ted Kennedy helped me articulate my predilection into my 10th rule of chutzpah.

The concept of working with all serious allies is foundational to getting things done. Case in point: Long after Ted Kennedy had passed away in 2009, I used this 10th rule of chutzpah to lead the effort in 2018 to secure a 10-year extension in the CHIP Act, with his own former partner, Orrin Hatch.

Even so, bipartisan efforts are easily distorted. This is especially true in today's political environment, when even a discussion, let

RON'S RULE
OF CHUTZPAH

10

WORK WITH
ANYBODY WHO IS
SERIOUS ABOUT
MOVING FORWARD

alone a negotiation, with members of another party is deemed by the noisiest and most extreme partisans as a sacrifice of one's own bona fides. For such reasons, bipartisanship today is considered risky. Powerful special interests see these alliances as threatening, primary opponents start salivating, and leadership prospects can start melting away.

Yet bipartisanship is not a sacrifice of principle, not if the first principle is furthering the greater good. What's more, principled bipartisanship fits well with the structure of the U.S. Senate, where ideas and coalitions built around them are so vital. It also aligns with my personality: It's much easier for me to push positive change than act like a son of a bitch trying to growl his way to victory.

I rattled sabers everywhere with Arizona Republican John McCain, the Senate's Mr. Chutzpah himself. A military hero long recognized for his expertise in foreign policy, McCain also had a low tolerance threshold for BS artists, bureaucrats, and special pleaders in domestic policy. When I came to the Senate he had just become Chair of the Commerce Committee, and I got a thrill teaming with him to fight the sleazeball leaders of the corrupt energy company Enron, the trial lawyers who hoped to sue everyone that moved over the much-hyped Y2K bug, and the prevaricating tobacco lobby. I was particularly proud when, during the 1998 hearings that were part of his effort to craft the multi-billion settlement by which tobacco companies would be forced to pay for the decades they spent knowingly killing Americans, McCain and I got the executives to recant the lies they'd famously told me about tobacco's addictiveness only four years before in the House. (On a less contentious note, we also together wrote, with Spence Abraham, the bill that legalized electronic signatures on Government documents, saving Americans countless hours of unproductive waiting and repetitive strain injury–inducing hand-signing. I even signed the contract for this book electronically!)

In 2011, I brought principled bipartisanship back to fights over the Internet. The motion picture industry and their allies had been pushing passage of one bill after another meant to cripple the new technologies and cement their power for another generation. Their latest bill was a step too far. The problem was, they were wrong. So wrong that the policy they were advancing would have forced a redesign of the Internet's underlying architecture, compromising the security of the entire network and embedding censorship in a mechanism that was designed to empower the frictionless spread of information around the world. This time it wasn't just one censorious Senator but legions of the Washington influence swamp pushing the Stop Online Piracy Act and the Protect IP Act—SOPA/PIPA—claiming that this was the only way to stop counterfeits and file sharing.

"There's no question that people who sell fake Rolexes or tainted Viagra or movies they don't own are bad actors," I told the *Washington Post*. "But…to solve this problem by doing damage to the Internet, which has been a juggernaut for job growth and innovation and free speech, is a mistake."

The industry had lined up 40 Senate sponsors and support of the Chamber of Commerce and AFL-CIO—what should have been an unstoppable force. At the time, viral online campaigns were largely unknown. But if ever there was a time to organize one, this was it. Jeff Michels, my Chief of Staff, arranged for several pro-Internet-freedom user and civil liberties groups to meet in my office every week; I began a phone campaign to the leaders of all the Internet's major user-centric sites, I put a "public hold" on PIPA, to make it hard to advance it on the Senate floor; and I started doing lots of interviews with the news media (even though many of their own companies were backing the bill, the news media always like a fight).

But I did not have one component that's crucial when you're taking a battle against entrenched power to the Senate: a Republican partner. Fortunately, because I had been born in Kansas and I had read about Internet companies gravitating to Kansas City, I was able to make a successful pitch to Kansas Republican Senator Jerry Moran that he join me.

Majority Leader Harry Reid had scheduled a January 24, 2012, vote on whether to override my hold. Moran and I were a classically *chutzpadik* pair: We were taking on leadership, colleagues, and powerful industries, all to assure a future for hundreds of tiny companies and millions of mostly young digital citizens who had never raised their collective voices for...anything.

Thanks to our organizing, on January 18, 2012, just days before the vote, tens of thousands of websites, including the influential Wikipedia, blacked out their home pages in protest of the legislation. Thousands more Americans emailed, texted, and phoned their opposition to the legislation—the first mass Internet organizing campaign in history. Having just discovered a new, enormous pressure group of which they previously were unaware, Senators began withdrawing their support. Four days before the vote, Harry Reid called me to say he'd canceled it. First for the first time, users had defeated corporations to promote Internet freedom.

My favorite example of principled bipartisanship, however, is my alliance—and later my deep friendship—with Gordon Smith, the Republican I narrowly beat to win my seat in the Senate.

The 1996 Oregon special election to replace Robert Packwood was beyond bitter: Until I took mine off the air, our TV negative ads were brutal about each other. Mine said Gordon was poisoning our families, fish, and communities by dumping waste from his pea-packing plant; Gordon said I represented the worse of Big Government, and intimated that if I was elected, I—the former Gray Panther!—would kill Medicare and drive vulnerable seniors into poverty. Unlike many campaigns, where candidates can compete roughly but still get along personally, we grew to loathe each other.

When Oregon's senior Senator, Mark Hatfield, announced his retirement, Gordon, armed with a softer approach on the environment, won the race to succeed him. That meant that Oregon would be going from a state represented by two powerful committee chairs to two new Senators in their forties with zero institutional power. I started rethinking the Gordon-Ron relationship from scratch.

I congratulated Gordon on his victory and invited him for coffee in a dark restaurant in downtown Portland. Gordon's response was perfect: "Glad you called Ron, I was going to call you." We shared a laugh as to how the "senior Senator" designation would work, since we were elected less than a year apart and neither of us had a lick of power. When Gordon arrived to Washington in January, we hosted a party for him and his staff; he thanked me by giving me a beautiful pair of cowboy boots that I still enjoy wearing 27 years later.

We decided to have weekly breakfasts on Thursday in the Senate dining room (they made a bronze plaque identifying our spot as The Oregon Table). We put out a schedule of joint priorities at the beginning of each Congress. And then we did something almost unheard of: holding "Ron and Gordon" town hall meetings. When I went to eastern Oregon, Gordon and his gracious wife, Sharon, hosted me for an overnight at their beautiful Pendleton home.

We came to be known—positively—as The Oregon Odd Couple. And what started as professional became personal. When Gordon and Sharon's son, Garrett Lee Smith, who had been battling depression for years, committed suicide in 2003, the day before his 22nd birthday and a year after my brother Jeff's passing, we shared a tearful bond over our families' mutual struggles with mental health. We were with the Smiths as they grieved and I was proud to be a lead co-sponsor of the Garrett Lee Smith Memorial Act, which allowed college campuses, Native American tribes, and states to receive grants for suicide prevention efforts.

Gordon and I teamed countless times during his two terms in the Senate—to make sure the vulnerable poor had access to Medicaid, advance nanotechnology research, fund rural schools and roads, protect the Portland Air Base, and more. The friendship endures, with catch-up dinners at the legendary RingSide Steakhouse on the west side of Portland. He is in my personal pantheon of Mormon mensches.

∽

I needed some odd coupling if I was going to get the elderly prescription drug coverage under Medicare. The Republicans now controlled Congress. Unless you team up you might as well declare yourself in semi-retirement when the other party takes over the Government. Besides, my philosophy about health-care reform was that the political predispositions of both liberal Democrats and conservative Republicans consisted of too many empty platitudes. Neither expanding benefits nor containing costs alone would help Americans, particularly the elderly. Why? Because if you spend health-care dollars inefficiently, especially on new benefits, the burden inevitably will fall on middle-income taxpayers, who will eventually rebel and reject the reforms, ultimately leaving less money available to help those who, through no fault of their own, cannot secure care.

Philosophically as well as practically, any grand *and successful* health-care reform initiative would have to draw from both classic Democratic and Republican biases. Put simply, health-care reform in the United States must twine together the public and private sectors into a stronger combined force, both to offer benefits and control costs.

That seems like the simplest and most pragmatic principle on earth, so you might well wonder why so many find it so hard to assimilate. I attribute it to a fundamental flaw in the ideology of 21st-century conservatism. As articulated in the very first issue of his influential journal of opinion *National Review*, the pundit William F. Buckley Jr. defined a conservative as one who "stands athwart history, yelling Stop." But his definition begs the most essential question: At what point in history do you yell "stop," to whose benefit, and at what cost? Would today's conservatives have yelled "stop" when the United States's Founders were rebelling against King George III's exploitative tyranny? When American biologists, chemists, and engineers were inventing a vaccine for polio, discovering the structure of DNA, and sending astronauts to the moon? The fact is there were conservatives yelling stop to all these things, but such overwhelming, reactionary sentiment has not previously dominated an entire political party.

Any philosophy premised on "stop" is by definition empty and meaningless. The very basis of the United States is progress, as embodied in the 33rd word of the second paragraph of the Declaration of Independence: This nation exists to promote "life, liberty, and the *pursuit* of happiness." My approach to principled bipartisanship honors the Founders' understanding that honest conservatives and true liberals can, should, and will debate not *whether* to stop or go, but *when* to stop and *when* to go.

Providing prescription drug coverage for the elderly was a perfect place to pursue such principled bipartisanship.

The booming economy of the late 1990s was dividing the nation's haves and the have-nots more starkly than ever. Drug prices during the late '90s were skyrocketing—rising by double digits every year, pressuring retirees and, if they still had coverage from their unions or from lifelong employers, their insurance plans, too. Indeed, many of the private "managed care" programs—the HMOs and preferred-provider organizations that had been added as options under Medicare Part C during that period, and which had initially offered drug coverage in their plans—were withdrawing from the market or reducing their coverage. So there was pressure on Medicare to fix that deep chasm in its coverage. The resources appeared to be there: The return of economic growth and full employment to the U.S. was transforming our chronic budget deficits into surpluses and contributing political will to add such outpatient drug coverage to Medicare. What's more, for the first time since its creation, the rate of growth in Medicare spending started to decline as the Government cracked down on fraud and inefficiency in the program, providing some running room to add new forms of necessary coverage.

Senator Snowe was the perfect partner with whom to take this on. Tough and fearless—orphaned at 9 years old, widowed at 26, she liked to remind people that her grandparents emigrated from Sparta, the ancient Greek home of fabled warriors—she was first elected to Congress at the age of 31, and was later declared by *Forbes* magazine the 54th most powerful woman in the world. As one of the last of the body's moderate Republicans, Olympia lived and breathed bipartisanship, holding it essential to getting things done in Congress. "There is not only strength in compromise, courage in conciliation, and honor in consensus-building," she believed, "but also a political reward for following these tenets."

In November 1999, we introduced SPICE—the Senior

Prescription Insurance Coverage Equity Act. It was modeled on something all our Senate colleagues knew intimately: the Federal Employees Health Benefits Plan, to which we all belonged. SPICE was not, as I told our fellow Senators in presenting it, "some alien, one-size-fits-all Federal price control regime," but, like our own Congressional health plan, a program that offered copious choices and alternatives. That was our model for a new entitlement that we were calling Medicare Part D: voluntary prescription drug coverage for seniors.

On the Senate floor, I read a portion of a letter I received from an elderly woman in Beaverton, Oregon. In this booming headquarters city of Nike, she and her husband were living almost entirely on Social Security income. Once they finished paying for their prescription pharmaceuticals, they had exactly $107.40 left each month to pay for everything else. Her last sentence was a heart-wrenching plea: "Can you help?"

From the start, Senator Snowe and I hammered home incessantly the language of bipartisanship. I used the term 13 times in introducing the bill. "I hope to be able to show the need in our country is enormous and to help catalyze bipartisan action," I stressed, threatening that "until we get comprehensive bipartisan legislation that provides the elderly real relief, I intend to keep coming to the floor of the Senate to talk about this issue."

Six months later, Congressman Bill Thomas joined the fray.

I don't think Ted Kennedy knew Bill Thomas all that well, because if he did, he probably would've warned me away. The Bakersfield, California, Republican, who'd grown up poor in a government housing development and was the first member of his family to graduate from college, had a reputation for irascibility; members and the media openly debated whether he was more irritating or irritable. He feuded with the press and with colleagues and was prone to outbursts of temper. A magazine survey of Congressional staff once rated him the second "smartest" member of Congress and the no. 1 "meanest." He also was as partisan a Republican as existed in Washington, infamous for once calling the Capitol Police to eject Ways and Means Democrats from a committee library they'd occupied after storming out of a hearing he'd commandeered. Why was he collaborating with a progressive Democrat like me to promote a new Federal Government entitlement program?!

That's the unpredictable beauty of politics. What seems impossible today becomes necessary tomorrow, as public awareness and public will blend in the stewpot of electoral reality, turning the once unpalatable into something that suddenly seems quite tasty.

It was now May 2000. The Republicans, having taken advantage of Bill Clinton's first-term missteps to win control of both houses of Congress, had overreached in their attempt to impeach him during a vibrant economic recovery, threatening both their Congressional majority and their hopes of regaining the Presidency the following November. Central to both parties' electoral hopes were senior citizens, whose percentage turnout outstrips every other cohort. Seniors historically had been aligned with Democrats, but through the 1990s they were edging more gingerly into the Republican camp. Republican leaders like Bill Thomas didn't want to stop that momentum by taking a pass on prescription drug coverage. "The initiative highlights a fundamental shift in approach for House Republicans," the *Washington Post* noted. "Once fixated on transforming and shrinking the federal government, they are now focused on blunting political attacks by adopting popular Democratic issues and reframing them in Republican terms."

In other words, Olympia Snowe, Bill Thomas, and I, together, were moving the bar on when to say "stop" to progress.

Bill Thomas and I stood together in one of the most famous chambers in the U.S. Capitol, Room EF-100, which is situated exactly midway between the House and the Senate. With lights on opposite walls signaling the votes in each body, since the 1960s EF-100 has been the site of hundreds of conference committee sessions. "It is obviously symbolic of the fact that we believe there needs to be a bipartisan, bicameral effort to move before the end of this legislative session Medicare modernizations, including putting prescription drugs into the Medicare program and available to all seniors," Representative Thomas said, unveiling our partnership to colleagues and the media that day.

We're going to "try to defy the odds," I agreed, "and the prognosticators and the talking heads that say you just can't get this done."

The initiative we put forward for the House mimicked what Olympia and I had introduced in the Senate and drew from both Democratic and Republican orthodoxy. The Republicans were insistent that private insurers would have to be a major part of the delivery system for any new drug benefit. This was a departure from the Clinton Administration's preference for a plan premised entirely on direct Government payments to seniors. Thomas, in turn, agreed to something that had long rankled me but his party had previously resisted: Pharma companies that used and then profited from early stage Government-funded research to bring blockbuster drugs to market would have to pay a return-on-investment fee to Medicare. He also agreed to a series of other provisions that were important to Democrats.

Prescription drug coverage would be an entitlement for any senior who wanted it. The Government would use Medicare's immense, pooled purchasing power to negotiate down the price of important pharmaceuticals. Those discounts would reduce premiums for everyone, allowing the Government to cover most of the expenses for those seniors whose drug expenses were the highest. And the new drug benefit would be overseen by the Department of Health and Human Services.

We were under no illusions it would be easy. As one unnamed Senate Democrat lamented to the *New York Times*, "This will blur the lines between Republicans and Democrats on what is one of the Democrats' best election issues." I don't disregard the political importance of issues like this—after all, you can't get things done if your team can't even take the field—but if you won't seize the opportunity to make real, positive change in people's lives, you don't belong here in the first place.

If I may draw an analogy from my sports days, trying to turn a big idea into the law of the land isn't a game—it's more like a season. You might even look at individual legislative proposals, like the ones we were asking the House and Senate to take up, as games unto themselves, each bill representing a slightly different starting team going up against a somewhat different set of opponents. An individual member of the House or Senate might even introduce multiple bills on the same subject, each aiming to push the body to embrace one important tenet or another, hoping that over time, the multiple proposals might coalesce into an integrated bill, with enough votes to start or encourage something great to happen. You won't win everything, ever. But if you're good—if you continue to roll that boulder incrementally up the steep hills you face—you'll build on your victories and learn from your losses, and ultimately take home the championship, in the form of a law that makes people's lives better.

There's at least one big, obvious difference between sports and legislation, however: In sports, your season is a known, fixed number of games, at the end of which victory is definitive. A legislative "season," by contrast, has no boundaries, and often no conclusion. Which is why defeat is easier to swallow. Because there's almost always a second chance.

Despite Bill Thomas's power in the House and Olympia Snowe's and my respect in the Senate, we were no match for both our parties' predilections and the power of the pharmaceutical lobby, particularly over the Republican Party. The prescription drug benefit failed to make headway in the last months of Bill Clinton's Presidency and fell prey to the all-consuming post-9/11 politics of George W. Bush's first term.

Then President Bush came alive. Eyeing seniors' votes in his own re-election campaign, Bush asked Bill Thomas in the House and Senate Majority Leader Bill Frist to introduce the Medicare Prescription Drug, Improvement, and Modernization Act of 2003. Although it created the Part D outpatient drug coverage that Thomas, Snowe, and I had fought for, the bills stripped away much of Olympia's and my proposal. The Administration offered $400 billion to seniors over 10 years, which would cover barely 20 percent of what they would be spending on prescription pharmaceuticals. Feeding Democrats' fears that any Administration plan would seek to gut traditional fee-for-service Medicare, in which nearly 90 percent of retirees were enrolled, the Bush White House tilted its benefits toward private plans "approved by" Medicare. State by state, coverage would vary wildly, based on what kinds of private plans were on offer.

Still, prodigious work by Senator Kennedy and Minority Leader Tom Daschle improved the Senate bill substantially. Their intervention helped force preferred provider organizations to offer catastrophic coverage and preventive services as well as the new drug benefit, on top of basic Medicare coverage. The retooled proposal passed the Senate on June 27, 2003, by a substantial bipartisan margin.

The House, by contrast, was a circus. Representative Billy Tauzin of Louisiana—the oil state corporate crony next to whom I'd "marinated" on the House Energy and Commerce Committee for years—had switched parties to become a Republican and was known as the pharma industry's go-to guy in Congress. He'd managed to insert provisions in the House bill that absolutely forbade the Government from negotiating drug prices with industry, gutting the cost control provisions that were central to my proposal. Further pushing cost containment to the side, Tauzin helped kill another provision to allow consumers to import pharmaceuticals from Canada and other countries where the prices were substantially lower. (One year later, Tauzin left Congress to become CEO of the Pharmaceutical Research and Manufacturers of America, the industry's primary lobbying arm, for a salary rumored to be $2 million annually.)

Eliminating price negotiations and import competition (in complete contravention to their oft-expressed "free-market" principles) wasn't enough for many Republicans, who fought hard for incentives that would draw seniors away from fee-for-service Medicare toward private plans. Incensed, House Democrats battled the bill. In the end, it managed to pass on by a single vote.

What followed were four months of bitter negotiations between the House and the Senate to reconcile the two bills. Bill Thomas's legendary temper got the best of him several times. Although both were Republicans, he and the lead Senate negotiator, Iowa Republican Chuck Grassley, clashed constantly, in no small part because Senator Grassley believed—accurately—that the discrimination against classic fee-for-service Medicare would harm residents of rural states, where private, managed care programs were much harder to access.

Thomas's exclusion of most House Democrats from the conference committee inflamed tensions even more, prompting House Speaker Dennis Hastert to replace him as the House lead.

As bad as the resulting bill was, though, to many it was still better than nothing. In November, the AARP—with more than 36 million members and $1 billion in revenues the nation's largest lobbying group—announced its support. "This is not a perfect bill, but America cannot wait for perfect," AARP Chief Executive William D. Novelli said.

Many of my Democratic friends, even my mentors, were apoplectic at what they considered the defection of a vital constituency one year before an election. Senate Democratic Minority Leader Daschle said, "When seniors see the details of the Republican plan, the AARP leadership will regret this ill-advised decision." Ted Kennedy said the Medicare Modernization Act was "using our seniors as guinea pigs." The legislative director of the United Automobile Workers called it "a bill that will make many seniors worse off in terms of their health coverage."

I voted for it.

As managed and mismanaged by the Bush Administration, the Medicare Modernization Act had a lot of flaws. The opportunity to rein in the pharma manufacturers' out-of-control prices looked to have gone *pffft*. It was pretty clear to me that seniors were going to suffer from some rude sticker shock. One health-care journal, noting how premiums and out-of-pocket costs would collide for seniors whose incomes made them ineligible for subsidies, assessed that a beneficiary with $5,000 worth of annual medicine costs would still have to pay between $3,300 and $4,000 a year for the new benefit.

I'd spent many town halls in Oregon getting senior citizens' opinions on Medicare reform, and they had told me that their highest need, which they affirmed over and over, was obtaining some relief to offset the soaring cost of drugs. Mainstream Democrats whom I respected—including the North Dakotans Kent Conrad and Byron Dorgan, whose state has a huge elderly population—supported the bill.

Would its passage help George W. Bush's re-election one year hence? Possibly. But you know, in Washington, DC, there's *always* an election looming; by the first Wednesday in November, next year's fund-raising calls begin. You can't let that distract you. Like AARP's Bill Novelli, I reasoned that it made no sense to let the perfect trump the value of getting started. With Medicare Part D now the law, we could go about fixing its flaws, rather than trying to invent it from scratch.

I thought then (still do) that I was channeling Ted Kennedy. Yes, he vigorously opposed the Medicare Modernization Act. But he never tried to argue me out of my vote. His philosophy, which he articulated to me over and over, was "always get down the road as far as you can, and then come back to finish the journey." He called it "the 70/30 principle," but I've always thought of it as "the Kennedy Rule": If you can get 70 percent of what you want, that's a damn good start, so take it, and make it clear you plan to come back and go for the rest. Or in reference to Ron's Rule of Chutzpah #9, each time you go back at it, you push the boulder a little higher up the hill.

Which was exactly my plan. Except I was going to map the rest of this journey along the road to universal health care. And I was going to get Republican support to make it happen.

TWELVE

THE CUISINE OF COMPROMISE

Reader, I married her.

Perhaps the greatest occupational hazard of leadership is that you can readily get caught up in the trappings of your position and lose touch with both your humility and your humanity. The syndrome is a particular affliction in the U.S. Congress, especially the Senate, where your ability to start good things and stop bad things and attach incentives and penalties to each draws "friends" from near and far. To borrow a phrase from sociologist David Riesman, you can fall into membership in the lonely crowd—surrounded by people, but alone.

I was fortunate in this regard. Maybe because team sports had been such a formative part of my upbringing, maybe because I never really had to claw my solitary way to the top of an organization, maybe because I was surrounded during my Gray Panther years by a panoply of *bubbes* and *zaydes* (that's Yiddish for "grandmothers" and "grandfathers") looking out for me, I've always had friends making sure I didn't check my humanity at the door or give up after the end of my first marriage. And one of the things they knew about me was that I really wanted to meet a nice woman who wasn't a lobbyist.

An old friend made the *shidduch*—that's Yiddish for "marriage matchmaking." A *shidduch* is among Judaism's highest *mitzvahs*—that's Yiddish for a "selflessly good deed."

"There's this wonderful woman who owns the Strand, the iconic bookstore in New York," my friend called to tell me. "She's coming to Portland, and you should meet her. Her name is Nancy Bass." He knew Nancy from their time together at the Aspen Institute, and he knew me because of our mutual interest in American-Israel relations.

That night, I watched summer league basketball on TV and thought about the upcoming stops scheduled on my grassroots election campaign trail. I pondered whether to call Nancy Bass.

"She owns a bookstore, she must've read every book in it," I told myself.

I sunk deeper into my torment. "What if she asks me the last novel I read?" I wondered if Federal Statute 18 U.S. Code 1821, which makes it illegal for non-dentists to ship dentures across state lines, qualified. It *sounded* fictional.

Finally, I came to my senses. "If my dad were alive, he would say, 'We Wydens have writing and books in our DNA, and what's not to like about meeting someone terrific who owns a beloved bookstore?'" I called Nancy Bass.

Two days later, we met in the lobby of the historic Governor Hotel in southwest Portland. The ostensible purpose of her trip was to visit Powell's, a literary emporium often referred to as the Strand of the West. I offered to show it to her.

As we wound our way to Powell's, we passed lots of people eating outside at small tables. Every couple of minutes, we'd get hit with vintage Portland friendliness. "Hey, Ron, got time to join us for a dessert, a drink, a snack?" "Hey, Ron, it's a beautiful afternoon. Can you join us and fill us in on what's happening in DC?" "Hey, Ron, your date is gorgeous and has a great smile. You are a lucky bachelor."

No, no one said that last line. But they were thinking it, of that I am sure!

My rebuffs were gentle. "You folks are great to ask us to join you. My date owns a bookstore back East, and we've got to get over to Powell's"—I smiled at Nancy—"so she can see why we have the league-leading bookstore right here."

Afterward, we went to dinner at Bluehour, near Powell's in the Pearl District. The restaurant, though now gone, remains magical to us, because it stands for that moment just before sunset when the sky is at its most colorful—that very moment when we sat down to dinner, that moment my courtship of Nancy Bass began.

The next day, I had a previously arranged small dinner fundraiser scheduled for 7 p.m. I wanted to take Nancy to Cannon Beach to show her the sunset. The drive is an hour-and-a-half from Portland. The sun tends to set late on the Northern Oregon coast in July, so there was no way I could get Nancy to the coast by sunset and still keep the scheduled time for dinner back in Portland. I asked my dinner host if we could move the time up since we were a small group. He said sure, proposing 6 p.m. I tried not to laugh and proposed 5 p.m. Knowing me well, he wondered what else was happening. I said I wanted to show off Haystack Rock in Cannon Beach, with its high trees, long shore, and crashing waves, to a guest from back East before sunset. I heard his smile. The small dinner was changed to 5 p.m.

The last stretch of road from Portland to Cannon Beach that parallels the shore and Haystack Rock is aptly known as Sunset Boulevard. Nancy and I reached it for a spectacular 8 p.m. Oregon summer sunset. We walked the beach barefoot and smelled s'mores over campfires. Because it was a day before the Fourth of July, fire-crackers were exploding.

A bit more than a year later, on September 24, 2005, we were married at sunset at Cannon Beach by Rabbi Ariel Stone, breaking the glass on the reflective wet sand. We had family and a handful of long-time friends.

Nancy's store, nearing 100 years old, is not just a New York landmark—it is a humming hive of retail activity, mobbed with tourists and locals alike. So after we were married, Nancy continued to run the Strand, and I continued to act like a human yo-yo, going back and forth from Oregon to DC. We constantly juggled schedules and figured we would figure things out. Years later, one of our three children wondered out loud if I lived part-time in an airport. The yo-yoing has never stopped.

The twins, William and Ava, were born in 2007, and our young-est daughter, Scarlett, followed five years later. All were delivered at Oregon Health and Science University by Dr. Mark Nichols—in the same room and mostly with the same medical team. Dr. Mark told us he would ensure the deliveries did not conflict with any previ-ously scheduled Oregon football games. (He came through—not that it mattered!) More seriously, though, I don't have adequate words for the feeling that enveloped me, seeing these three healthy, beautiful babies enter our lives. I felt...blessed—yes, of course...for-tunate beyond belief...and resolved, with new shots of energy to help me work harder so that they and their generation and the next could have as bright a future as the one Nancy and I were born into.

Before I met Nancy, I owned a small apartment in southwest Portland. It became too cramped when the twins came along. We wanted a home in the Eastmoreland neighborhood of southeast Portland, where the trees are green and spectacular; the sidewalks

are generous, for after-dinner walks; and the basketball courts are nearby, at Duniway Elementary School. Our initial drives around the area turned up nothing for sale. We were determined to try again, and this time we lucked out and saw a new but unfinished house. Nancy figured out who the developer was, and we pounced. Our place is three minutes from beautiful Berkeley Park, with swings and lit tennis courts. It has been home for more than 12 years. After a busy day, if there is no traffic outside the house, I can dribble a basketball down the center of the street, the neighbors doing play-by-play: "Ron is headed down the lane to the basket." (It takes something more than chutzpah to still dream of playing for the Blazers at my age.)

Throughout Nancy's and my courtship, through George W. Bush's second term in the White House, I dwelled on the dilemma of

American health care. As big as creating a prescription drug benefit for retirees was, it wasn't big enough. After nearly 35 years fighting health-care battles, I'd concluded that the system's essential problem was that too many of its parts were intricately and directly connected with the others. Worse, as many commentators at the time noted, the entire system was like a balloon: Squeeze it in one place, like prescription drugs, to save money and it would bulge out somewhere else, all the while continuing to inflate beyond what families had ability to pay. The balloon needed to be deflated without bursting it.

The biggest part that needed to be reshaped was our essential misunderstanding of the problem: We were focused on curing the sick, whereas our primary attention ought to be having fewer sick people. America requires a health-care system that's oriented first and foremost toward illness prevention.

The second enormous challenge we needed to address was the dominance within the medical-industrial complex of middlemen—unnecessary yet amply compensated intermediaries between consumers and their hands-on health-care providers.

Middlemen are the Whac-A-Moles of American health care—indeed, public policy in general. More often than not the lobbies with a substantial presence in Washington (and the state houses) represent middlemen of one stripe or another. In health care I'd been beating them down for decades as they popped their heads up, such as with their scammy Medigap plans that didn't (as they claimed) fill holes in seniors' Medicare coverage, and pharmacy benefits managers who didn't (as they claimed) offer the lowest prices on medicines. A wise man once said, "Half the human race is middlemen and they don't take too kindly to being cut out." This was going to be quite a fight.

The third, and perhaps most controversial, component that required complete change was the health insurance system's dependence on the biggest and most inefficient middleman of all: employers.

The greatest misconception in America's century-long debate about health care is that it's a contest between the private sector and the Government. That's just wrong. Both are vital. Without Government funding and provision, there would be no basic medical research and far less applied research, and accessibility would suffer, especially in poorer and more rural areas. Without Government oversight and regulation, scams would proliferate, costs would skyrocket, and price-insensitive monopolies would consolidate control of medicine, to the detriment of families everywhere. Without the private sector, there'd be no competition to bring new drugs to market nor incentives to improve treatments or lower costs.

More material than the simplistic debate about the Government versus the private sector is the role of employers versus the rest of the private sector as the central conduit for the financing and provision of medical care.

Employer-based health care is an artifact of World War II wage-and-price controls that didn't make sense 10 years after the war's end, let alone 70 years. No other nation in the Western industrialized world put health coverage on the backs of employers; our singular reliance on them was dragging down the United States' competitiveness. Too many Americans were taking jobs they didn't want and staying in jobs that didn't elevate them merely to obtain and keep insurance coverage. As bad, or worse, too many Americans couldn't get any insurance at all, because they were self-employed or worked for companies too small to offer it.

Reliance on employers was a two-dimensional drag on the nation's economy, pouring too much of our national wealth into inefficient sickness care and militating against entrepreneurialism and business development. It needed to be replaced by some form of Government-guaranteed universal coverage that was built on a private-sector foundation, each side providing a check and balance on the other, to assure that care would continually improve as costs remained in check.

On December 13, 2006, I announced the Healthy Americans Act, the name chosen deliberately to highlight its emphasis on health over illness. I opened with a warning; "Employer-based coverage is melting like a popsicle in the summer sun," I said at a crowded press conference. Only 63 percent of Americans were then covered by their companies' plans, down five percentage points in only four years.

Underscoring both the pending crisis and the coalition politics that at last made it resolvable, I was joined by Steve Burd, the CEO of Safeway, the 91-year-old, 200,000-employee-strong grocery chain; and Andy Stern, the president of one of the nation's largest labor groups, the 1.8-million-member Service Employees International Union.

"You didn't have that picture in 1994," I said, pointing at Stern and Burd, and referencing the failed Clinton effort to bring universal health care into existence. "There was a picture this morning that did not exist the last time Congress took a run at this."

For all its complexity the plan was a simple one guided by Jeff Michels and my able Legislative Director Josh Sheinkman. We were keeping the parts of the system that worked and throwing out those parts that drove up costs, misdirected subsidies, and let profiteers sap the public purse. The Federal Employees Health Benefits Plan, the system that covered all Federal employees across the country, including members of Congress, was a part that worked. Costs were low; choices were many and varied, in both price and coverage across the FEHBP exchanges; and it kept the population it covered healthier. Our bill made that structure available to all Americans with an exchange in each state while guaranteeing that health care was held to an affordable share of a family's budget.

I did away with all the various Federal health-care systems for people under 65 (except for the VA, which cares for a unique population with specialized needs) and put the Portland janitor, the Austin coder, and the Miami developer in the same health-care system as their Congressman and Senators. So that no one was left behind, for low-income Americans who needed extra support we provided appropriate "wraparound" social support benefits to ensure they would be able to get to a doctor and could follow up with preventative care.

Famed economist Milton Friedman, in his younger, more creative days, designed the Social Security payroll withholding system, widely regarded as the most efficient economic transfer mechanism ever created. Despite his reputation as a scourge of every progressive policy, we adopted Friedman's idea to cut out the middlemen so as to ensure every American's premium payment was affordable and guaranteed. Those payments would come from reallocating all the existing money being inefficiently spent on employer health-care premiums and a multitude of government programs. In place of premiums, which Steve Burd and virtually every other employer complained were skyrocketing and unsustainable, all employers would pay a new, graduated tax, designed to reflect a company's fair share of a healthier, more productive American workforce. This was one of Jeff Michels's innovations, and it was the first tax ever designed around corporate ability to pay. Companies such as Google or a Wall Street firm, which earned millions of dollars per employee, would pay the most, whereas a labor-intensive business like Safeway, earning only thousands of dollars per employee, would pay far less—but all would contribute a share—and no more than they were already spending. In this way, we could transfer nearly $300 billion a year, enough to keep health-care costs below 15 percent of income for every single American family and eliminate the drag on jobs, worker mobility, and innovation that the existing system imposed.

The twisted balloon monster had been reshaped. "This has a real chance of having a successful conclusion," labor leader Stern told the crowd.

Now, let's stop for a moment and do a reality check.

Andy Stern was absolutely right: the Healthy Americans Act (which I formally introduced in the Senate in January 2007) had a real chance of success. But neither he, nor I, nor Safeway CEO Steve Burd, were under any illusion that anything would or could conclude quickly. The Presidential election was a mere 10 months away. What I was doing—what we were all doing—was laying down markers that all the Presidential candidates would have to dance across on their way to their parties' nominations and, thereafter, the White House. Candidates understandably try to operate their campaigns from 35,000 feet, nodding supportively in the direction of a big idea but not committing to specifics. As a legislator, my job is to try to nudge them toward, and if possible embrace, some details, thereby building as much momentum as possible while also acknowledging that any proposal must be subject to revision in return for support. That latter is one of the most misunderstood aspects of leadership, be it in politics, business, or any other field. This is especially true today, as the concept of compromise has grown to become reviled and is considered by ignorant commentators (particularly in the MAGA brigades) to be a sign of weakness. It's anything but: Compromise isn't about horse-trading bad ideas for each other; it's about blending good ideas together into a whole that's better than the sum of its parts.

With the George W. Bush Administration facing its term-limited end and a new President fated to surface, I determined to do something unusual, if not unheard of: visit all 99 other U.S. Senators individually in their offices to offer my draft, ask their input, and seek their collaboration. Most were cordial.

Bob Bennett, though, leaned in. "Let's talk about specific policies," said Bennett, a conservative Republican from Utah and, like me, a second-termer and a policy wonk.

I leaned in even further. I liked Bennett. If he was going to buy the bit, I wanted to make sure he understood exactly what its premises were (as they said in vaudeville about a successful routine, "Buy the premise, buy the bit"). "Look," I said, "the Dems are *right* to be for universal coverage. Because if you don't get everyone covered, there'll be too much cost-shifting and not enough prevention, and it'll be another version of the mess we have now.

"But get this," I continued. "The Republicans are right, too: There *should* be a role for the private sector. We already have a good model—the health insurance you and I get as members of Congress. We could just say that anyone who's not in the military or on Medicare should have the same coverage we and every other Federal employee has."

"Let me think about it," Senator Bennett replied.

> **RON'S RULE OF CHUTZPAH**
>
> **11**
>
> COMPROMISE ISN'T ABOUT HORSE-TRADING BAD IDEAS FOR EACH OTHER; IT'S ABOUT BLENDING GOOD IDEAS TOGETHER INTO A WHOLE THAT'S BETTER THAN THE SUM OF ITS PARTS

Nine times out of 10, when a member of Congress says, "Let me think about it," they will come back later with a no—if they even bother to respond at all. Bob Bennett was the 10th member. "Okay," he said in a phone call a few days later. "I want to be your Republican. Let's do it."

His participation, announced in May 2007, was a stunner. Bennett wasn't just any Republican. He was a member of Majority Leader Mitch McConnell's leadership team and hereditary Republican royalty: the son of a U.S. Senator, the grandson of the seventh president The Church of Jesus Christ of Latter-day Saints, and the great-grandson of two mayors of Salt Lake City. Having him join as co-author of the first-ever bipartisan universal health-care coverage bill in the history of the U.S. Senate—the first to try to sever the chain that had adversely bound together employers and health—was a Nixon-in-China moment.

I emphasized that point at St. Joseph's University in Philadelphia, when Bennett and I started touring the nation to tout our plan. "Isn't this great!?" I burst—smiling at the memory from decades earlier, when Gonzaga University tried to recruit me to play basketball for them. "A Jesuit university hosting a Mormon fellow and a Jewish fellow to fix health care!" The progressive journal the *American Prospect* dubbed Bennett and me—me for maybe the 107th time—a "political odd couple." (Who was Oscar and who was Felix, they didn't say.)

Bob and I went about seeking additional co-sponsors for what was now being called the Wyden-Bennett Healthy Americans Act. We quickly lined up a dozen influential allies, six from each party. The Congressional Research Service validated that it was the largest bipartisan coalition ever put together for a universal health-care bill.

Arguably our most important call, though, was not to a Democratic or Republican colleague, but to the nonpartisan Congressional

Budget Office, the watchdog body launched by Congress in 1974 to provide rigorous and unbiased economic analyses to the legislative branch. In May 2008, just six months before the election, the CBO wrote to Bennett and me that "our preliminary analysis indicates that the proposal would be roughly budget-neutral in 2014.... For the years after 2014, we anticipate that the fiscal impact would improve gradually, so that the proposal would tend to become more than self-financing and thereby would reduce future budget deficits or increase future surpluses."

We now had a pole position in the second most important campaign in America during that election year: the Presidential influence race. "The process Wyden and Bennett have kicked off is by far the most promising development in health reform," wrote journalist and pundit Ezra Klein at the time. "It's more important than anything the presidential candidates have proposed, more important than anything done in the states." Klein was optimistic: "It's conceivable that, by the time the next president is elected, they will have created a legislative working group that can actually pass health reform—something we've never had before."

The campaign was historic—the first election in 80 years when neither party had an incumbent President or Vice President vying for its nomination—and the field was crowded with candidates and reform proposals. Survey after survey showed that Democratic voters considered health care the most important issue in the election; for Republicans, it was no. 2, after immigration. "There are a bunch of issues that candidates can take a pass on. This [health-care reform] is not one of them," said Democratic pollster Geoffrey Garin.

As the Democratic field winnowed, I remained neutral. I figured my role was to keep both leading candidates focused on the goal of universal coverage, and not get sidetracked by campaign politics.

Chief among those was the question of mandates. The requirement that all Americans buy health insurance on their own if they didn't receive it from their employer had been a feature of the Clinton Administration's comprehensive reform proposal that went down in flames 14 years before.

In 2008, the candidates were still skittish. Barack Obama flat-out opposed any form of personal mandate and figured he could pay for universal coverage by reversing the Bush Administration's tax cuts on businesses and the wealthy. Hillary Clinton eventually disclosed that she still favored a mandate, but—scarred by her earlier experience—took a long time to make that clear.

Me, I wanted them to ignore it. The ballyhoo about Hillary wanting a mandate and Obama not wanting a mandate was, in my view, an overly simplistic media-goaded cage match that missed the most important part of the discussion: Should Americans take any personal responsibility for their own health care?

For both moral reasons and on economic grounds, I believed the answer was absolutely yes.

Like nations, personal behavior has borders that, when they erode, make innocents unsafe. Indulging in unhealthy behaviors—smoking cigarettes, gorging on saturated fats, refusing to exercise—are an individual's right. People have the constitutional right to be foolish, but they don't have the right to put the costs of that foolishness on others. Those trillions of dollars the United States already was spending on doctors, hospitals, and drugs, all of it ultimately was coming from the pockets of taxpayers. By far the simplest and best way to assure that the few don't bankrupt the many was to promote personal responsibility, by requiring everyone who could afford it to insure themselves.

I have always said that a large part of my job as a public servant is education. As the candidates argued over their health-care reform differences, I barnstormed Oregon and much of the rest of the country teaching the ins and outs of universal coverage. What I learned from these encounters is that mandates themselves weren't an issue for most voters. Americans participate in all manner of important mandates. We pay property taxes and income taxes to our town, state, and Federal governments to finance national defense, police and fire protection, kids' educations, and road and bridge repair. We accept TSA screening to secure air travel, driver's licenses to ride our roads, passports to enter the country, and vaccinations to attend schools. Required insurance—from auto insurance in order to get behind the wheel of a car, to life insurance to help qualify for a mortgage to buy a house—is part of the landscape of life.

The politicization of health-care requirements was rife with hypocrisy. The concept of a universal health insurance requirement was first recommended by the conservative Heritage Foundation think tank in 1989 and was first turned into state law—quite successfully—in 2006 by Massachusetts' Republican Governor Mitt Romney. Even Milton Friedman endorsed the mandate.

Conservatives' subsequent demonization of mandates had nothing to do with any opposition to Government coercion—after all, they had no problem trying to force women into health-care regimes where abortion was illegal—and everything to do with not allowing "the other side" a victory on health-care reform. That's why I wished Barack Obama and Hillary Clinton would move on and reframe the issue as what it really was: a question of personal responsibility.

That mandates could inflame the debate even in a Democratic primary, though, highlighted the thornier problem: Most people don't understand insurance. The most frequent question I'd encounter in town meetings was, "Where in the Constitution does it say

I have to buy health insurance?" Rather than browbeat a constituent with a pre-cooked answer, I'd meet the question with a question: "Okay, tell me how you'd do it."

"If I get hurt skiing Mt. Bachelor, I'll buy insurance then," I heard back at one Oregon town hall.

As gently as I could, I said, "Well, that's not how insurance works," I explained. "If people bought it only after they needed it, the insurers would quickly go broke and disappear. Insurance only works when large pools of people buy into it: The many are both subsidizing the few who will need it and assuring that if you end up among those unlucky few, you'll have the support you require. That's the whole premise underlying the phrase 'mutual insurance.' I mean, if people only bought homeowner's insurance the day after they had a fire, pretty soon no one would be able to get homeowner's insurance." To all this, my town hall questioner gave a thoughtful head tilt and said, "Yeah man, that's really cool!" (Perhaps the best reaction insurance-related humor has ever gotten.)

Whenever I tell the story that way, I always get at least one person coming up to me afterward to say, "Thanks—I was always too afraid to ask before, and never understood this until now."

The politics only became more heated when Barack Obama won the Democratic nomination and then defeated Republican Senator John McCain for the Presidency. On his third day in the job, he invited me to a private meeting in the Oval Office.

I admired President Obama. How couldn't I? It takes enormous chutzpah when, barely two years into your first term in the U.S. Senate, you announce your candidacy for President—and then go on to win after a campaign marked by consideration, conciliation, and intelligence.

I'd been to the Oval Office before, but usually as part of a planned

Presidential schedule for a press event or a many-on-many negotiation. This meeting was shrouded in mystery. I was given no agenda; I was told to follow a different entry route than I'd ever taken before; and there was no press gaggle. When I arrived, I was met only by the new President and one old ally—Philip M. Schiliro, whom I knew from his decades of service to the Democratic Party as Representative Henry Waxman's Chief of Staff, Senator Tom Daschle's Policy Director, and Staff Director for the Senate Democratic Leadership Committee.

Now Phil was President Obama's Director of Legislative Affairs, and issue no. 1 for the two of them was health care—and it was clear that what they wanted to know, without being pushy, was if I would be with them or against them.

"Mr. President," I replied quickly, "this bill will not be called Wydencare. It will be named after you. I am convinced, based on our previous talks, that you want a major bill, and I would be thrilled to work with you on it!"

The ice thus broken, President Obama got down into the details, saying, "Ron, I agree with 90 percent of what you and Bennett have done." Specifically, he intended to propose a bill that pulled important provisions from the Healthy Americans Act. It would legally bar insurance companies from discriminating against customers with pre-existing conditions. Not only that, he was open to accepting an insurance mandate, and what I called "shared responsibility."

The 10 percent on which he disagreed was pretty substantive, however. He did not want fundamental reform of massively inefficient employer-based coverage system. "Ron, you are a great leader on health, but you are just ahead of the times on employer-based coverage," Obama told me. In a later interview with the *Oregonian*, he detailed his hesitancy. "There are a lot of good concepts to what

Ron's proposing," the President said. But a "radical restructuring" of health care away from an employer-based system would meet "significant political resistance."

I tried gently to persuade him otherwise—having a quarter-century more tenure than him in Washington and more than three decades in the health-reform trenches, I did offer some additional thoughts.

"Mr. President," I responded, "we Democrats are good at expanding benefits, but not so good at containing costs." Home builders and software companies, I said, simply are not health-care experts, nor do they have the power, individually or collectively, to keep costs in check. I suggested to him that one of the Democrats' oft-invoked tactics to sell the concept of universal coverage to voters—that they could "keep what you have" if they liked their current employer-provided plan—had a time bomb ticking away inside it, for if a provider leaves an insurance network, consumers almost inevitably get hit with higher costs when their employer's new plan coalesces. *The system of employer-based insurance simply is not sustainable,* I said.

He told me what he later told the press. "Families who are currently relatively satisfied with their insurance but are worried about rising costs...would get real nervous about a wholesale change," he said.

Despite our disagreement, I told him I'd work vigorously with him for passage of his Affordable Care Act. The bill he wanted to sign indeed had many of my priorities, although I believed that Obama's tilt in the traditional Democratic direction of a government-dominated program lacking market-based incentives for cost containment would lead to a massive fight in Congress, despite the significant Democratic Senate majority that came in on his coattails. Liberal pundit Jacob Weisberg channeled my concerns, lamenting in *Newsweek*: "Democrats are poised to pass legislation that spends an additional trillion dollars, fails to restrain spending, and shores up an anachronistic employer-based system."

The President got his bill...and his fight. Senate Minority Leader Mitch McConnell, as wily as he is coldhearted, organized the Republicans' opposition, which centered on the "mandate." He and the right-wing Tea Party, a force then burgeoning in his party, frightened even longtime supporters of personal responsibility into submission. Iowa's Chuck Grassley did a full 180-degree flip-flop in only three months: In June 2009, he had told *Fox News* that just as states require drivers to purchase automobile insurance, "the principle ought to lie the same way for health insurance"; but the following September, he told the same network that "individuals should maintain the freedom to choose whether to purchase health insurance coverage or not." Eventually every Senate Republican voted that the mandate was unconstitutional.

As gratified as I'd been that I was able to get Democrats to accept the Republican concept of an insurance mandate, I was shocked by the Republicans' reversal on their very own issue. "I would characterize the Washington, DC, relationship with the individual mandate as truly schizophrenic," I told Ezra Klein.

What was more dispiriting was how the Republicans and the Democrats colluded to abandon one of the equally important concepts of the Healthy Americans Act: freedom of choice.

Throughout the battle to win passage of the Affordable Care Act, it was becoming clearer and clearer that freedom of choice in health insurance was an endangered species. Since the bill was going to set up exchanges in every state, as Bennett and I had proposed, I pushed to allow every person to be able to take the money their employer paid for their insurance to those exchanges—while the employer kept the tax benefit of providing coverage. We called this Free Choice Vouchers. This idea would, much less efficiently, offer the choices of the Healthy Americans Act.

But even that came under furious fire from big business and labor. A substantial share of the power of both labor and big business comes from being the only secure source of health coverage for their members and/or workers. Other than salary increases, which had become hard to come by in recent years, the primary win the unions had to deliver for their membership in contract negotiations was health benefits. With the increasing cost of health care it wasn't even better benefits, per se, just better and cheaper than the folks who didn't have the good fortune to be represented by a union. The same was true with corporations: Health insurance might have been a pain in the butt to manage, but it made their workforce far less mobile, so even the horribly inefficient cost of managing health care internally was less than the many tangible and intangible costs of lower employee retention.

This "feature" of the employer-based system was in many ways its most pernicious. While developing the Healthy Americans Act, I called it the entrepreneurship tax. In pure economic terms, employer- and union-provided health insurance decreased the mobility of labor, reducing the bargaining power of workers versus management at every level. A highly skilled engineer at Intel in Hillsboro, Oregon, could leave the company to start their own chip company and, freed from bureaucratic management, might innovate an entirely new architecture that would help our country leap ahead in manufacturing. But if that same engineer has a spouse and kids who rely on their excellent health coverage for challenging medical conditions, that is a leap that, all too often, the engineer wouldn't take.

Even for lesser skilled labor the constant siphoning of wages into paying for health-care benefits was a huge drag on take-home pay for millions of working Americans. In fact, it's difficult to compare wages from the 1950s with the 2000s since so many of the gains were for "benefits" rather than cash income—benefits that were important but that didn't pay for housing, food, or children's education, making those costs an ever-increasing bite out of a family's budget.

The political reality that captive workforces were important to both big business and organized labor resulted in strident political attacks on me personally.

Three labor unions that had been strong supporters of my other work poured money into ads in Oregon attacking me and my Free Choice Voucher proposal. The national Chamber of Commerce and Business Roundtable mobilized their hordes of contract lobbyists around Washington to throw stones at me and the idea of freeing workers from the chain of immobile health coverage.

The business and labor campaign was filled with lies and half-truths. "The Free Choice proposal has run into a buzz-saw of special interest opposition," the *New Republic* reported. "Employers don't like it, benefits managers don't like it, unions don't like it—in each case, because it means these groups have less control over, or stand to derive less loyalty from, workers over health-care decision-making."

Having taken on progressive god Ralph Nader a decade-and-a-half earlier when I was first running for the Senate, I wasn't about to succumb to this new round of bullying. So I did something that is rare in politics, I took out my own advertisements to counter the claims of all the special interests.

"It's not true—Wyden's plan gives middle-class taxpayers a break..." my ads said. "Employers would still help pay for coverage, but we'd make our own choices. If you like the coverage you have, you can keep it or choose another plan—and every American is finally covered for life, even if they change jobs or get laid off."

Labor and I agreed 90 percent of the time throughout my Congressional career. But if they were going to beat me about the head and neck, damned if I wasn't going to fight back. My ads closed with the narrator saying, "When you've got a health-care plan that is being attacked by insurance lobbyists and some DC labor unions, you must be doing something right," followed by me announcing: "I'm Senator Ron Wyden and I approve this ad because I won't let DC lobbyists stop health-care reform again—not this time."

The unions backed down in Oregon, in no small part because they saw polls that showed my support going up. But many of my Democratic colleagues on Capitol Hill took the opposition of big business and labor to heart. Finance Committee Chair Max Baucus invited representatives from the big-corporate lobby Business Roundtable into his office to tell Jeff Michels and Josh Sheinkman why Free Choice Vouchers couldn't be in the bill. When that didn't work, he organized a rare, coordinated attack on my amendment to add Free Choice Vouchers to the Affordable Care Act by the senior members of the committee.

It is understandable why the members joined this attack—my amendment strategy relied on the support of those Democrats who understood the policy and supported what I was trying to do for American workers *and* the Republicans who were hoping that by adding such a groundbreaking provision they could kill the entire legislative enterprise. I knew they were wrong about killing the bill, but I was happy to take their votes.

The objections weren't substantive. During the Committee session they publicly worried (or said that the large companies worried) that they would have people shifting in and out of their plans and they would lose stability—even though the bill already restricted switching to the same "open-season" period that the Senators and their staffs were restricted to. They worried that offering people choice with subsidies would somehow encourage them to buy less than they needed—an objection that was never offered with any supporting evidence, real world or theoretical. Chairman Baucus mused, "If we were to do this all over again, start from scratch, we might not have an employer-based system." But "to move away from the system would be destabilizing, it would cause such consternation in what we know as a country." Dogs and cats sleeping together— apparently, I was threatening the very fabric of the nation with this amendment. Sadly, with the clear message that the amendment was a threat to the overall bill, I lost the vote.

I refused to back down. "What is indisputable is over 200 million Americans—200 million Americans!—if they're getting hammered by their insurance company, if they are getting lousy service, we are saying that 'you are stuck.' *That* is indefensible," I warned my colleagues.

I did more than warn them. Teddy Kennedy had died just six weeks earlier, a few months after being diagnosed with a malignant brain tumor. After 40 years in the trenches I was one of the Senate's longest-standing authorities on health care. I knew that without a personal mandate and freedom of choice to shop for insurance, the plans offered under the Affordable Care Act would become increasingly *un*affordable. Getting rid of vouchers wasn't a compromise; it was a garden variety bad idea. So after my beatdown, I went to Senate Majority Leader Harry Reid (a fabled, tough-as-nails former boxer) and swung back: Without Free Choice Vouchers in the bill, I wouldn't vote for it.

Having decided, against my advice, to battle for Obamacare strictly on partisan grounds, the Administration needed every vote. Reid put my vouchers in the bill, as part of the leader's amendment—it is the right of the Majority Leader to jump the queue and be the first to offer amendments, substitutes, and motions for the Senate's consideration. During the meeting he pointed a finger in the face of Jeff Michels, and said menacingly, "You—I don't like you."

For all the misplaced and deliberately stoked ire, the Affordable Health Care for America Act squeaked through the House 220–215 on November 7, 2009, and—as the Patient Protection and Affordable Care Act—passed the Senate (by the slimmest of margins, since it required 60 votes) 60–39 on December 24, with my "aye" vote, just after Hanukkah, and in time for Christmas. President Obama signed it in March 2010.

On January 1, 2014, Obamacare began offering coverage to 20 million Americans who previously lacked insurance. It was filled with provisions drawn from my Healthy Americans Act: a health insurance exchange modeled on my concept where at least some Americans can shop from among competing private health plans...a ban on insurers' discrimination against people with pre-existing conditions...incentives for states to innovate their own solutions that can improve on the Federal requirements...enhanced coverage for home care of the elderly suffering from multiple chronic conditions...continuing Medicare payments for seniors in hospice care... and personal responsibility, in the form of the individual insurance mandate.

It lacked my Free Choice Vouchers, which were stripped in a secretive midnight budget deal among Democrats, Republicans, and a multitude of special interests in 2011. Three hundred thousand people who were slated to gain choice in affordable coverage under the law were now going to be denied it. It was meant to be a foot in the door: Once choice had made it available to some, I expected it to be demanded by more.

But nobody said great things happen overnight. As I offered when Obamacare passed: "We've always known that the path to reforming the nation's health-care system was going to be long...So while it's important to celebrate how far we've come, let's remember this is only a start."

Or as the Rolling Stones put it, articulating Ron's Rule of Chutz-pah #11 better than I can: *No, you can't always get what you want... But if you try sometimes, you'll find you get what you need.*

THIRTEEN

THE LONG GAME, PART II

You must realize that the reactionary right wing never gives up. Whether motivated by religious zealotry, racial prejudice, or a sheer determination to dominate others, they will persist in their efforts to subvert Americans' freedoms.

This reactionary impulse kicked in after the 13th Amendment to the Constitution abolished slavery in 1865; little more than a decade later, the right's subversive reaction launched the nation into 90 more years of Jim Crow laws, segregation, and lynching of Black Americans. It happened after the post–World War II exposure of the Nazi death camps promised to end prejudice against Jews in the United States when, only 77 years after the anti-Semitic bile of Father Charles Coughlin was forced off American radio, MAGA marchers—President Trump's "good people"—were stomping through Charlottesville, Virginia, chanting, "Jews will not replace us." The far right's reactionary speed is accelerating: It was just eight years after the Supreme Court affirmed gay marriage as the law of the land that Florida Governor Ron DeSantis and his legislative lackeys passed their "Don't Say 'Gay'" law, making it illegal to discuss gender identity in the state's public schools.

The far right is and always was an extremist faction, disdainful of democracy, subversive to its core. In their modern incarnation, their malignant craftiness has only grown. They exploit existing laws and customs to subvert the rest of us, manipulating the tax code to build allegedly nonpartisan nonprofit organizations devised to subjugate minorities; teach false histories at fake colleges; and then hand-pick from them to employ future leaders of their fifth column as they ascend their tax-sheltered positions; staff Republican Presidential Administrations; control administrative agencies; and pack the courts. They are well financed by billionaires—both hereditary and self-made, a few of them are defiantly public, but most are anonymous—who are motivated overwhelmingly by the passion to hold on to their wealth, regardless of what the rest of us pay in taxes, and are heedless of our rights. For this movement, the extremism is just a way to win over the working class to preserve their privileged economic position. They are secure in the belief that they'll always have enough money to buy an abortion, private schooling, or an antitrust exemption if they need it.

The right calls this legal warfare. And that is what they unleashed on the safe and effective abortion medicine mifepristone the moment it became available in the United States.

Even before mifepristone's approval, I saw the furious counter-reaction directly. It was 1996, and I'd just become the first Oregon Democrat in 28 years elected to the U.S. Senate, replacing Republican Bob Packwood after his ouster in a sex scandal.

Soon after my election, I was asked by women's health leaders in the midsized city of Bend to help organize an effort to get the first Planned Parenthood clinic in central Oregon. Bend today is a sophisticated metropolis renowned as one of the most delightful and congenial places to live in the United States. Yet in those days, it was still pretty rural. It had taken nearly 80 years since Planned Parenthood's founding for the women's health organization to make its way there. The night was cold, and my staff and I, in those pre-GPS days, were having trouble locating the place. The Planned Parenthood team hadn't wanted to print the address in the newspaper; they and the local police were concerned about security. Our discussions took place inside a private house.

It was another example to me that when opposed to the far right's extremist impulses, freedoms are not fully won, not ever. They must be continuously secured.

But even though you can perceive the silhouette, you don't always see the portrait. The outline of how Senator Mitch McConnell and his ultra-conservative allies were going to stuff anti-science and anti-women judges on Federal courts by turning abortion rights into a litmus test for receiving a nomination was clear. Frankly, knowing that alone, we Democrats should have moved decades earlier to codify Roe v. Wade into Federal law. Sadly, there were never the votes to overcome the inevitable filibuster.

This is why my good friend, Oregon Senator Jeff Merkley, has written his own book specifically about the filibuster. It's an important tool that I used to publicly stop right-wing attempts to override the will of Oregon voters and to raise alarms about the direction of our nation's energy policy. The filibuster is now used in secret to gum up the works of the Senate and make it impossible to address critically important but controversial issues like choice.

Still, by early 2023 my staff's own monitoring alerted me to a more devious and potentially more destructive tactic the right was now deploying in their war against women. They were going to challenge mifepristone's legality—more than two decades after its approval—by subverting the legal principles that also underlay virtually every important national civil right established in the U.S. during the past hundred years.

Validating the menace to Federal rights was a new claim by the Republican attorneys general of 20 states. They asserted that the Supreme Court's ruling six months before in Dobbs v. Jackson Women's Health Organization—the infamous decision that eradicated women's national right to abortion—already gave them the authority to force legal medicines off the market in their jurisdictions. In early February, they sent letters to executives at the national chain pharmacies Walgreens and CVS threatening legal action against them and declaring they were in "direct violation of federal law"—specifically, an obscure 150-year-old censorious law, the Comstock Act, that prevented the mailing of "obscene" materials through the U.S. Postal Service.

The Comstock Act had largely been declared unconstitutional, and its application to birth control explicitly had been repealed by Congress in 1971. But it was the right's new, preferred instrument for their anti-abortion campaign because, a month before, the FDA had issued new rules that, among other things, would allow women to get their prescription mifepristone by mail.

Vitiating the First Amendment's guarantee of religious freedom, a cherished goal of some anti-mifepristone crusaders, wasn't far beneath the surface of the anti-abortion brigade's latest round. Drawing on anti-Semitic tropes that had been circulating for years on the far right, Danny Bentley, a Republican member of the Kentucky House of Representatives, noted pointedly and falsely in a legislative debate that RU-486 and the Nazi death camp drug Zyklon B were the same thing, and the "person who developed" it "was a Jew."

All these extremist fever dreams came together on the desk of an obscure Texas judge—one of 650 Federal judges—whom the right had fed, nurtured, and put in place to formalize their goals.

Matthew Kacsmaryk is the only Federal judge working in Amarillo, Texas. A crew cut 45-year-old, he was raised in Fort Worth by two born-again Christian parents, attended a church that preaches the literal interpretation of Scripture, and received his undergraduate degree at Abilene Christian University, where he attended daily chapel services. None of this is in the least disconcerting in a pluralistic country whose founding principles include freedom of religion, assembly, and speech.

Except Judge Kacsmaryk firmly believes that the United States is a Christian nation, decrying those who have "facilitated the demise of America's Christian heritage" and mounted a "contemptuous assault on the traditional family." He has cited religious texts to justify legal decision-making, arguing that the Catholic "Catechism holds that 'homosexual acts are intrinsically disordered,' 'contrary to the natural law,' and 'do not proceed from a genuine affective and sexual complementarity.'"

Kacsmaryk caught the eye of national conservative leaders when he was still the undergraduate leader of his College Republicans, and then at the University of Texas School of Law, where he joined The Federalist Society, the billionaire-financed conservative legal organization that produced six of the nine current Supreme Court Justices and 43 of Donald Trump's 51 Appellate Court nominees. Through his schooling and beyond, into service as an assistant U.S. attorney and then as a deputy general counsel for the First Liberty Institute, a conservative religious organization, his faith was his "driving force," his sister told the *Washington Post*.

Sex and personal freedom were rarely far from his thoughts. "The erotic desires of liberated adults" were a scourge, he wrote. He advocated on behalf of employers who refused on religious grounds to allow their employees' health insurance plans to cover birth control. He opposed marriage equality, and when the Supreme Court upheld the right of gay people to marry, he supported local government workers who rejected marriage license applications from gay couples. Gay marriage, he declared, was "a road to potential tyranny." In my state, Oregon, he had defended the owners of a bakery who had invoked their religion to refuse to make a wedding cake for a gay couple.

Nominated to the Federal bench by President Trump in 2017, Kacsmaryk transparently lied about his judicial philosophy, telling my colleague Senator Richard Blumenthal of Connecticut that he couldn't recall any instance where he observed a judge imposing their religion on a ruling, and declaring "for the record, it is inappropriate" for a judge to do so.

Later, the *Washington Post* discovered that after his nomination but before his confirmation hearings, Kacsmaryk had privately asked the *Texas Review of Law and Politics*, a conservative law journal at his alma mater, to remove his name as the primary author of an article affirming that physicians had a religious right to refuse to treat women seeking medical abortions. Such doctors "cannot use their pens to prescribe or dispense abortifacient drugs designed to kill unborn children," he wrote.

Kacsmaryk's entire career, based on legally baseless, emphatic reversals of Constitutional logic and jurisprudence, seemed to jump from the pages of George Orwell's *1984*. A modern-day invocation of its fascist government's mantra, "War is peace, freedom is slavery, ignorance is strength."

This is what drove me to the floor of the Senate on February 16, 2023. I understood that Judge Matthew Kacsmaryk was the right-wing's hand-picked vehicle for undoing the entire legal under-pinning of the concept of Federal civil rights, beginning—but most certainly not ending—with the repeal of the FDA's decades-old approval of mifepristone.

In most states, Federal court cases are randomly assigned to judges, but Texas allows plaintiffs to maneuver cases to specific members of the judiciary. So *The Handmaid's Tale* Republicans made sure that any challenges to Federal laws guaranteeing women's reproductive freedom not only were filed in Texas, but got assigned to Judge Kacsmaryk.

The plaintiffs in this newest case, a radical right-wing physicians' front group called the Alliance for Hippocratic Medicine, had no standing to bring the suit in the first place. The "Alliance" had incorporated only a few months before; its "members" were four anti-abortion organizations and a quartet of doctors; its mailing address was in Tennessee; and it had only a "registered agent" in Amarillo.

More fundamentally, to establish the right to sue, a plaintiff must show that it has been harmed or injured directly by or because of the direct actions of the defendant. Since mifepristone has been used legally and safely for more than two decades, and because the statute of limitations only allows challenges to FDA drug approvals for six years, the plaintiffs could not claim standing under current law.

But attempting to void the venerable legal concept of standing has been another hallmark of the extreme right, and they did it again in this case: In its filing in Amarillo, the Alliance made the ludicrous and unconstitutional claim that some unknown future patient might someday take mifepristone, experience a highly unlikely side effect never documented in decades of study and practice, and then specifically walk into one of their member doctors' exam rooms for treatment. That, they claimed, would "injure" the physician by forcing them to help a patient who had engaged in an act—taking a prescribed pill—the doctor found distasteful.

If a standing claim that ridiculous and overly broad passes muster, then it's time to rip up all the legal textbooks in America and start over, for it would mean that anybody could wander into a Federal court and seek relief against anyone else, based on wild, dreamed-up scenarios hypothesizing that they might somehow be injured one day in the future by…something.

As designed, Judge Kacsmaryk accepted the case, hearing it in March 2023. And, in April 2023, as designed, Judge Kacsmaryk ruled in favor of the Alliance. And, as designed, the ruling was challenged—all the way to the U.S. Supreme Court.

I call this gambit courtwashing, a term I introduced that winter day in the Senate. Its aim is to give the appearance of judicial legitimacy to actions that undermine the rule of law. In the Supreme Court case, U.S. Food and Drug Administration v. Alliance for Hippocratic Medicine, the authoritarian right was wagering that courtwashing in Texas would get mifepristone outlawed in every state. A large part of their bet was that any appeal of Kacsmaryk's ruling would land at the equivalently activist Fifth Circuit Court of Appeals (spoiler: it did). That's the same court that had repeatedly attempted to ban abortion nationally before the Supreme Court ruled in Dobbs v. Jackson Women's Health Organization. With the support of this rogue Appeals Court, any Kacsmaryk ruling to take away legal access to mifepristone nationwide, no matter how spurious, would likely be in effect for years before the Supreme Court finally had to rule on this legal malpractice. At least, that was their plan.

"That's what good lawyers do," an executive at the conservative Heritage Foundation told the *Washington Post*. "They consider,

'Where might we have a venue that maximizes the chances of victory?'" That's a sly way to express an Orwellian twist of norm-breaking into business as usual.

So how do you fight a lawless judge, picked by litigants with no standing to bring a case that should be barred by the statute of limitations and has absolutely no merit? With chutzpah: the demand that the President and the FDA repudiate the bogus plot, expose Judge Kacsmaryk for the religious activist he is, and—not incidentally—promise the nation a bigger, better, deeper, more meaningful, and more far-reaching Constitutional crisis than the one the right had spent 20 years painstakingly fomenting.

Or, as I put it on February 16, 2023, "There are moments in history where Americans and their leaders must look at circumstances like this one and say, 'Enough.' Not 'Let's see how the appeals process plays out,' or 'Let's hope Congress can fix this down the road.' Just 'Enough.'"

The principle of judicial review is a crucial norm within the checks and balances that make our system work. A judge indeed has the power to limit the actions of the executive branch or declare a law passed by Congress unconstitutional. But for a judge to ignore more than a century of precedent that should have prevented him from even hearing the case—much less rule on it, and in so doing take away a drug crucial to the health care of millions of American women—the only just response is to vitiate the false "norms" he erroneously claims empower him.

This is a lesson that goes far beyond one case. When some choose to violate the norms that constitute our civil society in order to gain power and wealth for themselves and their supporters, good people must stop them with every tool at their disposal. Which was the exact counter-strategy I delineated on the Senate floor: "The FDA should go on just as it has for the last 23 years since it first approved mifepristone. The FDA needs to keep this medication on the market without interruption regardless of what the ruling says. Doctors and pharmacies should go about their jobs like nothing has changed."

I wasn't singing solo. Behind my team's tactics lay hours of conversation with a score of legal experts and Constitutional scholars, who validated our thesis that the most powerful way to avert the judicial coup Judge Kacsmaryk and his patrons were initiating was to cue the separation-of-powers chart-topper I was now spinning.

There was a considerable bit of inside-the-Beltway strategy involved. Washington, like most company towns—like most companies, for that matter!—runs on its own version of what the writer Christopher Buckley, in his comic novel *Thank You for Smoking*, terms "argumentation." Or, as his lead character, a thoroughly amoral tobacco industry lobbyist, says, "If you argue correctly, you're never wrong."

Put another way, in Washington, if you simply raise an issue plausibly, the idea behind it by definition must be credible. And if it's credible, it becomes part of the conversation. And if it becomes part of the conversation, it's possible. And if it's possible, all the people who need to worry about it *will* worry about it, since Washington is all about protecting your position and warding off every possible negative outcome.

In the case of mifepristone (not to mention the downstream cases of IVF legality, food safety laws, interracial marriage laws, and all the other rights Americans take for granted that were threatened by the Kacsmaryk ruling), the person we wanted to worry was Supreme Court Chief Justice John G. Roberts Jr. Because of the financial, ethical, and political shenanigans among his fellow conservative Justices, his Court already was confronting a crisis of legitimacy unlike any the Supreme Court had faced in its history. I saw no reason not to remind him that the stakes included his own legacy as Chief Justice.

"The power of the judiciary begins and ends with its legitimacy in the eyes of the public," I reminded him from the Senate floor. "It does not have the military backing of the executive branch or Congress's power of the purse. A judge's rulings stand because elected leaders and citizens have agreed that abiding by them is right and necessary to uphold the rule of law."

To this observation I appended a warning: "But the judiciary must uphold its end of the social contract, too," I said. "It must follow the rule of law and earn the confidence of the American people continually, every day, every month, every year."

Pointing explicitly at Matthew Kacsmaryk, I told Chief Justice Roberts and President Biden, both out there in the C-SPAN ether: "Parts of the judiciary have morphed into a mob of MAGA extremists, conspiring with and willing to do the bidding of every right-wing group or former President that appears before it, no matter the cost to life and liberty." I needed to impress upon them that these extremists are not part of the establishment, despite their positions; they are a threat to its very foundations.

That was my answer, too, to the cautious cabal in my own party who urged me, both before and after my speech, not to rock the Constitutional boat too violently, lest some future autocratic President uses it against us. Their tactic (which younger folk today call concern trolling) is a variation of argumentation. By going on the Sunday chat shows (or by having well-placed allies in powerful places call you directly) to register their "concern" with your activity, they are attempting to delegitimize you—signaling that you've gone rogue, and are certainly not attuned to the complexities of modern politics. It's not that they have direct power over you—the "drop that bill or we'll kill your treasured dam project" caricature went out with Lyndon Johnson, if it ever existed at all. It's more about pressure: When they called me or my Chief of Staff Jeff Michels to register their "concern" over my insistence that the President stand up to a Federal judge who was exceeding his authority, what they were really trying to do was convince me that I might not appreciate the long-term cost of losing their trust.

They'd tried that on me before. Back in 1995, when I became the first Democratic candidate for the U.S. Senate (and soon enough, the first U.S. Senator) to endorse gay marriage, a vow they thought might sacrifice the election and the Democrats' potential Senate majority, many party elders and interest-group bigwigs registered their "concern" that I was too far ahead of the public on the issue. As I said, my response then was, "If you don't like gay marriage, then don't get one."

My response today to similar concerns about abortion rights is the same: If you're in this politics business—if you're in any business—you have no choice but to do the right thing.

Like my original effort 33 years earlier to legalize mifepristone against a politically pressured FDA, my new campaign to keep it legal against a renegade, religiously juiced judge picked up allies. Many of them we sought out, like my University of Oregon School of Law classmate Ellen Rosenblum, now the Attorney General of Oregon, who on March 12, 2023, stood with me, two ob-gyns, and a Planned Parenthood nurse-practitioner outside a Portland CVS pharmacy. Unlike Walgreens, CVS had refused to buckle to pressure to withhold sales of mifepristone. "We are not going to back down!" Ellen declared.

Some allies were unrecruited—such as Alexandria Ocasio-Cortez, a key leader of the House progressives: "Senator Ron Wyden has already issued statements advising what we should do in a situation like this and I concur, which is that the Biden Administration should ignore this ruling," AOC told CNN.

As expected, the echoing uprising did not dissuade Judge Kacsmaryk from his scheme. As we'd foreseen, disregarding centuries of precedent about legal standing and Federal authority; invoking deliberate misreadings of the Comstock Act, among other laws; ignoring decades of medical trials and the actual medical experiences of millions of women worldwide; and abusing his authority as a Federal judge, on Friday, April 7, 2023, he issued a preliminary injunction against further distribution of mifepristone.

Like the FDA three decades earlier, which had prevented mifepristone from entering the United States because it "just felt" that people might misuse the medicine, Kacsmaryk based his ruling in part on "myriad stories" he'd heard.

Our months of strategizing, messaging, ally-gathering, and threats culminated with another ruling by a second Federal judge on April 13, 2023, just short of a week after Matthew Kacsmaryk's legal jihad. In a case filed by 17 states' attorneys general who did not want Kacsmaryk's opinion to block their citizens' right to obtain a safe, effective, Federally approved medicine, U.S. District Judge Thomas Rice of eastern Washington State said the FDA could not refuse access to mifepristone in those states.

On December 13, 2023, the U.S. Supreme Court agreed to hear the case.

Two dueling rulings.

Two incongruent interpretations of the Constitution.

Two distinct views of whether national civil rights exist and can be enforced.

Chief Justice Roberts had the issue in his hands. As I counted on in mounting my rhetorical campaign, he chose to protect the legitimacy of the courts by retreating in this case and falling back on the issue of standing. The fact that a case with such a clear lack of standing made it this far, past levels of Federal courts, shows what a fig leaf that reasoning was, serving to preserve the anti-precedent, anti-science, anti-choice, anti–civil rights argument for another day.

To be clear, his movement has not given up on the the idea of using the courts to strip millions of Americans of their rights, but realized they could not get away with it so transparently.

This means you and I must be even more vigilant against these reactionary forces in the days ahead.

FOURTEEN

SPENDING POLITICAL CAPITAL

won't lie: The battle over Obamacare was painful.

I'd been involved in tremendous policy conflicts in my then three-plus decades in public life. But few had reached the depths of special interest pandering I'd seen and experienced during the six-year campaign to bring comprehensive health-care reform—as eventually realized in the Affordable Care Act—into existence.

Let's be clear: Much of the wish list that I'd incorporated into my own, earlier Healthy Americans Act and for which I'd fought fiercely did make it into the final law and has uplifted Americans' lives for the past decade. Insurers' discrimination against people with pre-existing conditions—gone! Higher insurance rates for women and the elderly—ended! At least 54 million—and possibly as many as 129 million Americans—no longer have to fear losing their coverage for a chronic illness or because they weren't born healthy, white, and male. Preventive services such as colon and breast cancer screening, cholesterol and blood pressure testing, vitamin-deficiency screening for pregnant women, and help for smokers who want to quit tobacco—the "healthy" part of the Healthy Americans Act—are now covered, as are routine childhood vaccinations, pediatrician visits, and obesity counseling for kids. That helps 88 million people who didn't have these services before Obamacare became law. The nation's tiniest businesses—those with fewer than 25 employees—are now eligible for tax credits to enable them to pay for their employees' coverage. That's another 20 million previously uninsured people who now have access to health care.

Senior citizens, the cohort to whom I'd dedicated my life and career since my early 20s, have seen a raft of new benefits. The "doughnut hole" in drug coverage, which forced seniors to pay thousands of dollars for pharmaceuticals once they reached $2,800 in expenditures—closed! Screenings for diabetes, cancer, and other chronic conditions—covered! So are annual wellness visits to doctors. Private Medicare Advantage plans that used to gouge seniors undergoing chemotherapy or dialysis—stopped dead! Nursing home transparency—strengthened! For the first time, inspection reports, complaints against care facilities, staff turnover, and patient care investments now must be fully reported and made publicly available.

But I did not win on two very important issues the nation needs in health care: a unified program to enlist the public and private sectors in containing costs, and breaking for good the antediluvian linkage between employment and health coverage. Without these changes, health care in the United States will continue to wallow in complexity. It will continue to discriminate against the self-employed and unemployed and suck more and more of our national wealth. In consequence it will provide ongoing ammunition for cruel conservatives and their billionaire backscratchers to attempt to galvanize public will against our moral obligations to both the middle class and the disenfranchised.

The battle to shape the Affordable Care Act reinforced my conviction that several of Ron's Rules of Chutzpah are just plain indispensable. You've got to show up every day prepared to play; when you're being attacked by giant corporations and labor unions alike, you certainly have to be on your game.

Embrace the unscripted moments? When you're subject to a public beatdown by your own team, that's an opening to play jujitsu with them, turning their attacks into opportunities to strengthen your own case before the broader public.

Which, of course, requires you to make noise. Lots and lots of productive noise.

My biggest regret coming out of my meeting with President Obama in the Oval Office on day three of his Presidency was my inability to persuade him to make enough noise on sweeping health-care reform. I wish I could have convinced him to give a big speech on health-care reform that would have put the special interest groups on their heels. Given the fact that he'd considered me important enough to make the outreach, I might have been able to make that sale. He had all the tools and skills—a terrific orator, at the top of his game, a coalescing figure if ever there was one. He was better positioned than any President since LBJ to lay out the choices Americans faced on health care: We're spending too much. We're not spending it in the right places. We Democrats are good at handing out benefits, not good at containing costs. Republicans have some good ideas on containing costs, and if we work together, we can get the country not just what it needs but what every American deserves.

I knew and liked Rahm Emanuel, President Obama's Chief of Staff. Emanuel's brother Zeke had written op-eds on health care with Obama, and I knew Rahm had the horsepower to make comprehensive reform a reality. Unfortunately, early on, he was talking about hoarding the President's political capital by pursuing a kid's-only health-care reform plan. The White House staff was apparently recommending against a big, national address, the kind that would frame Obama's Presidency, preferring that he go small-bore. I don't know why they were recommending this approach, although I suspect his staff, so deeply experienced in the ways of Washington, may have wanted to protect a young, new President, thinking he'd get outgunned by Big Pharma, the giant hospital chains, and other monied interests in the medical-industrial complex.

Politicians are, by definition, protective when it comes to the support and positive feelings they receive from the fact that they are a Congresswoman or a Senator or a President. That good feeling is known as political capital, and politicians hoard it like Midas hoarded gold. The desire to stockpile political capital is why so many politicians shy away from picking fights over policy. In their eyes, the rare victories aren't worth the cost of angering friends or interests who find themselves on the other side of a policy disagreement. So rather than seeking to do something with the election certificate the voters have given them, they hunker down and focus on the next election. The problem is, unlike its economic namesake, political capital doesn't earn interest—if you don't spend it, it wastes away. Hence, Ron's Rule of Chutzpah #12—Political capital doesn't earn interest and is worth nothing if you don't spend it. If history gave me a redo, it would be to urge President Obama to go straight to the American people and make the case.

RON'S RULE OF CHUTZPAH

12

POLITICAL CAPITAL DOESN'T EARN INTEREST AND IS WORTH NOTHING IF YOU DON'T SPEND IT

History doesn't give redos, of course. That said, a leader learns more from partial victories than from outright wins or complete losses. A total conquest discourages introspection. An absolute defeat can be excused as a really bad day. Having been subject to a level of national scrutiny, praise, and criticism during the Obamacare years unlike anything I'd experienced previously—and having observed a President whom I admired undergo it as well—I learned a few more things about bringing complex policies and ideas to life.

President Obama hadn't spent his life fighting in the health-care trenches. He wasn't immersed in the complex interdependencies among the states, the Federal Government, insurers, companies, labor unions, doctors, hospitals, and human beings that resulted in the jerry-rigged employer-based system we were dealing with. This left him exposed in his 2008 primary campaign, especially in going up against a more experienced opponent, Hillary Clinton, who had spent years in the health-care trenches. So Obama fell back on what he knew, the traditional ideas for uniting the left and center of his own party and win him the Democratic nomination. His later flip on the personal mandate, his decision to go full-bore on a national public option, failing to address the cost drivers, plan choice, and the wasteful employer-based system may have helped politically, but not policy-wise.

As keen as his political instincts were, President Obama and his advisors made a serious error, assuming the Democratic Party would unite behind his plan. As Will Rogers said, "I don't belong to an organized political party—I'm a Democrat." The Democratic Party is more like a family—we vehemently and unalterably disagree on some things, but we stick together when it counts. Agreement on policy needs to be won, and elections don't confer assent from the Democratic base.

The Obama Administration's conscious decision to pursue a partisan path with their bill doomed the potential of my earlier effort with Bob Bennett to craft a big, bipartisan bill. The Administration's choice was understandable; it meant they wouldn't have to negotiate with Republicans on politically fraught topics like tax policy or universal coverage. Unfortunately, like every attempt to do something along party lines they were still going to have to negotiate with conservative Democrats who represented some of the same interests as the Republicans and had many of the same red lines they refused to cross.

A President can, in rare circumstances, rely on his own party to make things happen. But even Lyndon Johnson, with his massive Congressional majority and overwhelming goodwill in the wake of President Kennedy's assassination, required bipartisan support to pass his monumental Civil Rights Act, Voting Rights Act, and Medicare.

Political parties—and the Democratic Party most certainly—are coalitions, united by general principles (as I learned from the years I spent in the middle of Dingell-Waxman wars in the House of Representatives) but frequently divided by the needs and interests of their divergent constituencies and their personal philosophies. My colleague Senator Bob Casey of Pennsylvania, one of my closest allies and friends on the Senate Finance Committee, is personally pro-life. But he is deeply committed to a foundational principle of the Democratic Party: People's liberties are sacrosanct. That takes enormous courage. Imagine being a practicing Catholic like Bob and going into a church in a state where 44 percent of your constituents are pro-life, and explaining why you're committed to protecting choice. But that's who we are, as Democrats: We support the individual's freedom to choose their own path through life, as long as it doesn't confound the rights of others.

That philosophy translates into the way we manage politics in Congress. Having an allegedly filibuster-proof 60 votes in the U.S.

Senate isn't as meaningful as the civics textbooks would have it. Sure, Dems are generally and reliably united around civil rights and civil liberties. But when it comes to potentially transformative finance and economics legislation, assembling those five dozen votes to move a big bill forward can be like pulling a donkey through the eye of a needle. That's why bipartisanship is not a greeting-card homily, but a necessity of productive policy, whether in politics, business, or other spheres of life.

I am well aware that many of my Democratic colleagues roll their eyes at the "odd couple" alliances I habitually assemble. I fully appreciate that when other Democratic Senators and their staff say "that's just Ron," what they're actually saying is they think I'm a cockeyed optimist channeling some mythical Golden Age when members of Congress happily cut cross-the-aisle deals and then repaired to cigars and whiskey (neither of which I partake in) with each other to celebrate their harmonious coexistence.

Yes, I'm an optimist. I'm also very much a realist. If you cannot find common ground, if you can't find your way to some sort of bipartisan agreement, if you are forced to eke out your victories by one or two votes, then as sure as the night follows day your opponents will return and take your victory back when they are in control. The tortured implementation of the Affordable Care Act—with Republicans and the Trump Administration conspiring to limit access, reduce enrollment, exempt states from participating, and lower quality standards for insurance plans on the exchange—sadly proves the principle.

As my Chief of Staff Jeff Michels laments to this day, Obama "lost the opportunity to win a good policy with bipartisan support— finally goring some of the bloated sacred cows of the health-care industry that members of both parties were otherwise willing to protect." You need look no further than the fact that Utah Republican Bob Bennett, as honorable and consistent a leader as ever graced the halls of the U.S. Capitol, felt compelled to vote against the personal mandate that had been part of our own bill: Once the Obama Administration had abandoned bipartisanship in health-care reform, it was pretty much the only choice he had.

The point is this: In order to lead within a willful, messy, ornery, and vibrant coalition of individuals and interests, you've got to be attentive, act creatively, embrace your adversaries, and possess the risk-tolerance of a circus acrobat.

These were the qualities I determined to bring to my next giant crusade: reversing climate change. It would prove to be the ultimate test of all 12 of Ron's Rules of Chutzpah.

FIFTEEN

THE COACH'S JOURNEY

For decades, climatologists have tracked rising worldwide temperatures, increased greenhouse gas retention, longer and more severe droughts, tropical storms of historic ferocity, and rising sea levels devastating coastal communities. Nobel Prizes have been awarded on the subject. Best-selling books on it date back more than a half-century.

In 1969, Daniel Patrick Moynihan, later a Democratic Senator from New York and a special friend and mentor to me, but then a senior advisor to Republican President Richard M. Nixon, wrote a memo to Nixon's aide John Ehrlichman warning him of the "apocalyptic change" the world was undergoing.

"Recently man has begun to introduce instability through the burning of fossil fuels," Moynihan wrote to the President's domestic affairs chief. "It is now pretty clearly agreed that the CO_2 content will rise 25% by 2000. This could increase the average temperature near the Earth's surface by 7 degrees Fahrenheit. This in turn could raise the level of the sea by 10 feet. Goodbye New York. Goodbye Washington, for that matter."

Warning upon warning followed the Moynihan memo. Seven

years after it, Congress held its first hearing on climate change. In 1987, declaring that "even a small rise in temperature could disrupt the entire complicated environment that has nurtured life as we know it," then-Senator Joe Biden sponsored a bill to create a Federal task force on global warming. The next year, NASA climate scientist James Hansen told the Congress, "The earth is warmer in 1988 than at any time in the history of instrumental measurements."

During those decades and thereafter, various tax and regulatory ideas had been floated to combat climate change. But all fell to early deaths when smacked by the killer combination of special-interest lobbying, legal and mechanical complexity, and the inability of public officials to marry the urgency of the climate challenge to passable legislation.

I was long past "marinating in oil." Not only hadn't I been won over by the petroleum industry during my years as a House Energy Committee backbencher, as I'd playfully suggested to Jim Wright when I was campaigning for that appointment, but the sector's long history of absurd government subsidies had turned me into one of their greatest opponents. As late as 2006 I held a filibuster of the Senate's energy bill to try to block oil subsidies. Ultimately the bill passed 99-1, with my lone opposition.

After the failure of the Obama Administration's "cap-and-trade" initiative at the very peak of Democratic Congressional power, it was clear a different approach was needed. Chutzpah time!

⌐

On the surface, me taking on global warming was arguably futile, even nuts. Some of the biggest personalities Washington had ever seen—Al Gore, Pat Moynihan, Presidents Nixon through Obama, and five of the most prominent members of the U.S. Senate and

House of Representatives—had come in with all manner of ballyhoo and hadn't managed to pull off anything that looked like it might halt or even slow the Earth's slide to climate hell. I was in a senior position on the Energy Committee and I was only just becoming more senior on the Finance Committee. I didn't yet control any traditional levers of power. Any reasonable political hand would say I was setting myself up for failure.

Yet I had to make the effort. Part was my innate drive to make productive change happen. Over the course of the past 15 years I had gone from being an urban Portland Congressman to representing an entire state full of environmental gems. I had managed to pass strong laws to protect Oregon's land, air, and water—places like the Copper Salmon and Spring Basin Wildernesses, and later the spectacular Devil's Staircase Wilderness in southwestern Oregon. All of these treasures were threatened by global climate change.

But there also were mammoth practical considerations. The emotions exposed by the state's "timber wars"—the battle between environmentalists and the logging industry and its workers over the fate of the Spotted Owl in our old-growth forests—were still raw when I was elected to the Senate in 1996. While that conflict was conventionally viewed as an unwinnable standoff between elitist "greens" versus old-line industry and its unionized workers, it actually exposed a far more alarming reality: Oregon's Spotted Owl was the advance guard of global climate change, chased into our dense forests by predators whose own migratory patterns were shifting because of rising temperatures. In the past hundred years, Oregon's average temperature has risen about two degrees, as carbon dioxide and other greenhouse gasses trap heat in Earth's lower atmosphere. Snowpack is melting earlier in the year and summer meltwater is decreasing, resulting in more acidic coastal waters, warmer streams, and more wildfires. Climate change was devastating to our then-half-billion-dollar commercial fishing industry and a forestry sector that employed more than 60,000 Oregonians. By 2010, whether I was ready or not, it was past time to act.

Let me step back for a moment to address two related questions you've probably been asking for quite a few chapters by now: What took it so long? And what took *me* so long? Or more specifically, if climate change was first identified as a Federal priority in 1969 and the Oregon timber wars began circa 1989, why did it take the Senate and me another 20 or 30 or 40 years to start addressing the issue seriously?

The most obvious answer, frustrating as it is, is that the Federal Government was designed to move slowly. The overwhelming concern, appropriately so, of the Framers of the U.S. Constitution was tyranny. Whether wielded by an individual king or by a plurality of the population bent on ruling over the remaining minorities, tyranny is an ever-present threat in governments of men. The Framers were intent on designing a society and a governing structure of many competing yet interlocking components that would force interests to be balanced. As James Madison, the Constitution's primary author and later the fourth President of the United States, wrote in Federalist 51: "[I]n the federal republic of the United States…all authority in it will be derived from and dependent on the society, the society itself will be broken into so many parts, interests, and classes of citizens, that the rights of individuals, or of the minority, will be in little danger from interested combinations of the majority." Mirroring society, the government's "several constituent parts" would be "the means of keeping each other in their proper places."

Even under the ideal circumstance of one-party control of both houses of Congress and the Presidency (which is "ideal" only if it happens to be your own party!), Madison's architecture has guaranteed that big changes in policy take a long while to pass through the sluice gates of American society and government. And that ideal circumstance is, historically, rare. Unified governments have occurred in time blocs, with Lincoln's Republicans controlling the White House and Congress from 1860 to 1874 and again during the booming Gilded Age of 1896 to 1910, while Democrats had two decades of hegemony under FDR and Truman from 1932 to 1952. In between and thereafter, divided government has been the norm.

What's more, as I noted in other chapters, the whole notion of party unity is something of a fiction; the gulf between reactionary Republicans and the few remaining moderates and traditional conservatives is wide, and the chasm between liberal and conservative Democrats is even wider. Government gridlock may have increased in recent years but to one degree or another, gridlock is a feature of the system, not a bug. "These big national policies, whether it's Social Security, Medicare, Civil Rights Act, Voting Rights Act, the Clean Air Act in the 1970s—those are the exception rather than the rule," says University of Washington political scientist Jacob Grumbach.

As aggravating as this designed-in sloth might be, it also creates safeguards. It's one thing for a private company to rush to market with a new product or new product category. Assuming it's not, say, a commercial airliner, if it fails the only ones hurt are the company's investors, who knowingly took risks with their own money. Social and economic policies, by contrast, can disrupt vast numbers of lives, sometimes for the worse, if appropriate consideration and care are not applied. Although I am beyond impatient about the slow pace of legislation, I also have come to appreciate that, to be successful, important political, social, and economic changes usually have to be built over time, like great cities, not raised hurriedly, like the Tacoma Narrows Bridge.

In this regard, Government isn't that different from the private sector, where it often takes decades of building, one innovation on top of another, before a transformative change starts to move cultures and economies. It took 32 years from the Wright Brothers' first flight in Kitty Hawk, North Carolina, in 1903 before McDonnell Douglas was able to weave together five separate innovations (the variable-pitch propeller, retractable landing gear, lightweight molded unibody construction, radial air-cooled engines, and wing flaps) to make commercial aviation viable. From Arpanet to the Netscape browser—two among many crucial inventions that enabled the consumer Internet—took 35 years.

I've learned as well that, its vaunted hustle notwithstanding, more frequently than not the private sector also responds to innovation quite slowly—a phenomenon documented by such economics and management scholars as Joseph Schumpeter and Clayton Christensen. Schumpeter, the Nobel Prize–winning mid-20th century economist, coined the term "creative destruction" to represent the often-lengthy process by which inventions—a new idea or process or technology—become innovations (that is, the applications of the invention in the real world), and finally diffuse widely, transforming sectors of the economy. Harvard Business School Professor Christensen's addition to Schumpeter's scholarship was to show how, very frequently, the inventions that disrupt industries and societies emerge slowly from the low end of a sector: They often are less expensive solutions with fewer features than the dominant technologies already in the market. They take hold explicitly because their cheapness *both* enables them to spread widely *and* limits any upside an established firm might realize if it pursued the new innovation. That's a central reason one generation's giant may be toppled by a pipsqueak—as mainframe computer megalith IBM fell to

RON'S RULE OF CHUTZPAH

2

IN A WORLD WHERE EVERYONE THINKS AND ACTS FOR THE SHORT TERM, ALWAYS PLAY THE LONG GAME

personal computing disruptors Apple and Microsoft—which become the next generation's giants.

Schumpeter's and Christensen's research explains how the newspaper industry began to die because it clung to black-and-white photography and mechanical presses long into the era of color television and, later, the Internet. It describes how, despite three decades of advance notice, the television industry failed to pay heed to the disruptiveness of streaming video. My point is not to excuse the sluggish speed of Government, but to show that almost all revolutions are built on evolutions, whether in politics, business, or societal relationships. And that deliberateness and iteration—the long game on which I was now preparing to embark to reverse the scourge of climate change— aren't diseases of Washington but features of virtually every sector.

So, to act, I started by observing, listening, and recruiting.

The historian Doris Kearns Goodwin's concept of the "team of rivals" stands as a far more accurate model for how giant advances in culture, society, politics, and economics occur than any of the hoary old "great man" theories. (If I were to fault one predilection of the Democratic Party, it's the tacit conviction of our faithful that electing a single God-like figure as President of the United States is the most important means to effect change. The Republicans, by contrast, understand that change can be successfully propelled by figureheads.)

For me, all this analysis led in one direction: In deciding to take on global warming, I needed to act less like LBJ and more like Clem Wiser. I had to recruit a team, assess their talents and predispositions, respect them by learning from them, and earn their trust by building a solution with them.

I began my...let's call it The Coach's Journey...with Clem Wiser's principle of rigorous honesty about diagnosing problems. I sounded out my Republican colleagues John McCain (with whom I had worked closely when he chaired the Commerce Committee) and Lindsey Graham, because I knew they believed climate change was a real problem, yet they'd both withdrawn from the much-touted cap-and-trade legislative solution. Why?

RON'S RULE OF CHUTZPAH

3

LEADING IS COACHING: YOU'VE GOT TO BRING PEOPLE AND IDEAS TOGETHER AROUND A SHARED GOAL.

Both men told me directly that all previous climate change solutions had run afoul of the Republican Party's distaste for taxes, mandates, and the complexity of "pricing energy." When moderate Democrats told me the same thing, I knew that our half-century of emphasis on trying to bully through a cap-and-trade solution or other punitive tax-like legislation was a non-starter.

What could replace them? I pulled together past statements my colleagues had made about climate change, and newspaper articles and journal papers about the politics of climate policy and why past proposals failed. I dug deeply into climate science to see if I could find ways to meet my colleagues where they were, with possible solutions that were both scientifically sound *and* politically viable.

Everywhere I went, my research showed both from a science standpoint and a politics standpoint the key player to attract onto the starting team was Democrat Joseph Manchin III. A former Governor of West Virginia, the nation's no. 2 coal-producing state, Joe was sworn into the Senate in November 2010, as a ballyhooed but complicated bipartisan climate-change bill designed by Democrats John Kerry and Joe Lieberman and Republican Lindsay Graham was collapsing. One of Manchin's campaign commercials depicted him shooting a rifle into a Congressional climate-change proposal. He certainly didn't look like an ally—we obviously had very different views on a host of issues, but looking at all the complex cross-currents of the Senate I knew it would be impossible to pass legislation to take action on climate change without him. Your playbook is based on the team you have, not the team you wish you had.

As we neared the 2012 midterm elections, Majority Leader Reid made it clear that if the Democrats retained our majority, he was going to support me for chair of the Energy and Natural Resources Committee—my first Senate chairmanship. Senate Minority Leader Mitch McConnell indicated that if the Republicans could pull off an upset, Alaska's Lisa Murkowski would get his nod. Senator Murkowski has her own renegade reputation, which brings her great respect in Alaska but perennially puts her in the gunsights of her party's far right wing. She hadn't endeared herself to the cap-and-trade coalition because she wanted to dramatically expand oil drillers' access to the Arctic National Wildlife Refuge, which Democrats had spent decades protecting. I, on the other hand, thought her a perfect cross-aisle partner, because not only is she courageous, inquisitive, and independent, but her state, like Oregon, has been historically reliant on the economics of extraction industries but is also deeply affected by climate change. She would take the assignment seriously.

Lisa and I became quite close over the years. We met once a week at 8 a.m. for a working breakfast, and had dinners together as well (her husband Verne Martell is a world-class cook). I trusted her so much that I hesitated only slightly when, on a visit to Alaska to review the state's energy markets and their needs, she invited me to taste a graham cracker dipped in liquified natural gas. (What can I say? It does *not* taste like chicken.)

RON'S RULE OF CHUTZPAH

10

WORK WITH ANYBODY WHO IS SERIOUS ABOUT MOVING FORWARD

As much as I admired Senator Murkowski, though, I dearly wanted the Energy Committee's chairmanship for myself. In Congress, the most successful committee chairs act almost exactly like athletic coaches. Neither a chair nor a coach can do it all; you must work through other people. Your team members, in turn, must work through you: Both the coach and the chair control the floor, and determine who gets playing time (of which the Congressional equivalent is getting on the agenda). Unless you want to ride the bench (and yeah, there are loudmouths who are happy just to do that), that dynamic tension between the coach and the team (or the chair and the committee) is the raw material of progress.

So too, the committee chair, like the coach, must be completely attentive to the individual skills and interests of his team's members. In many ways, a Senator with designs on the Presidency is not unlike a college player with an eye on the NBA—and, without proper coaching, just as often they forget the needs of their current team. If you want to lead a team, you need to know what drives all your players, the better for you to harmonize them into a winning unit.

Joe Manchin joined us on the Energy Committee and went out of his way to develop a relationship with both me and Lisa. One of the first things he ever said to me was that he liked Oregon Governor Ted Kulongoski, a longtime pal of mine. We told jokes about

Ted. From such simple courtesies you can find opportunities to work together.

An experienced politician, Joe knew that, especially as chair, I could thwart or advance his priorities. He also understood, as I did, that Lisa Murkowski, whether as chair or as ranking member, would be a vital coalition partner on whatever any of us hoped to accomplish. It's a great merit of the Senate: Especially under the body's unanimous consent arrangements, by which both parties agree to waive the rules to expedite floor action on legislation or other measures, you are forced to work with people with whom you might otherwise never associate.

Joe invited Lisa and me to West Virginia to see the importance of energy to his constituents—which ran from the expected (coal, strip mines, and natural gas) to the surprising (hydro, solar, and wind). Underlying his invitation was his belief that many Democrats couldn't see his state as anything other than a backward-leaning obstacle to their environmental goals, while many Republicans might just see him as an easy, unthinking vote for their anti-environmental policies. It was clear to me, Joe believed he could tackle big problems, shape a better future, and represent his constituents, all at the same time.

Manchin was so excited by our visit that his office issued a glowing press release announcing it. "For the first time," Joe said, "I am bringing leaders in both parties together to see how our state is an example of how to develop a comprehensive energy policy using all our domestic resources." His goal was "to bring lawmakers together around a commonsense energy policy to tour energy production sites that demonstrate the state's 'all-of-the-above' approach to energy."

"All of the above." He'd used this phrase with me before; the problem was that current policy was drastically skewed in favor of fossil fuel technologies. The path forward was technological neutrality, throwing out the old incentives and tying incentives to reducing carbon, cleaning the environment, and promoting energy independence. With our West Virginia road trip at hand, I read Joe's past energy statements and came to grips with his thinking: He wouldn't support a policy framework that forced the transition from coal, oil, and gas to renewables, but instead would favor one that allowed multiple alternatives to compete.

It's an elitist canard that all politicians are short-sighted hucksters, so concerned with their own political survival that they are unable to put the national interest ahead of their own parochial self-interest. Madison called devotees of this cynical critique (many of whom, I'm forced to conclude, are Washington journalists whose ornery independence immunizes them from the vagaries of political bargaining) "theoretic politicians."

They have "erroneously supposed that by reducing mankind to a perfect equality in their political rights, they would, at the same time, be perfectly equalized and assimilated in their possessions, their opinions, and their passions," Madison wrote in Federalist 10, of those who assumed political compromise was the redoubt of lesser humans. Hogwash, Madison countered: It's entirely rational for Senators, Governors, and House members to protect their state's key interests and constituencies. Self-interest, the Founders understood, is a feature of democratic capitalism. "The latent causes of faction," said Madison, "are thus sown in the nature of man." Resolving them through research, reason, debate, and negotiation is the very purpose of the Congress. "The regulation of these various and interfering interests forms the principal task of modern legislation, and involves the spirit of party and faction in the necessary and ordinary operations of the government."

RON'S RULE
OF CHUTZPAH

4

SHOW UP
EVERY DAY
PREPARED
TO PLAY

Which is to say, Joe Manchin's invitation to Lisa Murkowski and me to tool around West Virginia with him was a Madisonian example of the very purpose of Congress. I intended to take every advantage I could from it.

The three of us spent hours motoring around West Virginia in a big van, visiting a Marcellus Shale drilling pad, coal mines, a coal-fired power plant, a wind farm, and reclaimed surface mining locations. Each facility at which we stopped, Joe repeated his mantra: "Here's another example of 'all of the above.'" "Here's what I'm talking about when I call myself an 'all of the above' type of guy."

I gently twisted Manchin's words, to see if I was understanding him correctly. By "all of the above," I wondered whether he was saying that a "technology neutral" approach to energy production would be acceptable to him?

RON'S RULE
OF CHUTZPAH

7

IDEAS ARE THE
SEEDS OF CHANGE;
FIND THEM AND
PLANT THEM
WHEREVER AND
WHENEVER
YOU CAN

"No one can say in 2012 what or who the big carbon reducers will be in 2032," I said, adding: "A pro-science approach can drive innovation—and over time innovation can beneficially transform the economics of West Virginia, Oregon, and Alaska."

Joe reacted positively to the idea. He then asked specifically about whether this would apply to energy sources like carbon capture and hydrogen. I said yes—as measured by the degree to which they reduced carbon emissions each would reap benefits in the tax code.

I know technology-neutrality sounds like

energy-industry jargon. But translated into Coach Wiser's language, it meant making sure the players (technologies and those who would invest in them) knew their positions and understood our strategy and the path to victory, then getting them on the court to PLAY— their game, and ours.

At the press conference at the end of that West Virginia trip, I simply told the crowd that Joe, Lisa, and I had discussed using the tax code "to put people to work diversifying the country's energy portfolio." I held my breath, because so many energy proposals had died climbing the tax policy hill.

Neither Joe nor Lisa dissented. We had the makings of a team…and a playbook.

RON'S RULE OF CHUTZPAH

11

COMPROMISE ISN'T ABOUT HORSE-TRADING BAD IDEAS FOR EACH OTHER; IT'S ABOUT BLENDING GOOD IDEAS TOGETHER INTO A WHOLE THAT'S BETTER THAN THE SUM OF ITS PARTS

I chaired the Energy and Natural Resources Committee for barely a year while putting this game plan together before a far bigger and thoroughly unanticipated opportunity landed in my lap: the Chairmanship of the U.S. Senate Finance Committee.

"The Senate's most powerful committee," the *New York Times* deemed it, because it "helps dictate how the government raises almost all of its money, and spends nearly half of it," the Senate Committee on Finance has shaped the growth of the United States as much as any President in our history. Among its early Chairs were our nation's most potent constructors, Daniel Webster, Henry Clay, and John C. Calhoun, whose extraordinary influence over trade and tariffs laid the groundwork for America's eventual dominance over the world economy; such later Chairs as Harry Byrd and Russell Long were instrumental in creating Medicare and Medicaid. In between, the Finance Committee had overseen the bankrolling of the Civil War, the creation of the nation's first income tax, the development of paper currency, and the establishment of Social Security, unemployment insurance, and the G.I. Bill of Rights. A reminder that bad decisions can be as momentous as good ones, it was also the instigator of the 1929 Smoot-Hawley Tariff Bill that halted global trade, prolonged the Great Depression, and helped prompt World War II. For better and for worse, every American citizen since the body's invention in 1816 has been affected by the work of the Senate Finance Committee.

My ascendency wasn't supposed to happen. In the space of a few years Democratic Finance Committee members Kent Conrad and Jeff Bingaman retired (and they are missed); Obama pulled John Kerry from the Senate to succeed Hillary Clinton as Secretary of State. Arkansas's Blanche Lincoln lost her Senate seat, falling prey to a right-wing Republican due to her support for bringing affordable health care to her constituents. Then the President unexpectedly appointed the Committee's chair, Max Baucus of Montana, to become Ambassador to China. Finally, Jay Rockefeller, in his final term, graciously chose not to take a short turn as Chairman, leaving the job open for me.

My turn. No one was more surprised than me...but that's why you always show up ready to play.

My rise as Senate Finance Chair threw Washington into conniptions. Pat Moynihan aside, the Democratic chairs who had preceded me were not always known as bold policy innovators. Russell Long and Lloyd Bentsen, both from oil country, had been the architects of many of the tax loopholes that had gummed up energy policy for so long. Baucus, who aside from a four-year break when Republicans ruled the chamber, had chaired the committee since 2001 and was renowned for his quiet friendliness with business. He put forward modest proposals, even in his avowed area of interest, tax reform, and had more former aides working as lobbyists than any then-current member of Congress. It's fair to say that even the U.S. Chamber of Commerce Republicans who dominate much of the K Street lobbyist corridor had grown quite comfortable with the Finance Committee's Democratic leadership and direction.

Although I'd been in Washington for 35 years at the time I picked up the Committee's gavel, the power structure still couldn't fit me into its conventional boxes. "By any reasonable standard, Wyden is a bona fide liberal," the *New Republic* offered, "a staunch believer in universal health insurance, a more progressive tax code, and greater public investment." I had 95 percent ratings from the progressive group Americans for Democratic Action and the labor organization Service Employees International Union, and a zero ranking from FreedomWorks, the conservative advocacy organization. A major point of pride: I have one of the longest tenured staffs on Capitol Hill, and even when folks do depart the team, more often than not, they don't leave to go lobby.

But cock an eyebrow—conservatives were surprisingly (to some) open to me. "While there probably shouldn't be any Democrats on the Senate Finance Committee, if you have to have one, Ron Wyden would be a fine choice," quipped the powerful anti-tax activist Grover Norquist. And cock the other eyebrow—I had this infuriating habit of partnering with Republicans: a Government surveillance reform bill with Rand Paul, an education proposal with Marco Rubio, even (heaven forbid!) a plan to update the Medicare guarantee with former Republican Vice Presidential nominee Paul Ryan.

RON'S RULE
OF CHUTZPAH

6

EMBRACE THE
UNSCRIPTED
MOMENTS

A few seasoned observers understood the way my gears functioned. "His background is as a progressive, but a lot of the things that he's done don't necessarily fit," Congressional scholar Norman Ornstein said when I was appointed. "He has relentlessly, vigorously sought to find ways of creating innovative bipartisan approaches to different policies." But for the most part, the terms the various factions threw around to describe me and my proposals—"manic wonkiness," "often professorial," with "ambitious and complex policy ideas"—were the establishment's way of saying they didn't, *couldn't*, understand chutzpah. Not my version of it, anyway.

The lobbyists thought I was doomed. "It's one thing to write a bill with another senator or two that ultimately goes nowhere," several snickered to *Politico*, "and it's another to shepherd legislation through a panel so divided that markups have become rare."

My unforeseen chairmanship was my moment to prove them wrong.

⌐

Thanks to a song written by Oregon jazz maestro Dave Frishberg, the TV show *Schoolhouse Rock!* taught generations of children how a bill becomes a law:

> *Yes, I'm only a bill,*
> *And I got as far as Capitol Hill.*
> *Well, now I'm stuck in committee*
> *And I'll sit here and wait*
> *While a few key Congressmen discuss and debate*

Whether they should let me be a law.

Alas, that old-school portrayal of a Congress wrapped up in procedure, committee hearings, and conference committees is long gone. For political survival, if for no other reason, Senators spend less and less time in Washington and more time in their home states. Hearings, which aside from occasional "gotcha" moments were rarely good at uncovering truly useful information, are even less of a fact-finding exercise than ever and more of an opportunity for members and witnesses to score a few minutes of C-SPAN video to send to their respective constituencies. There are virtually no conference committees anymore. More frequently today, what happens is informal back-and-forth emails and document-trading, with very little human interaction or live debate among the members.

Power and control of the agenda has centralized in the Majority and Minority Leaders in the Senate. But as that power has concentrated, it has been diluted. First, it's just not humanly possible for, say, my friend and uniquely skilled Majority Leader Chuck Schumer to produce, let alone see through to victory, the large, complicated, and useful pieces of legislation a modern political economy requires. He doesn't have the resources—no one could with the funds we have to work with—be it the staff, the ideas, and the time.

Nor can Chuck, or for that matter other leaders like Mitch McConnell, command the undying fear and fealty of their members or the obedience of an entire city's power structure. There are too many bypasses around their authority, from rich PACs to global NGOs to wealthy campaign financiers to media moguls to YouTube influencers with 100 million followers. For Congressional leaders, theirs is now a daily slog of shoring up support, coddling egos, and herding the most disagreeable cats ever to have been corralled together under the Capitol's dome. The historically awful election and rapid defenestration of House Speaker Kevin McCarthy by his own Republican Party is a graphic example of how tenuous the individual's hold on power has become, just as the positions themselves have grown more powerful.

Congressional committee chairs still, obviously, have more authority than the average legislative bear. They're in the room when the bigger decisions get made. But if I could conjure the spirit of Dave Frishberg, I'd encourage him to rewrite his *Schoolhouse Rock!* ditty, to highlight the newer ways by which legislation moves:

> *You start with an idea*
> *Big enough that everyone can see ya.*
> *Then get your friends to sign their name*
> *So they can be in the game.*
> *(If they have any doubts*
> *Get the media to give them shouts.)*
> *Make it so the leaders adopt your position*
> *And turn it into the President's mission.*

On climate change, I already had the idea—technological neutrality, managed via a tax code swept clear of its myriad special breaks. I had one Senator of my own party in a pole position on the subject, Joe Manchin, who was willing to give a listen. I had talked to a number of Republicans who were willing to engage, notably the highly respected Lisa Murkowski. I now possessed a powerful committee Chairmanship. Now, like a 19th century Oregon homesteader putting a stake in the wilderness, I needed to clean out all the underbrush that had cluttered energy policy for decades, so we could build a sensible, comprehensive climate change policy on a firm, ideally permanent foundation.

When I think back on the Trump years, I'm moved to quote the final line spoken by Kurtz, the dying anti-hero of Joseph Conrad's novel *Heart of Darkness* (and Coppola's *Apocalypse Now*), as he reflects back on his life of racist, imperialist, colonialist exploitation: "The horror! The horror!"

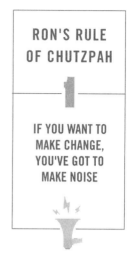

RON'S RULE OF CHUTZPAH

1

IF YOU WANT TO MAKE CHANGE, YOU'VE GOT TO MAKE NOISE

There was Trump's gag order preventing employees of the Environmental Protection Agency from saying anything publicly about climate change, the appointment of oil industry executives and lobbyists to key positions in the EPA and the Department of the Interior, the elimination of reporting requirements about environmental risks, the U.S.'s withdrawal from the Paris Climate Agreement by which 195 nations had agreed to reduce greenhouse gas emissions, and the weakening of fuel-economy standards that even the auto industry wanted kept intact.

It would be hard to pinpoint the most horrible moment, but an excellent candidate would be Trump's personal reaction to the 2017 National Climate Assessment report by hundreds of scientists from 13 Federal agencies. The voluminous study said that half the nearly one-inch rise in global sea levels over the past century had occurred just since 1993, driven by man-made causes; that the nearly two-degree rise in average global temperatures since 1900 was the "unambiguous" result of human activity; that 89 U.S. weather disasters in the previous five years alone had caused three-quarters of a trillion dollars in damage and taken 4,557 lives; and that it was going to get worse. A lot worse.

Trump's response: "I don't believe it. No, no, I don't believe it."

But y'know, sometimes horrors have the advantage of concentrating minds and energies. Every decision and action Trump made to rescind an Obama Administration environmental executive order, every treaty abandonment, every public denial of the scientific consensus on climate change unleashed furious counter-reactions among researchers, climatologists, advocacy groups, young people, and the broader citizenry.

What's more, there's something about being in a triple-minority—Republicans then controlled both houses of Congress and the Presidency—that, like being in a foxhole, enhances your own team's camaraderie. Having figured out the twofer—clean out the tax code *and* reinvent climate policy with a focus on goals rather than specific mechanics—we were ready to commit it to paper. On May 5, 2017, I introduced the Clean Energy for America Act. As I'd promised her, after me and Minority Leader Chuck Schumer, the first name among our 21 co-sponsors was Debbie Stabenow, the long-serving Senator from Michigan.

The draft bill encompassed the five years of spadework that began in the van in West Virginia. It replaced the overly complex and ineffective system of energy incentives with a dramatically simpler, technology-neutral set of incentives that fell into three simple buckets: domestic production of clean electricity, clean transportation fuel, and energy-efficient homes and office buildings. "These credits," I said in releasing the draft, "are open to all resources, including fossil fuels that reduce carbon or make efficiency improvements." If a mechanism, a process, or another innovation reduced carbon emissions, it would qualify for the tax credit—and the credit would stay in place until the emissions target was hit.

I drew on my experience with Chris Cox more than 20 years earlier, when we were designing Section 230 of the Communications Decency Act explicitly to get the Government out of the way of any innovations that could safely create new industries and new jobs. "This bill," I said about the Clean Energy for America Act, "is built around the proposition that the law ought to reward innovative energy technologies with incentives that spark investment in the private economy. These investments will shrink electric bills for American families and create new clean energy jobs in Oregon and across the country."

Citizen groups put wind at our backs. Led by Gene Karpinski, President of the League of Conservation Voters, and Jamal Raad, co-founder of Evergreen Action in Seattle, among many others, activists were beating the drum. With every hurricane, superstorm, and record-breaking hot summer day, they hit the streets with rage over the Trump Administration's refusal to act on climate change. They also adopted our language and philosophy.

This was no small matter. Go back to my earlier explanation about the two paths you can take to progress: Either you can start or encourage something good to happen, or you can stop or discourage something bad from happening. Since the dawn of the modern environmental movement in the 1960s, activists' focus had been largely on stopping industries and companies from polluting the air, water, and land, through tax penalties, civil liability, and criminal law. Known as "punitive ecology" or "punitive environmentalism," its fiercest promoter may have been the Stanford University ecologist Paul R. Ehrlich, whose 1968 book *The Population Bomb* argued that our "dying planet" required us to control population growth "hopefully through a system of incentives and penalties, but by compulsion if voluntary methods fail."

The stop-it-now school of environmentalism has undeniably been crucial in cleaning up polluted rivers and reclaiming damaged landscapes. Every time I see an eagle soaring above me in Oregon, I recall that when I was in law school, we were sure our national bird was on the verge of extinction. Spurred by Rachel Carson's magisterial 1962 book *Silent Spring*, the Federal Government's ban on DDT was the central contributor to the eagle's survival.

It's also undeniable that the caricature of the environmental movement as being opposed to progress, growth, and jobs—a misrepresentation fostered by firebrands like Ehrlich and inculcated over decades by industrial polluters and their lobbyists—has created political paralysis. I saw it during the Dingell-Waxman battles on the House Energy and Commerce Committee, and during Oregon's timber wars. Each side digs in, unwilling to listen, let alone find the mutual win inside the squabble.

Fast-forward from the 1990s, a new public positioning was coalescing, driven by Trump's virulent slash-and-burn evisceration of environmental protections: Instead of environmentalism destroying jobs, even the environmentalists were now speaking eloquently about *creating* jobs.

RON'S RULE
OF CHUTZPAH

5

THERE ARE
TWO EQUALLY
IMPORTANT PATHS
TO PROGRESS:
START GOOD
THINGS AND STOP
BAD THINGS

By far its most influential exposition came in a whitepaper published in late 2019 by the World Wildlife Fund in partnership with the Institute for Public Policy Research, a left-wing think-tank in the U.K. Titled "Putting People at the Heart of the Green Transition," the paper in many ways was a restatement of old and politically challenged sermons advocating for vast, Government-directed industrial policies. "The 21st century is increasingly being defined by the need to respond to major social, environmental and economic challenges," the paper stated. "Sometimes referred to as 'grand challenges', these include climate change, demographic challenges, and promotion of health and well-being. Behind them lie the difficulties of generating sustainable and inclusive growth. These problems are 'wicked' in the sense that they are complex, systemic, interconnected and urgent."

But high up in the piece was a kernel of simple brilliance that re-articulated what we were attempting in the Clean Energy for America Act. "Industrial strategy," it argued (and emphasis mine), "must be about *steering investment-led growth across different sectors towards solving problems that matter to citizens.*"

Seven years earlier, tooling around in a van across the mountains and valleys of West Virginia, Joe Manchin, Lisa Murkowski, and I talked nonstop about connecting climate policy to jobs. Now, here it was resurfacing in policy debates. Meanwhile, the cause had embraced an easy to grasp name: Green New Deal.

Senator Ed Markey and I worked with Congresswoman Alexandria Ocasio-Cortez, who was very much a leader in this cause, to map out the agenda of a Green New Deal, encapsulated in a five-page non-binding resolution that would meet the climate crisis with a "national, social, industrial, and economic mobilization." Launched on a cold February day in 2019, we were two old lions and one of our most promising new legislators announcing a new era of environmental innovation and progress.

As much as it pains me to say it, though, progressives just aren't great marketers; they fall in love with words and slogans that might fly in Palo Alto but won't land in Pendleton. "Green" is one of those words. I thought of it then—and still do today—that a far better term for our proposal was The *Renewed* Deal. Our bill, and the philosophy it represented, signaled a renewed commitment to working people by creating new jobs in new industries that would benefit from cleaning up our environment rather than polluting it.

In each Congress, I reintroduced my Clean Energy for America Act. Soon, my squad of sponsors climbed above 30 Senators.

We just needed two more things: A President...and a Senate majority.

We got the former on November 2, 2020, when Joe Biden defeated Donald Trump. We got the latter on January 5, 2021, when both Jon Ossoff and Raphael Warnock were elected in run-off elections as United States Senators from Georgia, which, with Vice President Kamala Harris's tie-breaking vote, delivered Democrats the Senate majority for the first time in six years. I was going to chair the Senate Finance Committee, regaining substantial authority over the tax policy provisions we would need to seal the deal on our climate change proposal.

Now I needed to knit together a plan for the Finance Committee to go where it had never gone before: Taking our draft of a bill that could materially reduce climate change and generate jobs...and passing it.

The most critical job of a leader in any field is to take abstract ideas and plans and to make them concrete. To turn a game plan into plays and assignments.

In the start-something-good form of political leadership, an idea doesn't become concrete until funds are allocated, people are hired, work is performed, and products or services result. A prerequisite, as I've outlined throughout this book, is the construction and passage of legislation that enables money to flow and work to occur. In Washington, as I've described, that legislative process, especially with society-shaping proposals, often takes years of socialization, using your bully pulpit, hearings, the media, relationship-building with your colleagues and their staffs, and all the other elements of chutzpah to increase people's comfort levels.

But even when you've done all that, more often than not, you still have to force the issue. And the most important place to force it is onto the Resolute Desk in the Oval Office of the President of the United States.

As a U.S. Senator, Joe Biden was a thoroughly congenial colleague. He did tilt to the right of center and was known for his work crafting controversial tough-on-crime legislation, and for overseeing the Judiciary Committee hearings that placed the right-wing apparatchik Clarence Thomas on the Supreme Court. As Vice President, he was a loyal, seasoned advisor, especially on international matters, to the less-experienced President Obama. But overall, in a Washington career that began in 1972, when he was elected to the Senate at age 30, Joe Biden had not been known as an activist on domestic policy.

So we were all surprised and gratified that he emerged from the pandemic-scarred Presidency of and campaign against Donald Trump with perhaps the boldest proposal any of us had seen in our professional lifetimes—a $4 trillion plan to reshape the U.S. economy by updating the nation's infrastructure, building schools, modernizing the auto industry, investing in clean energy and energy efficiency, and eliminating carbon pollution.

President Biden called it the "Build Back Better" plan. Its foundation, repeated like a mantra by White House officials at every turn, was straight from the Wyden playbook: It replaced mandates with incentives; it was government-enabled but private-sector led.

While a big part of it was already in the Clean Energy for America Act, now I had to

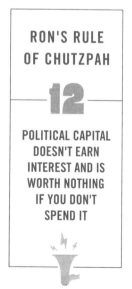

RON'S RULE
OF CHUTZPAH

12

POLITICAL CAPITAL
DOESN'T EARN
INTEREST AND IS
WORTH NOTHING
IF YOU DON'T
SPEND IT

design the plays and assignments that would make Biden's courageous concept the law of the land.

Presidents often will announce bold plans, only to back away if the power structure refuses—or fails—to align. If I could pass a bill out of Committee with substantial support from all corners of our often obstreperous Democratic Party, then Chuck Schumer would have something ready-to-go that he could force the House to accept and send to the President. It wouldn't suffer the fate of cap and trade, where it passed one chamber but failed in the other.

Lobbyists put its prospect of passage below zero percent. On hearing that I was moving ahead, Republican leader Mitch McConnell made the rounds of Republican Senators, unsubtly stating that Western Civilization would end if what I was proposing became law. Despite my lengthy history of bipartisanship, in this new environment of McConnell refusing to work with any Democratic President, I knew I would need every Democratic vote. The game plan was clear.

I made the kind of chart that is second nature to coaches, diagramming the interests of colleagues, each of whom, regardless of their seniority or lack thereof, owned an extraordinarily powerful possession: their vote. Several already were deeply committed because their priorities were covered in the bill. For my seatmate Debbie Stabenow of Michigan, the top priority was promoting electric vehicles; my newest colleague on the committee, Elizabeth Warren of Massachusetts, a beloved professor of commercial law and finance at the Harvard Law School before her election to the Senate, shared my desire to clean out the special-interest tax breaks for fossil fuels.

I was more concerned about how the Republicans' recalcitrance—particularly their by-now-routine, dishonest, but nonetheless effective, characterization of our work as a "tax-and-spend" initiative—would affect four very good Democrats on the Finance Committee. Each was going to face a tough re-election fight: Maggie Hassan of New Hampshire, Catherine Cortez Masto of Nevada, Sherrod Brown of Ohio, and Bob Casey of Pennsylvania.

Maggie and Catherine were already running for re-election in 2022, and I knew senior Republican Senators were trying to make it look like they were for hiking taxes—even though our bill had no tax increases. Sherrod and Bob had different challenges. Ohio is increasingly Red, and Sherrod, his working-class populist bona fides notwithstanding, was sure to have a tough race in 2024. Bob, in addition to representing a swing state, had what he called "coal communities" in Pennsylvania that were naturally concerned about how a clean energy bill would affect them. Bob knew he, too, would face a tough fight in his 2024 reelection campaign (and in fact got David McCormick, a wealthy former hedge fund founder, as his opponent).

I assigned our best tax staff to work with the Cortez Masto and Hassan teams to make sure we were ready to refute the false claims that we were hiking taxes. I assigned my key staffer, Sarah Bittleman, to work with Bob and Sherrod to provide whatever help their communities needed to grow under these new policies. Having done this for Oregon towns long dependent on timber, Sarah was up for the challenge.

Delaware Senator Tom Carper agreed to insert into the debate his argument that the bill should have bipartisan support, a way to push back against McConnell's falsehoods, and to serve as an invitation to Lisa Murkowski and other Republicans—who admitted to me that this was a solid idea—to join us when the ultimate vote came. Tom's credentials as a respected centrist, supporter of nuclear power and Chair of the Environment and Public Works Committee made him just the right person to offer this argument. Maria Cantwell, an expert on hydro power and renewable energy, and my longtime personal friend, had been a strong supporter from the bill's inception, and made the case to Senators on and off the Committee that I had earned their trust over a decade of hard work on the legislation.

On May 26, 2021, all 14 Senate Finance Committee Democrats voted for the first-ever comprehensive clean energy legislation reported by the Committee. In announcing the vote, I said the Committee had put America on the "path to achieve our emission reduction goals and help create hundreds of thousands of good paying clean energy jobs."

It was a team effort. I wish Clem Wiser had been alive so I could have shown him how much he'd taught me about coaching.

The rest...well, by definition, is history. I'll spare you the details as obsessively covered by the Washington press corps. Over a year of back-and-forth between my team, Chuck Schumer, and the White House on one side, and Joe Manchin and Arizona's Democratic

RON'S RULE
OF CHUTZPAH

8

PAY ATTENTION TO
YOUR FRIENDS,
BECAUSE THEY
CAN BE FAR MORE
UNPREDICTABLE
THAN YOUR
ENEMIES

Senator Kyrsten Sinema on the other, the ultimate bill's investment was whittled down from $4 trillion to a still hefty $900 billion. (If you want to know more about the arcane process called "budget reconciliation" by which giant, multi-disciplinary bills like President Biden's are passed, drop me a line or an email and I'll convene a webinar for all you budding policy wonks.)

Manchin ruffled plenty of feathers during the year it took to finalize the Act—diving in, backing out, and using every ounce of clout he had as one of the two Democratic holdouts to extract the concessions he said he needed. But to his credit, he was clear and communicative about his needs, right up until the time he said he was ready. Sinema, the other holdout, was even more challenging. Intelligent, mercurial, and tight-lipped, and always keeping her options open. But the Administration's experienced political team eventually secured her vote.

Because Manchin said he needed it to sell it to his constituents in West Virginia, he also forced the President and Schumer to change the legislation's name from the tolerable "Build Back Better" initiative to the inadequate and limited "Inflation Reduction Act." Yeah, I know—it ain't no "Renewed Deal."

But it *was* and *is* The Renewed Deal that America needs to survive—and thrive—through the 21st century and beyond, built around the two principles that came out of my trip to West Virginia: technological neutrality and economic incentives for carbon reduction.

The bill that President Biden signed on August 16, 2022, is expected to reduce America's carbon emissions by more than 40 percent of the levels needed to reach our goals. It "reshapes industry across the country and the world," as *Time* magazine put it, by directing nearly $400 billion through tax incentives, grants, and loan guarantees to clean energy production and carbon-emission reduction. About $250 billion of that aims to upgrade or replace existing energy infrastructure. This means jobs. More jobs than we will lose in the inevitable end of fossil field extraction and combustion, more good paying jobs that clean, rather than pollute, the world we are leaving for our kids and grandkids.

The legislation makes electric vehicles, energy-efficient appliances, rooftop solar panels, geothermal heating, and home batteries more affordable by offering consumers $43 billion in tax credits.

To assure the jobs generated by these incentives are good ones—and American ones—the legislation offers full tax credits only to companies that meet prevailing wage and apprenticeship standards, domestic production and procurement requirements, and trade agreements. Because it also imposes new minimum taxes on the largest companies and excise taxes on stock buybacks and additionally provides funds for the IRS to improve tax collection, the bill will lower deficits by nearly $240 billion over the next decade.

In just its first year, this Renewed Deal has supported theory with fact. Companies already have invested more than $270 billion in solar, wind, battery, and other clean energy projects, according to the American Clean Power Association. More than $130 billion has been invested in electric vehicle technology, generating 32,000 new jobs from Michigan to Alabama. The Department of Energy identified 114,000 clean-energy jobs created since the bill's signing, 93,000 of them in the nation's new "Battery Belt" comprising 91 new plants in Kentucky, Tennessee, Missouri, Louisiana, Georgia, and—a geographic outlier—New York. Eighty-four new wind and solar energy equipment plants dot the landscape from Florida to Pennsylvania.

All told, industry and Government analysts expect Joe Biden's Inflation Reduction Act to generate 1.3 million new jobs in the next 10 years, while reducing greenhouse gas emissions by 40 percent below their peak by 2030.

Oh, and there's one more thing—and this one is personal: President Biden's Inflation Reduction Act included the provision envisioned by Olympia Snowe and me more than 20 years earlier—to allow Medicare to negotiate some drug prices with the largest pharma companies. This, plus the bill's extension of several other Obamacare provisions, will cut Government health-care expenditures by $173 billion over the next seven years. "Senator Ron Wyden is the architect of the drug-price negotiation measure," the *New York Times* declared.

But more important to me than the credit is what's happening right now, for the nearly 30 million Americans diagnosed with diabetes: Because Medicare sculpts the shape of the entire medical-industrial complex, the cost of insulin for most Americans, regardless of age, will fall in 2024 to $35 a month from its average 2021 price of $98.70.

Which is exactly as I'd predicted when we were pushing this forward in 1999, and why I went back for more.

"Everything that made it into law," the policy expert David Dayen wrote in the *American Prospect*, "from tackling the climate emergency to improving the Affordable Care Act, from restaffing the IRS and taxing wealthy corporations to reducing the cost of prescription drugs, has origins like Wyden's van trip to West Virginia, an extended backstory rooted in learning from failures, building coalitions, sacrificing important elements, and sometimes waging furious battles to reach consensus."

Or, as I'd summarize it: It takes chutzpah.

RON'S RULE OF CHUTZPAH

9

DON'T PUSH ROCKS UP HILLS. PUSH BOULDERS. THEY WILL FALL BACK ON YOU, BUT YOU'LL GAIN THE STRENGTH TO GET TO THE TOP

THE FUTURE IS ALWAYS JUST 20 MINUTES AWAY

No matter when you are reading this afterword, I hope it will serve as a good measure of my rules of chutzpah. Today, though, I hope you will read it as a call to action—2 years from now, I believe it will be a good yardstick—and in 20 years—well, I hope it will be a litany of accomplishments we all share, not regrets.

First and foremost, we must continue the fight to limit and ultimately eliminate human-caused growth in atmospheric carbon. Without it, I can virtually guarantee that you—and certainly your children's generation—will be forced to move from riverfront or seafront towns, face rebuilding after repeated, unprecedented weather disasters, or suffer from diseases that migrate and flourish as the climate changes. Despite vast scientific consensus on these facts, there is enormous ideological opposition to doing anything about climate change, manifesting in counties and states voting to make renewables deployment more difficult. Such resistance is certifiably insane—literally a sacrifice of lives and livelihoods on the altar of right-wing political correctness. The good news: As of this writing the Clean Energy for America Act / Inflation Reduction Act has been a smashing success, and major projects enabled by the Inflation Reduction Act are being built in even the Reddest states. Those projects and many more like them will get us most of the way toward carbon neutrality in the United States.

But that only gets us part of the way if we're going to stop a warming globe for future generations. Global agreement on carbon reduction is a game for diplomats that will be neither enforceable or effective. However, the same mechanism that fueled global growth over the past 50 years can enforce carbon reduction worldwide. The U.S., with Canada and Mexico, and the EU must draw a customs border around their enormous consumer economies that puts a high price on carbon. Producers can either pay the tax or cut their carbon output—human nature will accomplish what the diplomats cannot. If we dither trying to get India, China, Saudi Arabia, and Indonesia to reduce the carbon in their economies, all of Florida will be treading water. It takes chutzpah to draw this line, but failure in global carbon reduction is not an option.

At the same time, we need to ensure that the minerals necessary to support a zero-carbon economy are—to the extent possible—mined where they are used. It is neither just nor smart to put the burdens of mining on less developed nations simply because their environmental and labor protections are weaker. There will always be opposition to mines—they are not warm and fuzzy neighbors—but mining can be done in a safe, sustainable way, with respect for the miners, and the environment. When the minerals are available, that is best done at home. We must also address the needs of energy transmission and local, distributed generation so that clean, zero-carbon energy is available where it is needed to support health and welfare while driving productivity and innovation. That's a bold goal, but the right one. Remember: *There are only two paths you can take to progress: Start good things and stop bad things.*

The greatest challenge that we face strictly on the home front is protecting and preserving our income security system for a second century. There are forces that have been trying to kill Social Security since it began (according to these misguided souls, President Roosevelt was a communist) and they are seizing on a failure in our tax system—not in Social Security itself—to take their next shot.

In 2034 the Social Security system is going to be forced to cut benefits to all recipients by 20 percent. This is not due to the fact that you haven't paid enough payroll taxes. It is the failure of repeated Administrations since Ronald Reagan and Tip O'Neill worked together, to adjust the tax system to account for the changing ways wealth is made and accumulated.

The problem is not that there are an increasing number of unfathomably wealthy individuals, but that many of those individuals are vastly underreporting their taxable income. They tell the Government they're tantamount to paupers when they're actually cruising around the world on their ever-larger yachts. According to tax documents uncovered by the investigative reporting organization ProPublica, Jeff Bezos, the richest man in the world, reported less income in a recent year than one of his Amazon.com middle managers or *Washington Post* copy editors. In some years the same publication uncovered that he, Elon Musk, and George Soros paid no income or Social Security tax at all.

The tax system has not kept up with the games people play to avoid it, and while the average wage-earner can't avoid taxation, billionaires and mere multi-millionaires have often managed to avoid paying their share. We are seeing the consequences in Social Security, the national debt and deficit, and a number of other Government functions that keep our society whole. One of our greatest Supreme Court Justices, Oliver Wendell Holmes, noted that "taxes are the price we pay for a civilized society"—and it's a price of which too many are not paying their fair share.

Before 2034 we must have the chutzpah to reform the tax system so that no income is hidden and all income is taxed fairly. When we do this, we can prevent 100 percent of those 2034 Social Security cuts without raising the retirement age, cutting cost of living increases, or playing any other games with these insurance benefits that every American has already paid for—benefits that support millions of American jobs and keep our seniors out of poverty.

At the other end of the income security system is wage insurance. In the opening chapter of this book, you read about the bold change to unemployment insurance I forced on the Trump Administration during the early days of the Covid-19 pandemic. Folks living paycheck to paycheck are going to do what they must to keep food on the table and a roof over their heads, and without the Covid-19 emergency payments large swaths of the wage-earning public would have defied stay-at-home orders and reported to work out of necessity, making the pandemic far worse than it was. It is a national embarrassment that our wage insurance system was not able to protect people, or the nation, without dramatic intervention. The difficulty many Americans had in accessing those temporarily increased benefits through creaky, state-based bureaucracies compounds the embarrassment.

We must have the chutzpah to sweep away the crazy quilt of unemployment insurance, disaster aid, and trade adjustment assistance, and we must take on the challenge of restructuring wage insurance so that it can respond to disasters and dislocations, natural and man-made. What we create should improve the minimal protection against unemployment now offered so poorly and with so much red tape. It should provide rapid, flexible response to natural disasters. And it must offer more effective support for disruptions from technology, trade, and related changes that can eliminate professions and decimate industries. Rest assured, just as automation and globalization eliminated American manufacturing and mining jobs, AI will eradicate untold numbers of law, accounting, media, and finance positions. Yes, it is more efficient and ultimately better for our economy to let trade and innovation disrupt, but it takes the very opposite of chutzpah to allow those disruptions to afflict our fellow man without lifting a finger to cushion the blow.

The ultimate cushion in everyone's life is good health. As the saying goes, if you don't have your health, you don't have anything. As of this writing, the Affordable Care Act—Obamacare—has guaranteed health coverage to millions of Americans who might have lost it due to changing jobs, divorce, or "pre-existing conditions." It has even slowed the increase in some health-care costs. But it has not transformed a system that still costs too much to do too little. True transformation takes chutzpah.

Both Democrats and Republicans need to come down off their ideological soapboxes and shape a health-care system that provides average citizens care without sending them to the poorhouse. We need progressives to see that there is a role for marketplace forces to appropriately provide better, faster, less expensive care. And as for the Right? They've got to stop running all those expensive ad campaigns decrying "government interference" in health care when they are the very ones fighting tooth and nail against free-market reforms.

An efficient free market presumes perfect information on both sides of a transaction. But the moguls of health care, some of whom are now Senators, fight to hide from you how much things cost, how effective they are, what doctors you can see, and what you will pay. To them, market forces are great when they make more money by having better information, but awful when increased transparency, competition, and educated consumers means they will make less.

We need to assure the Government performs its proper role and brings better, complete information to all parts of the health-care marketplace—and ensures that any middlemen who are interposing themselves are actually needed and are not just profiteering at the public's expense. No more ghost networks where mental health coverage is offered, but no actual care is provided. No more surprise bills or hidden fees, no more dropping doctors from a plan because they're providing higher quality care, no more "the devil is in the details" coverage that tricks people into thinking they are safe only to find out after the fact that they are uncovered and financially ruined. And finally, let's let everyone choose their health plan like members of Congress, so that health insurers are really competing for who can make their customers healthy for the lowest cost. It is both asinine and immoral that the Government provides its own elected leaders coverage options it refuses to provide the citizens of Keizer, Kokomo, and Key West.

Blocking bad ideas is as important as advancing bold new ideas. Sure, it lacks glamour and requires spending a great deal of personal and political capital—especially when you're forced to fight against friends who are stepping, unknowingly or unthinkingly, onto dangerous ground.

My work in technology has been the embodiment of many of the 12 Rules of Chutzpah. And I'll tell you, it took old-fashioned chutzpah as a U.S. Senator to vote against a bill, called SESTA/FOSTA, that purported to protect kids from sex trafficking. Why did I take that vote? Because the bill would not do what it promised (and it hasn't, it's just made it harder and more expensive to catch these criminals), and it would do great harm to those already living at the margin of society (which, sadly, it has).

We need to continue to work together to protect innovation and innovators from those who attack it for political or personal gain, or defend outmoded but personally profitable ways of doing business, or just out of ignorance or fear of change. It is damn hard to be the advocate for change—for that's what innovation is—because change means uncertainty, and the easiest thing in the world to sell is certainty.

If you ever wonder why it's so hard to convince folks of commonsense, good ideas like civil rights for women and minorities, even to some women and minorities; better and cheaper health care versus "what you have"; or even democracy versus fascism—it's because the other guy is selling certainty. The promise of certainty—economic, social, or physical security—is a powerful drug that stands in the way of improving the world and can even drag us backward. Too many are willing to suffer the certainty of poor circumstances rather than risk the uncertainty of change, choice, and progress. That fear of, or simply opposition to, change is what underlies the resurgence of ultra-right-wing reactionary movements, MAGA and the rest, in the U.S. and around the world.

I'll be damned if I'll give up one ounce of liberty for a little, ephemeral, security. And if you've read this far, I know you feel the same way. Liberty is the wellspring of all good things and we must defend it in all its forms—innovation not the least of them.

That doesn't mean we don't stand against uses of technology that are designed to hurt people for fun or profit. If something is illegal to do without technology, no use of technology should allow folks to get away with it. Racial discrimination, rental price fixing, monopolization, slander, libel, and theft—all should be just as illegal for an algorithm to do it as it is for a flesh and blood crook to do it.

In change, in growth, playing the long game is essential. Understand that a simple innovation today can be the seed for monumental growth and opportunity in the future, so long as it is not quashed by the forces of fear, uncertainty, and doubt. We may very well lose millions of jobs in transportation and restaurant service, or accounting and coding, to the latest innovations in AI and automation—but that doesn't mean we stop the innovation, rather it means we smooth the way to more and better jobs in the future.

Nor does it mean we leave the rest of us behind. Our rural economies are still the foundation of the modern technological society. Rural people and businesses, rural industry and organizations, grow our food and lumber, mine our minerals, are the source of much of our clean water, and increasingly generate our clean, renewable energy through wind, solar, and geothermal. Technology has reduced the number of people needed to do all of those things, but it cannot eliminate the need for people. It is long past time to recognize that rural communities have earned support, just like urban ones do, but that the safety nets of the last 70 years have left them behind. Even worse, the 100-year-old safety nets known as revenue-sharing arrangements between the Federal Government, extraction industries, and rural places have not kept pace with technological change.

It will take chutzpah to do away with these old arrangements, but we must create a budgetarily stabilizing endowment for these rural places, funded by the benefits our rural communities provide to the nation as a whole. This endowment can ensure that the education, law enforcement, and infrastructure needs of rural communities are fully funded for generations, not funded piecemeal a year or even a month at a time. Much in the way big corporations can weather recessions while many small businesses go under, our current system favors the big cities and populous counties while leaving our rural areas to founder during difficult times. They should not have to come hat-in-hand to Congress, and our system must be redesigned to recognize their contributions and their necessities.

The romance of the rugged individualist timber or mining town, and the boom or bust cycles that have become part of their culture, don't hold up against a modern world where the ore and lumber are part of the global economy. There is still romance in being a miner and logger—but the infrastructure needed to support these ever more sophisticated professions can't simply be abandoned the next time prices fall. Stabilized county budgets will do more to keep our mills and mines working than any of the deregulatory schemes floated by Wall Street. This is the way to maintain a part of America long celebrated in novel, song, and poem—a part as necessary now as it has been in our national mythology.

Much of this is about having the chutzpah to make our society a greater society, for the benefit of all. Saying this, I am forced to reflect that many of the greatest societies in human history—Persian, Arabic, Chinese, each responsible for a sizable share of human progress— are currently afflicted by authoritarian regimes that are crushing the promise of their people. We would do well to remember, too, that the European philosophies that were among those that laid the foundations for the United States and other modern democratic republics also formulated the ideology and tools of fascism that allows these authoritarians to maintain their grips on power. Many today fail to remember how close the West came to falling to that same self-perpetuating tyranny.

We must all remember, and we must constantly resist these forces. Modern technologies make the jobs of every aspiring Goebbels and Himmler that much easier—and they only need to win once. Only in fantastical fiction can the scrappy band of rebels topple an established fascist regime. In reality, the strength of fascism over its feudal and strongman predecessors is its ability to perpetuate itself generation after generation; whereas those previous systems could fall at every transition of power. Fascism can only be defeated when an outside influence acts upon it. That is our challenge with China.

We are not trying to defeat the Chinese people. We are trying to prevent a fascist regime from dominating the world the way the Axis nearly did in my father's generation. The best possible outcome of this confrontation would be a vibrant, free Chinese society still competing with America culturally and economically, but one that is no longer trying to extend the shroud of tyranny across the entire world.

Winning this battle requires having the chutzpah to realize that our freedom is our strength. In confronting both the Axis and later the Soviets, it was the unbridled freedom of our press, our people, and our economy that allowed us to prevail. No fascist regime can tap the vibrancy, the self-correcting resiliency, or the sheer productivity of a free people. The concentration of power within "The Party" in those regimes results in corruption, waste, and inefficiencies that give us the edge we need. Their trains may occasionally run on time, but those tracks will not lead them to the future.

We must unleash the power of our workers, employers, and entrepreneurs to compete on a level playing field. In the same way the democratic republics of the world must erect a customs border that puts a proper price on carbon, we should ensure that the non-market advantages of a Government-run economy, cheap capital, oppressed workers, and state-controlled technology, are not allowed to swamp those who are playing by the rules. "Free trade" never should have been about freedom from rules, and it's time the international trade regime fostered the ideology of individual freedom that gave it birth.

Inevitably our freedom enables admirers of the deceptive strength of the fascists within our own society. American newspapers of the 1920s are replete with fawning portrayals of Benito Mussolini's "strong leadership"—and so we should not be so surprised that, 100 years later, there are in the United States admirers of Vladimir Putin, Viktor Orban, and even Kim Jong Un.

To keep such admiration from becoming repetition, we must fight not only the ideas of fascism—demonizing minorities, promoting grievance, deifying strength—but also the tools: propaganda, government control, and surveillance.

Government surveillance is the foundation of tyranny. This is why I will fight to my last breath every attempt to limit privacy and expand the power of Government with new technologies that swallow our privacy and allow surveillance Orwell only dreamed of. There is no space in this book to explore this idea with the depth it demands. I ask that you have the chutzpah to object to each and every effort to intrude on personal privacy, by laws, courts, or technology; and I promise I will be right there with you.

ACKNOWLEDGMENTS

For years all I wanted to do was play professional basketball. When it became clear that wouldn't be possible, I owe thanks to the many friends and staff (so many of whom are both) who helped me all along the path to a life of public service.

Never having been elected to anything, I had the chutzpah to believe at age 29 that I could be elected to Congress. That first campaign brought me so many good friends, Merrie and Ron Buel, Lois and Jimmy Davis, Ray Wilkeson, Walt Mintkeski and Al Panek. The Kohnstamm family, Warren Rosenfeld, Matt Chapman, Gert and Tim Boyle, Duncan Campbell, Jordan Schnitzer, Joe Angel, Jay Zidell, Michael and Alice Powell, Ron Herndon and Nan Heim, and so many others helped introduce me to business and community leaders.

My first Congressional Office was helmed by the talented Gary Conkling. Danny Saltzman led our environmental work, Janice Yaden ran point on health care and Rich Brown handled business and housing. Steve Jenning, a superb ex-*Oregonian* business writer, led our investigations work at the House Small Business Subcommittee. A big tip of my hat to the Chair of that full Committee, John LaFalce of New York who had the chutzpah to let me lead the investigations. Wendy Greenwald did a superb job in that Office, in comms and then as Chief of Staff. And to Lou Savage, who along with our staff gave me the best Congressional district office in the country. Lou, a keen student of the importance of the rule of law to a democracy, continues to be my key advisor on judicial appointments to this day.

In my campaign for the Senate, Josh Kardon and Amy Chapman masterminded our way to a narrow victory over my friend Senator Gordon Smith. Josh, my first Senate Chief of Staff, has been a revered personal friend for decades. Josh lovingly helped navigate Nancy's wheelchair when she, I, and the twins were leaving Oregon Health and Science University—where Dr. Mark Nichols also brought Scarlett into the world.

Helping Amy and Josh put that upset win together were Chris Warner and Barbara Smith Warner (later State Representative), Lisa Grove, Curtis Robinhold, and again, Al Panek. And my very dear friends Joan and Tom Moore who kept me going on so many occasions. And to the late great, Mary Gautreaux, my "ambassador" of Oregon. Also, Lisa Rockower of Eugene, an inimitable force of good heart and great intellect who has now for over two decades kept our Oregon operations humming with 1,100 open to all town hall meetings and maintained a staff that is respected across the state. (Added perk, being lucky enough to be invited to join a meal for the Jewish holidays at Lisa's.) And Jocelyn Tyree, whom my kids lovingly refer to as Aunt Jocelyn.

Drs. Frank Baumeister and John Moorehead were hugely helpful in bringing me together with the health-care field in the first Senate campaign. Around the country many friends took my late-night calls as I worked to find my footing in the Senate. They included Keenan Wolens and Melissa Landaw in California. Stuart, Janice, and Marissa Shorenstein, Danny Mintz and Meredith Berkman, Dr. Carey and Ellen Dolgin, and Lisa Kohl in New York, Edna and Kenny Adelberg in Philadelphia, and Steve and Lisa Schatz in San

Francisco. And my rabbis at Portland's Congregation Beth Israel, first the late Rabbi Manny Rose, and today my friend Rabbi Michael Cahana, who have always been incredibly generous with their time and counsel. Kent Hinckley, one of Palo Alto's true basketball greats, who spent hours reminiscing with me about our mutual admiration for a special coach, Clem Wiser.

Great early Senate staffers, Carole Grunberg who led my legislative team, Stephanie Kennan, Emily Katz and Elizabeth Jurinka in health, and Geoff Stuckart, Tom Towslee, and Carol Guthrie in communications, Scott Bolton who established a vital presence in Central Oregon, and Wayne Kinney and Kathleen Cathey in Eastern Oregon, as well as Jane Hill, Molly McCarthy, and Juine Chada and for so many years Loretta Smith in Portland.

Steve and Brenda Forrester, friends for 40 years, continue to sustain me when I'm holding town halls on the Oregon coast with hot sandwiches and warm tea—we've seen our families grow up on the sands of our beautiful beaches. Those breaks often include Hank Stern, with whom I've traveled to all of our 36 counties: Hank has brought savvy and a wicked sense of humor to our travels. Peter Sage and Debra Lee have been wonderful friends and eyes and ears in Southern Oregon, and the King family has done the same in Lane County.

As readers will learn more about in this book I've always known that health care was the most important issue, because if you don't have quality, necessary health care, everything else is subordinate. Doubly so for women, whose health-care needs receive decidedly short shrift. Working with stellar experts in Congress like Senator Mazie Hirono, North Carolina Congresswomen Kathy Manning and Deborah Ross, and California Congresswoman Sara Jacobs has been vital to our good work. Senator Patty Murray of Washington deserves special mention for her more than 30 years of advocacy for women's health.

My inestimable current staff, including Josh Sheinkman and Tiffany Smith at the Finance Committee and Sarah Bittleman and Isaiah Akin in the office, also John Dickas and Keith Chu who have been vital in policing privacy and intelligence abuses by the Federal Government. Along with them is a team too large to mention individually, but whose skills and dedication make me confident that we can get things done for Oregonians and the American people in the coming years.

I close by mentioning two wonderful friends without whom this book would not have climbed out of the literary crib. Randall Rothenberg, friend of 40 years, is a journalist-turned-business executive-turned consultant I first met when he was a writer and reporter with *Esquire* magazine and the *New York Times*. Randy's good ideas, research, and, most importantly, his enthusiastic collaboration with me on the page was indispensable in making this book a reality.

Finally, Jeff Michels, who I first met when I was thinking of running against Bob Packwood and who put together the war chest that allowed me to enter the primary for that seat two years later with the wind at my back. He joined me in the Senate handling technology, finance, and foreign policy and took over for Josh Kardon as my Chief of Staff. He has given me more wit, innovation, and political savvy mixed with common sense and a determination to do good then I ever could have hoped for. No one in American politics has a better grasp of the intersection of politics and sound public policy that he has. His wife, Susan, is a valued counselor in all my efforts. A typical night often ends with Jeff putting his two beautiful daughters, Verity and Honor, to bed, and washing dishes while answering a dozen hypotheticals from me. Without him this book would not be possible.

I hope the pleasure you get from reading this book is even a fraction of how much I got from writing it. Even more, I hope it inspires you to put your own chutzpah to work and do some good.

REFERENCES

INTRODUCTION

Mitch McConnell showed how little compassion he had for working Americans:
For details about the pandemic's impact on the American workforce, and Senate testimony and debate about the CARES Act, see "Wyden Responds to GOP Opposition to Supercharging Unemployment Insurance: An Extra $600 Per Week for Laid Off Workers Will Not End Western Civilization," March 25, 2020, https://www.finance.senate.gov/ranking-members-news/wyden-responds-to-gop -opposition-to-supercharging-unemployment-insurance-an-extra-600-per-week-for -laid-off-workers-will-not-end-western-civilization; "May 2020 to September 2022 supplemental data measuring the effects of the coronavirus (COVID-19) pandemic on the labor market," https://www.bls.gov/cps/effects-of-the-coronavirus-covid-19 -pandemic.htm; "Labor Secretary Scalia Testimony on Economic Impact of COVID -19," https://www.c-span.org/video/?472836-1/labor-secretary-scalia-testiimony -economic-impact-covid-19; "Senate GOP Says Fix Need for Unemployment Benefits Error in Economic Relief Bill," https://www.c-span.org/video/?c4863775 /senate-gop-fix-unemployment-benefits-error-economic-relief-bill; and "Trump Had One Good Response to Covid-19. His Party Killed It," by Paul Krugman, https:// www.nytimes.com/2020/08/31/opinion/trump-coronavirus-economy.html.

CHAPTER 1: MAKING PRODUCTIVE NOISE

My father, all joyful cheek: Although he never wrote a memoir per se, Peter Wyden wrote extensively about himself and his family in *Stella: One Woman's*

True Tale of Evil, Betrayal, and Survival in Hitler's Germany (Simon & Schuster, 1992) and *Conquering Schizophrenia: A Father, His Son, and a Medical Breakthrough* (Alfred A. Knopf, 1998).

The author Robert Caro: Power is the ability to "get things done": "The Power Broker—III: How Robert Moses Got Things Done" by Robert A. Caro. *New Yorker*, August 4, 1974. https://www.newyorker.com/magazine/1974/08/12/the -power-broker-iii-how-things-get-done; "Robert A. Caro on the Means and Ends of Power," by David Marchese, *New York Times Magazine*, April 1, 2019. https://www.nytimes.com/interactive/2019/04/01/magazine/robert-caro-working -memoir.html; and https://wtcs.pressbooks.pub/introsociology2e/chapter/power -and-authority/.

One of the 20th century's most prominent public philosophers, Walter Lippmann: For more on Lippmann and his theories about media, democracy, and representative government, see *Public Opinion* by Walter Lippmann (Harcourt, Brace, 1922) and *The Phantom Public* (Harcourt, Brace, 1925). Also see "The Unattainable Ideal: Walter Lippmann and the Limits of the Press and Public Opinion" by Amy Solomon Whitehead. Louisiana State University and Agricultural and Mechanical College. https://repository.lsu.edu/cgi/viewcontent .cgi?article=3281&context=gradschool_theses.

"The 24 hr news cycle has destroyed Congress": "With the World in Crisis, House Republicans Bicker Among Themselves" by Carl Hulse. *New York Times*, October 12, 2023. https://www.nytimes.com/2023/10/12/us/politics/house -republicans-bicker-world-crisis.html.

Chutzpah meant "enterprise, audacity, brazen impudence and cheek": "On Language; Chutzpah at Camp Greentop" by William Safire. *New York Times Magazine*, March 18, 1990. https://www.nytimes.com/1990/03/18/magazine /on-language-chutzpah-at-camp-greentop.html.

Joseph Goebbels, said chutzpah "means unlimited, impertinent, and unbelievable impudence and shamelessness…": "Mimicry," by Joseph Goebbels. https://research.calvin.edu/german-propaganda-archive/goeb18.htm.

Steve Bannon, and his anarchic acolytes in the Republican House Freedom Caucus: "What Is Broken in American Politics Is the Republican Party," *Politico Magazine*, October 6, 2023, https://www.politico.com/news /magazine/2023/10/06/republican-leaders-mccarthy-expert-roundup-00120170.

Jewish scholars do recognize that there is such a thing as "bad chutzpah": I'm indebted to the incisive and delightful analysis of chutzpah by Rabbi Tzvi Freeman, a senior editor with Chabad, which can be found here: https://www .chabad.org/library/article_cdo/aid/1586271/jewish/Chutzpah.htm.

The moral philosopher Harry Frankfurt: See *On Bullshit* by Harry G. Frankfurt (Princeton University Press, 2005).

As the great salesman Dale Carnegie said, "To be interesting, be interested": *How to Win Friends and Influence People* by Dale Carnegie (Simon & Schuster, 1936).

CHAPTER 2: THE LONG GAME, PART I

A global battle by scientists committed to women's health against religious fanatics who wanted to keep a life-changing medicine out of the United States: Among the many excellent sources on the history of mifepristone, I have found the following particularly useful: "The Father of the Abortion Pill" by Pam Belluck. *New York Times*, January 17, 2023. https://www.nytimes .com/2023/01/17/health/abortion-pill-inventor.html?smid=nytcore-ios -share&referringSource=articleShare; "The Complicated Life of the Abortion Pill" by Lauren Collins. *New Yorker*, July 5, 2022. https://www.newyorker.com /science/annals-of-medicine/emile-baulieu-the-complicated-life-of-the-abortion -pill; "A Political History of RU-486" by R. Alta Charo, K. E. Hanna, ed. Institute of Medicine (US) Committee to Study Decision Making, 1991. https:// www.ncbi.nlm.nih.gov/books/NBK234199/; "The Story of Abortion Pills and How They Work" by Chris Baraniuk. *Wired*, May 25, 2022. https://www.wired .com/story/abortion-pills-how-they-work/; "Justices Uphold Federal Seizure of Abortion Pill" by Philip J. Hilts. *New York Times*, July 18, 1992, https://www .nytimes.com/1992/07/18/us/justices-uphold-federal-seizure-of-abortion-pill

.html; "The Abortion Pill's 1992 Supreme Court Battle and the Woman Who Started It" by Timothy Bella. *Washington Post*, April 8, 2023. https://www .washingtonpost.com/politics/2023/04/08/abortion-pill-mifepristone-leona -benten/; and "How Safe Is the Abortion Pill Compared with Other Common Drugs?" by Annette Choi and Way Mullery. CNN, December 13, 2023, https:// www.cnn.com/health/abortion-pill-safety-dg.

We heard from a panoply of physicians, patient advocates, and patients themselves: In addition to the sources above, coverage of the hearings in 1990 and subsequently can be found at "Hill Holds Heated Hearing on RU-486" by Curt Suplee. *Washington Post*, November 19, 1990. https://www .washingtonpost.com/archive/politics/1990/11/20/hill-holds-heated-hearing -on-ru-486/19f4cb31-db18-4b2d-9c1c-d3d6bef6c7d0/; https://www.c-span .org/video/?15059-1/import-ban-ru486; "The Effect of Federal Ban of RU 486 on Medical Research, New Drug Development, and Pharmaceutical Manufacturers." https://books.google.com/books?id=aG0VsP2JhiMC&pg.

CHAPTER 3: CRYING WITH PURPOSE

You might say I was to the manor—and the manner—born: The Jews of Capitol Hill by Kurt F. Stone (Ktav Publishing House, 2000).

CHAPTER 4: LEADING IS COACHING

John McPhee…in his classic 1965 New Yorker *magazine profile of Bill Bradley:* "A Sense of Where You Are" by John McPhee. *New Yorker*, January 25, 1965. https://www.newyorker.com/magazine/1965/01/23/a-sense-of-where-you-are.

All of which put me on the radar screen of a mensch named Clem Wiser: Among the best sources on the history of Palo Alto and its people, especially during the postwar period, are the websites Palo Alto Online, https://www .paloaltoonline.com, and Palo Alto High School's Paly Journalism Online, https://palyjournalismarchive.pausd.org.

He invented a special salute for his ersatz political movement, which he dubbed The Third Wave: The story of Ron Jones and the Cubberley High School "Third Wave" movement can be found at "The Wave that changed the world: Fifty years ago, a Palo Alto teacher's lesson on fascism took on a life of its own," by Linda Taaffe, March 17, 2017, https://www.paloaltoonline.com/news/2017/03/17/the-wave-that-changed-history/ and "The Third Wave (experiment)." https://en.wikipedia.org/wiki/The_Third_Wave_(experiment).

The fervor that surrounded us peaked on April 15, 1967: My references for the antiwar and civil rights movements in Palo Alto include "A War Without End: What Palo Alto Can Tell Us About the History of Curriculum Conflicts" by Amann Mahajan. Medium, September 12, 2023. https://medium.com/@amannsmahajan/a-war-without-end-what-palo-alto-can-tell-us-about-the-history-of-curriculum-conflicts-ddf78a03d641; "From Race Riots to Strength in Diversity" by Sana Sheikholeslami. *M-A Chronicle*, January 26, 2016. https://machronicle.com/from-race-riots-to-strength-in-diversity/; "Ravenswood High School, 1958–1976," https://ravenswood.sequoiaalumni.net/about_rhs.htm; and "Ravenswood High School (East Palo Alto)," https://en.wikipedia.org/wiki/Ravenswood_High_School_(East_Palo_Alto).

The University of Michigan management scholar Noel Tichy: "Noel M. Tichy: The Thought Leader Interview" by Randall Rothenberg. *strategy+business*, February 14, 2003. https://www.strategy-business.com/article/8458; and https://fs.blog/stretching-yourself-to-learn-new-things/.

"How do you teach people how to win?" muses Larry Bossidy, the former CEO of Honeywell: "The CEO as Coach: An Interview with AlliedSignal's Lawrence A. Bossidy" by Noel M. Tichy and Ram Charan. *Harvard Business Review*, March-April 1995. https://hbr.org/1995/03/the-ceo-as-coach-an-interview-with-alliedsignals-lawrence-a-bossidy.

CHAPTER 5: TAKING HITS, BOUNCING BACK

He deemed the hapless invasion of Cuba early in the Kennedy Administration "Waterloo staged by the Marx Brothers": The Bay of Pigs: The Untold Story by Peter Wyden (Simon & Schuster, 1979).

Seeing Oregon for the first time was the second inflection point in my young life: The definitive histories of Oregon and Portland were written by the masterful historian Kim MacColl, including *The Shaping of a City: Business and Politics in Portland, Oregon, 1885–1915* by E. Kimbark MacColl (Georgian Press, 1976); *The Growth of a City: Power and Politics in Portland, Oregon, 1915 to 1950* by E. Kimbark MacColl (Georgian Press, 1979); and *Merchants, Money, & Power: The Portland Establishment, 1843–1913* by E. Kimbark MacColl with Harry H. Stein (Georgian Press, 1988). Other favorite sources for the history and culture of Oregon include *That Balance So Rare: The Story of Oregon* by Terence O'Donnell (Oregon Historical Society Press, 1988); *Portland: An Informal History and Guide* by Terence O'Donnell and Thomas Vaughan (Oregon Historical Society, 1984); and the *Oregon History Project* by the Oregon Historical Society, https://www.oregonhistoryproject.org/.

Blacks were not allowed to be within its borders after dark: "Sundown No More," *Medford Mail Tribune*, Medford, Oregon, July 18, 1963. https://www .newspapers.com/article/medford-mail-tribune/29370669/; and "A Look Back at How White Supremacists Sowed Seeds of Hate in Oregon in the 20th Century" by Kami Horton. Oregon Public Broadcasting, March 14, 2022. https://www .opb.org/article/2022/03/14/rise-of-klan-white-nationalism-hate-racism-oregon/.

Oregon elected Joseph Simon, a Jew, as U.S. Senator in 1898, until then only the fourth Jewish Senator in American history: "Joseph Simon: Pioneer Jewish Lawyer, State Senator, and U.S. Senator from the State of Oregon," Jewish Museum of the American West. https://www.jmaw.org/simon-jewish-oregon/.

If you read profiles of Wayne Lyman Morse: My sources for the life of the late U.S. Senator Wayne Morse include "U.S. Sen. Wayne Morse," Oregon Public Broadcasting's *Oregon Experience*. https://www.opb.org/television /programs/oregon-experience/article/wayne-morse; "Wayne Morse (1900–1974)," the Oregon Historical Society's Oregon Encyclopedia, https://www .oregonencyclopedia.org/articles/morse_wayne/; "Boss of the Waterfront: Wayne Morse and Labor Arbitration." University of Oregon. https://expo.uoregon .edu/spotlight/boss-of-the-waterfront; "Oregon Sen. Wayne Morse Dies at 73, July 22, 1974" by Andrew Glass. *Politico*, July 22, 2017. https://www.politico

.com/story/2017/07/22/this-day-in-politics-july-22-1974-240682; "Wayne Morse
Sets Filibuster Record," United States Senate, https://www.senate.gov/about
/powers-procedures/filibusters-cloture/wayne-morse-sets-filibuster-record.htm;
"The Foreign Policy of Senator Wayne L. Morse" by Larry Ceplair, *Oregon
Historical Quarterly*, Spring 2012, https://www.jstor.org/stable/10.5403
/oregonhistq.113.1.0006?read-now=1&seq=10#page_scan_tab_contents; "Wayne
Morse," University of Oregon, Wayne Morse Center for Law and Politics. https://
waynemorsecenter.uoregon.edu/wayne-morse; "Bernie Sanders's Political
Ancestor, Wayne Lyman Morse" by Jeffrey Frank. *New Yorker*, May 24, 2016.
https://www.newyorker.com/news/daily-comment/bernie-sanderss-political
-ancestor-wayne-lyman-morse; "Leadership as Political Mentorship: The
Example of Wayne Morse" by Lee Wilkins. *Political Psychology*, March, 1986.
https://www.jstor.org/stable/3791156; and "Oregon: The Reign of Wayne." *Time*,
January 5, 1968. https://time.com/archive/6647963/oregon-the-reign-of-wayne/.

*An open "Declaration of Conscience" decrying the anti-Communist witch
hunt of the right-wing Wisconsin Senator Joseph McCarthy:* "Declaration of
Conscience," by Margaret Chase Smith, July 1, 1950, edited and introduced by
David Krugler. Teaching American History, https://teachingamericanhistory.org
/document/declaration-of-conscience/.

CHAPTER 6: THE COURAGE TO ENCOURAGE AND DISCOURAGE

*But senior rights—that really hadn't crossed the threshold of public
consciousness:* For the rise of intergenerational activism, particularly the
work of Maggie Kuhn, Ruth Haefner, and the Gray Panthers, my sources
included "Gray Panthers Challenge Stereotypes," *The Rural Tribune*, Hillsboro,
Oregon, February 1976. https://heritage.lib.pacificu.edu/files/original
/fb0087245d6069f205003ead7b6c277578d92861.pdf; "Distinguished Alumni
Award: Ruth Haefner 18BA, 1978 Achievement Award," Iowa Center for
Advancement, http://www.pa.state.us_www.givetoiowa.org/daa/daa-profile
.php?namer=true&profileid=212; and the daily journalism of Walli Schneider
in the *Oregon Journal*, which can be found at *The Oregonian*'s OregonLive
website, https://oregonlive.newsbank.com.

CHAPTER 7: EMBRACING UNSCRIPTED MOMENTS

Representative Henry Waxman's relentless 35-year campaign to get Big Tobacco to pay for killing millions of Americans: "Portraits in Oversight: Henry Waxman and Big Tobacco" by the Carl Levin Center for Oversight and Democracy. Wayne State Law School, Detroit, MI. https://levin-center.org/what-is-oversight /portraits/henry-waxman-and-big-tobacco/; "Tobacco CEO's Statement to Congress 1994 News Clip: 'Nicotine Is Not Addictive.'" https://senate.ucsf .edu/tobacco-ceo-statement-to-congress; "The Master Settlement Agreement and Its Impact on Tobacco Use 10 Years Later: Lessons for Physicians About Health Policy Making" by Walter J. Jones, PhD, and Gerard A. Silvestri, MD, FCCP. *Chest Journal*, March 2010. https://www.ncbi.nlm.nih.gov/pmc/articles /PMC3021365/; https://www.c-span.org/video/?56038-1/oversight-tobacco -products-part-1#.

Claude was a living, breathing model of chutzpah: "Courtly Champion of America's Elderly" by John Egerton. *New York Times Magazine*, November 29, 1981. https://www.nytimes.com/1981/11/29/magazine/courtly-champion-of -america-s-elderly.html.

John D. Dingell Jr. of Michigan was among the most powerful members of Congress ever: "Portraits in Oversight: Rep. John Dingell, Jr., an Oversight Champion" by the Carl Levin Center for Oversight and Democracy, Wayne State University, Detroit, MI. https://www.levin-center.org/rep-john-dingell/; "John Dingell: What Ex-Michigan Lawmaker Was Like in Private" by Todd Spangler. *Detroit Free Press*, February 8, 2019. https://www.freep.com/story/news/local /michigan/2019/02/08/rep-john-dingell-michigan-congress/2811318002/.

As Presidential historian Richard E. Neustadt affirmed: Presidential Power and the Modern Presidents: The Politics of Leadership from Roosevelt to Reagan by Richard E. Neustadt (The Free Press, 1990).

Once, conducting a hearing on the illegal activities of Drexel Burnham Lambert: "Enduring a Congressional Investigation" by James F. Fitzpatrick. *Litigation*, Summer 1992. https://www.jstor.org/stable/29759555.

The Clean Air Act, first passed in 1970, was a favorite scapegoat of Ronald

Reagan: For more on the environmental battles between John Dingell and Henry Waxman, see "The National Press Club Luncheon with John Dingell." June 27, 2014. https://www.press.org/sites/default/files/20140627_dingell.pdf; "Fairness in Water Quality: A Descriptive Approach" by Katrina Smith. Duke Environmental Law and Policy Forum, 1994. https://scholarship.law.duke.edu /delpf/vol4/iss1/4; "An Overview of the Clean Air Act Amendments of 1990" by Henry A. Waxman. *Environmental Law*, Lewis & Clark Law School, 1991. https://www.jstor.org/stable/43266224?read-now=1&seq=4#page_scan_tab _contents.

CHAPTER 8: IDEAS MATTER

The Dutch leadership expert Dr. Marij Swinkels of the Utrecht University School of Governance: "How Ideas Matter in Public Policy: A Review of Concepts, Mechanisms, and Methods" by Marij Swinkels. *International Review of Public Policy*, 2:3, 2020. https://journals.openedition.org/irpp/1343.

Chris's and my shared appetite for technology, innovation, and action landed squarely on a newfangled invention called the Internet: Of the tens of thousands of pages devoted to the history of Section 230 of the Communications Decency Act, by far the best narrative and analysis is *The Twenty-Six Words That Created the Internet* by Jeff Kosseff (Cornell University Press, 2019), a legal and public policy scholar.

It's hard to overemphasize how strange the Internet was in 1995: "Jurassic Web" by Farhad Manjoo. Slate, February 24, 2009. https://slate.com /technology/2009/02/the-unrecognizable-internet of 1996.html.

"One of the hottest new markets to develop in years," according to Morgan Stanley: "From clip art to Comic Sans, screenshots show how different the internet looks 25 years later," *Business Insider*, July 24, 2021, https://www .businessinsider.com/web-from-1996-internet-25-years-ago-screenshots-2021-7.

Capitol Hill was getting its paws into the Internet: "Was the 1996 Telecommunications Act Successful in Promoting Competition?" by Stuart N.

Brotman. Brookings, February 8, 2016. https://www.brookings.edu/articles/was
-the-1996-telecommunications-act-successful-in-promoting-competition/.

Chris wrote in a later retrospective: "Section 230: A Retrospective" by
Christopher Cox. The Center for Growth and Opportunity at Utah State
University, November 10, 2022. https://www.thecgo.org/research/section-230-a
-retrospective.

The case, Stratton Oakmont, Inc. v. Prodigy Services Co.: In addition to Jeff
Kosseff's book, Brookings has published a very good analysis of Section 230
and the preceding case law, "Interpreting the Ambiguities of Section 230" by
Alan Z. Rozenshtein. Brookings, October 26, 2023. https://www.brookings.edu
/articles/interpreting-the-ambiguities-of-section-230/.

*The Supreme Court voted unanimously in Smith v. California that a state law
banning the selling of "obscene" books violated the First Amendment:* "Smith
v. California (1959)" by Elizabeth R. Purdy. Free Speech Center at Middle
Tennessee State University, January 1, 2009. https://firstamendment.mtsu.edu
/article/smith-v-california/.

*Scholars have estimated that those 26 words have injected $1 trillion of new
wealth into the global economy:* "A Bit of Internet History, Or How Two
Members of Congress Helped Create a Trillion or So Dollars of Value" by David
Post. *Washington Post*, August 27, 2015. https://www.washingtonpost.com
/news/volokh-conspiracy/wp/2015/08/27/a-bit-of-internet-history-or-how-two
-members-of-congress-helped-create-a-trillion-or-so-dollars-of-value/.

*In 2020, the Internet economy contributed $2.45 trillion to the United States'
$21.18 trillion gross domestic product:* The data on the growth of the Internet's
contribution to the U.S. economy is from "The Economic Impact of the Market-
Making Internet: Advertising, Content, Commerce, and Innovation: Contribution
to U.S. Employment and GDP" by John Deighton and Leora Kornfeld, IAB.
https://www.iab.com/wp-content/uploads/2021/10/IAB_Economic_Impact_of
_the_Market-Making_Internet_Study_2021-10.pdf.

CHAPTER 9: FACING FORMIDABLE FOES (AND FRIENDS)

I never much cared for Robert Packwood: For background on the 1995–96 campaign for the U.S. Senate, see "Forest Economics Top Issue in Senate Races" by Roberta Ulrich. *Oregonian*, April 22, 1992. https://oregonlive.newsbank.com /doc/news/0EB08732C8AB6354; "Taking on Packwood by the Numbers" by David Sarasohn. *Oregonian*, April 24, 1991. https://oregonlive.newsbank.com /doc/news/0EB0867F55C98075; "In Packabucks, Lucky Number Is 1992" by David Sarasohn. *Oregonian*, August 11, 1991. https://oregonlive.newsbank.com /doc/news/0EB086A0B08D6921; "Vietnam Isn't Issue in Oregon—Wayne Morse Is" by Robert M. Krim. *Harvard Crimson*, October 11, 1968. https://www .thecrimson.com/article/1968/10/11/vietnam-isnt-issue-in-oregon-/; "Burning the Candle at Both Ends," by Steve Duin, *Oregonian*, March 26, 1991, https:// oregonlive.newsbank.com/doc/news/0EB086767A912F01.

The Federal Government owns more than half our state's 61 million acres: For more on the timber industry and the "timber wars" in Oregon, see "Oregon's Forest Economy." Oregon Forest Resources Institute. https://oregonforests.org /economics; "Owl Bites Both Sides." *Oregonian*, April 2, 1989. https://oregonlive .newsbank.com/doc/news/0EB085D34FB2D528; "This Land, Oregon" by William G. Robbins. Oregon Historical Society, Oregon History Project. https:// www.oregonhistoryproject.org/narratives/this-land-oregon/; "Oregon History: The Gaps Widen." Oregon Blue Book. https://sos.oregon.gov/blue-book/Pages/facts /history1/gap.aspx; "What's Changed in Oregon Since the Timber Wars?" by Ed Jahn. *Oregon Public Broadcasting*, September 30, 2020. https://www.opb.org /article/2020/09/30/whats-changed-in-oregon-since-the-timber-wars/.

Less than three weeks later, a bomb dropped: For more about the sexual harassment charges against Bob Packwood and his resignation from the U.S. Senate, see "Packwood Accused of Sexual Advances." *Washington Post*, November 22, 1992; https://www.washingtonpost.com/archive /politics/1992/11/22/packwood-accused-of-sexual-advances/ee1934bf-2e24 -4291-bd63-5842147526eb/ "Packwood's Alter Ego: One Tough Woman" by Roberta Ulrich and James O. Long. *Oregonian*, December 13, 1992. https:// oregonlive.newsbank.com/doc/news/0EB0877A0C702DE3; "Packwood Offers

Apology Without Saying for What" by Martin Tolchin. *New York Times*, December 11, 1992. https://www.nytimes.com/1992/12/11/us/packwood-offers -apology-without-saying-for-what.html; "Packwood: Behavior Was 'Wrong'" by Helen Dewar and Florence Graves. *Washington Post*, December 10, 1992. https:// www.washingtonpost.com/archive/politics/1992/12/11/packwood-behavior-was -wrong/6a4fdff6-fa3d-4db8-8fc2-923c1085bc72/; "Chief Justice Rejects Packwood Diary Plea" by Rose Ellen O'Connor and Dee Lane. *Oregonian*, March 3, 1994. https://oregonlive.newsbank.com/doc/news/0EB0884305BEC85D; "The Packwood Case: Statement from Senate Ethics Committee." *New York Times*, September 7, 1995. https://www.nytimes.com/1995/09/07/us/the-packwood -case-statement-from-senate-ethics-committee.html; "Packwood Fights On" by Rose Ellen O'Connor and Brent Walth. *Oregonian*, September 7, 1995. https:// oregonlive.newsbank.com/doc/news/0EB0891804494553.

Nader unleashed his attack on me: "Nader Blasts Wyden, Accuses Him of Selling Out" by Scott Sonner. *Oregonian*, November 2, 1995. https:// oregonlive.newsbank.com/doc/image/v2%3A11A73E5827618330%40NGPA -ORO-1786097EB3D2107A%402450024-17853DD9050F43F2%4024 -17853DD9050F43F2%40?search_terms=ralph%2Bnader%2B1995 &date_from=1995&date_to=1996&text=ralph%20nader%201995&contentadd ed=&pub%25252525255B0%25252525255D=ORGB&sort =old&pub%252525255B0%252525255D=ORGB&pub%2525255B0%2525 255D=ORGB&pub%25255B0%25255D=ORGB&pub%255B0%255D= 11A73E5827618330&page=2&pdate=1995-11-02; "Ron Wyden: Serious, Awkward, Driven, Idealistic" by Gail Kinsey Hill and Steve Suo. *Oregonian*, January 14, 1996. https://oregonlive.newsbank.com/doc/news /0EB0896AF97A0E11.

President Clinton also had managed to make a hash of gay rights: For a history of the "don't ask, don't tell policy," its antecedents and aftermath, see *Sexual Orientation and U.S. Military Personnel Policy: An Update of RAND's 1993 Study* (National Defense Research Institute, 2010). https://www.jstor.org/stable/10.7249/mg1056osd.10?seq=2; "How Ron Wyden Became the First U.S. Senator Ever to Endorse Marriage Equality" by Kari Chisholm. BlueOregon. https://www.blueoregon.com/2013/03/how-ron -wyden-became-first-us-senator-ever-endorse-marriage-equality/.

There were more than 1,000 Federal rights and responsibilities to which gay couples did not have access: "The Journey to Marriage Equality in the United States." The Human Rights Campaign. https://www.hrc.org/our-work/stories /the-journey-to-marriage-equality-in-the-united-states.

Political attack advertising had been creeping into public consciousness for several years: "The 1990 Election: Usual Flurry of Election Ads on Television Becomes a Blizzard This Year" by Randall Rothenberg. *New York Times*, October 21, 1990. https://www.nytimes.com/1990/10/21/us/1990-election-usual -flurry-election-ads-television-becomes-blizzard-this-year.html; "Accentuate the Negative: Contemporary Congressional Campaigns" by Ronald D. Elving. *PS: Political Science and Politics*, September 1996. https://go.gale .com/ps/i.do?p=AONE&u=googlescholar&id=GALE|A18796143&v=2 .1&it=r&sid=bookmark-AONE&asid=9450f44d.

CHAPTER 10: PUSHING BOULDERS

Sickness consumes families: Background sources for this chapter include "Health Care Spending in the US Is Nearly Double That of Other Wealthy Nations: Report" by Chia-Yi Hou. *The Hill*, January 31, 2023. https://thehill .com/changing-america/well-being/prevention-cures/3836252-health-care -spending-in-the-us-nearly-double-of-other-wealthy-nations-report/; "The Real Cost of Health Care." KFF.org, February 21, 2019. https://www.kff.org /health-costs/press-release/interactive-calculator-estimates-both-direct-and -hidden-household-spending/; "Health Insurance Coverage in the United States: 2021" by Katherine Keisler-Starkey and Lisa N. Bunch. United States Census Bureau, September 13, 2022. https://www.census.gov/library /publications/2022/demo/p60-278.html; "Health Insurance Coverage of the Total Population." KFF.org. https://www.kff.org/other/state-indicator/total -population/?currentTimeframe=0&sortModel=%7B%22colId%22:% 22Location%22,%22sort%22:%22asc%22%7D.

Medicare...had become a victim of its own success: For background on the history of employer-provided health insurance and the evolution of Medicare, see "Employer-Sponsored Health Insurance and the Promise of Health Insurance Reform" by Thomas C. Buchmueller and Alan C. Monheit. National Bureau of Economic Research, April 2009. http://www.nber.org/papers/w14839; "Remarks of Senator John F. Kennedy at the Memorial Program Honoring the 25th Anniversary of the Signing of the Social Security Act, Hyde Park, New York, August 14, 1960." https://www.jfklibrary.org/archives/other-resources/john-f -kennedy-speeches/social-security-25th-anniversary-hyde-park-ny-19600814; "The History of Medicare." National Academy of Social Insurance. https:// www.nasi.org/learn/medicare/the-history-of-medicare/; "How Medicare Was Made" by Julian E. Zelizer. *New Yorker*, February 15, 2015. https://www .newyorker.com/news/news-desk/medicare-made; "Medicare Matters: Building on a Record of Accomplishments" by Marilyn Moon. *Health Care Finance Review*, Fall 2000. https://www.ncbi.nlm.nih.gov/pmc/articles/PMC4194692; "What to Know About Medicare Spending and Financing" by Juliette Cubanski and Tricia Neuman. KFF.org, January 19, 2023. https://www.kff.org/medicare /issue-brief/what-to-know-about-medicare-spending-and-financing/.

The result has been longer lives and higher costs: For details on health-care cost inflation, see "How Does Health Spending in the U.S. Compare to Other Countries?" by Emma Wager, Matthew McGough, Shameek Rakshit, Krutika Amin, and Cynthia Cox. KFF.org. https://www.healthsystemtracker.org /chart-collection/health-spending-u-s-compare-countries/; "NHE Fact Sheet." CMS.gov, Centers for Medicare & Medicaid Services. https://www.cms.gov /data-research/statistics-trends-and-reports/national-health-expenditure-data /nhe-fact-sheet; "Lobbying Expenditures and Campaign Contributions by the Pharmaceutical and Health Product Industry in the United States, 1999–2018" by Olivier J. Wouters. *JAMA Internal Medicine*, May 2020. https://jamanetwork .com/journals/jamainternalmedicine/fullarticle/2762509.

CHAPTER 11: PRINCIPLED BIPARTISANSHIP

Providing prescription drug coverage for the elderly: For background on the SPICE Act and prescription drug coverage, see "A Political History of Medicare and Prescription Drug Coverage" by Thomas R. Oliver, Philip R. Lee, and

Helene L. Lipton. *Milbank Quarterly*, June 2004. https://www.ncbi.nlm.nih.gov /pmc/articles/PMC2690175/.

Senator Snowe was the perfect partner with whom to take this on: "Olympia J. Snowe," edited by Kerri Lee Alexander. National Women's History Museum. https://www.womenshistory.org/education-resources/biographies/olympia-j -snowe; "Olympia Snowe," *Bipartisan Policy Center*, https://bipartisanpolicy .org/person/olympia-snowe/; "Olympia Snowe: Why I'm Leaving the Senate" by Olympia J. Snowe. *Washington Post*, March 1, 2012. https:// www.washingtonpost.com/opinions/olympia-snowe-why-im-leaving-the -senate/2012/03/01/gIQApGYZlR_story.html.

Six months later, Congressman Bill Thomas joined the fray: "Bill Thomas, Rep. with a Rep" by Mark Leibovich. *Washington Post*, July 26, 2003. https:// www.washingtonpost.com/archive/lifestyle/2003/07/27/bill-thomas-rep-with-a -rep/23df043a-7e34-485a-a76e-ff007e8585b8/; "Before Kevin and Devin, There Was Bill" by Dorothy Mills-Gregg. *Capitol Weekly*, March 1, 2018. https:// capitolweekly.net/kevin-devin-bill-thomas/.

Seniors historically had been aligned with Democrats: "U.S. Seniors Have Realigned with the Republican Party" by Jeffrey M. Jones. Gallup, March 26, 2014. https://news.gallup.com/poll/168083/seniors-realigned-republican-party .aspx; "For House GOP, a New Prescription: Election Realities Spur Drug Benefit Plan, Medicare Reversal" by Juliet Eilperin. *Washington Post*, April 25, 2000. https://www.washingtonpost.com/archive/politics/2000/04/26/for-house -gop-a-new-prescription/3217dc3c-192c-4a64-921c-91cd9e098fc8/; "Bipartisan Effort on Drug Coverage Is Begun" by Robert Pear. *New York Times*, May 27, 2000. https://www.nytimes.com/2000/05/27/us/bipartisan-effort-on-drug -coverage-is-begun.html.

Then President Bush came alive: "The Medicare Prescription Drug, Improvement, and Modernization Act of 2003: Will It Be Good Medicine for U.S. Health Policy" by Susan Adler Channick. *The Elder Law Journal*, January 10, 2007. https://publish.illinois.edu/elderlawjournal/files/2015/02/Channick .pdf; "Editorial: The Drug Lobby Scores Again." *New York Times*, December 17, 2004. https://www.nytimes.com/2004/12/17/opinion/the-drug-lobby-scores

-again.html; "Medicare Plan Covering Drugs Backed by AARP" by Robert Pear and Robin Toner. *New York Times*, November 18, 2003. https://www .nytimes.com/2003/11/18/us/medicare-plan-covering-drugs-backed-by-aarp.html.

CHAPTER 12: THE CUISINE OF COMPROMISE

On December 13, 2006, I announced the Healthy Americans Act: For background on this legislation, see "Wyden Pushes for Universal Health Care Legislation" by Drew Armstrong. The Commonwealth Fund, December 13, 2006. https://www .commonwealthfund.org/publications/newsletter-article/cq-newsroom-wyden -pushes-universal-health-care-legislation; "The Healthy Americans Act Is No Laughing Matter" by William A. Galston. Brookings, April 14, 2009. https:// www.brookings.edu/articles/the-healthy-americans-act-is-no-laughing-matter/.

Bennett and I started touring the nation to tout our plan: "Health Care's Odd Couple" by Ezra Klein. *American Prospect*, February 15, 2008. https://prospect .org/article/health-care-s-odd-couple/.

The campaign was historic: "Health Care in the 2008 Presidential Primaries" by Robert J. Blendon, Drew E. Altman, Claudia Deane, John M. Benson, Mollyann Brodie, and Tami Buhr. *New England Journal of Medicine*, January 24, 2008. https://www.nejm.org/doi/full/10.1056/NEJMsr0708410; "2008 Candidates Vow to Overhaul U.S. Health Care" by Robin Toner. *New York Times*, July 6, 2007. https://www.nytimes.com/2007/07/06/us/politics/06health.html.

The politicization of health-care requirements was rife with hypocrisy: "The Tortured Saga of America's Least-Loved Policy Idea" by John E. McDonough. *Politico*, May 22, 2021. https://www.politico.com/news/magazine/2021/05/22 /health-care-individual-mandate-policy-conservative-idea-history-489956.

"There are a lot of good concepts to what Ron's proposing," the President said: For the battle to pass Obamacare, see "Obama Calls Wyden Health Plan Radical" by Dee Lane. *Oregonian*, July 2, 2009. https://www.oregonlive.com /politics/2009/07/obama_calls_wyden_health_plan.html; "We Are What We Treat" by Jacob Weisberg. *Newsweek*, July 17, 2009. https://www.newsweek.com/we-are

-what-we-treat-82021; "Sen. Bennett Loses GOP Nomination" by David Catanese. *Politico*, May 8, 2010. https://www.politico.com/story/2010/05/sen-bennett-loses -gop-nomination-036960; "Unpopular Mandate" by Ezra Klein. *New Yorker*, June 18, 2012. https://www.newyorker.com/magazine/2012/06/25/unpopular -mandate; "Key Facts About the Uninsured Population" by Jennifer Tolbert, Patrick Drake, and Anthony Damico. KFF.org, December 18, 2023. https://www.kff.org /uninsured/issue-brief/key-facts-about-the-uninsured-population/.

Three labor unions that had been strong supporters of my other work poured money into ads in Oregon attacking me: For background on the fight over Free Choice Vouchers, see "Liberals Dog Wyden on Bill" by Michael Falcone. *Politico*, July 28, 2009. https://www.politico.com/story/2009/07/liberals-dog -wyden-on-bill-025490; "Wyden Hits Back at Unions in Healthcare Fight" by Alexander Bolton. *The Hill*, May 22, 2009. https://thehill.com/homenews /news/17316-wyden-hits-back-at-unions-in-healthcare-fight/; "Senate Health Care Legislation Markup, Day 7, Part 4." C-SPAN, October 1, 2009. https:// www.c-span.org/video/?289239-4/senate-health-care-legislation-markup-day-7 -part-4; "Wyden on Warpath over Voucher Deal in CR" by Jennifer Haberkorn. *Politico Pro*, April 12, 2011. https://subscriber.politicopro.com/article/2011/04 /wyden-on-warpath-over-voucher-deal-in-cr-002627.

CHAPTER 13: THE LONG GAME, PART II

The right calls this legal warfare: "How Fighting for Conservative Causes Has Helped Ken Paxton Survive Legal Woes" by J. David Goodman. *New York Times*, May 26, 2023. https://www.nytimes.com/2023/05/26/us/ken-paxton -texas.htm.

Validating the menace to Federal rights was a new claim by the Republican attorneys general of 20 states: For details on the battle to overturn the legalization of mifepristone, see "20 Republican Attorneys General Warn CVS, Walgreens Against Selling Abortion Pills by Mail" by Christine Fernando. *USA Today*, February 2, 2023. https://www.usatoday.com/story/news /nation/2023/02/02/medication-abortion-abortion-pills-republican-attorneys

-general/11171581002/; "20 Attorneys General Warn Walgreens, CVS over Abortion Pills" by Jim Salter. AP, February 1, 2023. https://apnews.com/article /abortion-missouri-state-government-west-virginia-united-states-us-food-and -drug-administration-a1b1a387788bb5aaa39c9ce4128d77ab; "The FDA Finalizes Rule Expanding the Availability of Abortion Pills" by the Associated Press. NPR, January 3, 2023. https://www.npr.org/2023/01/03/1146860433/the-fda -finalizes-rule-expanding-the-availability-of-abortion-pills; "Kentucky Lawmaker Apologizes for Referencing Jewish Women's Sex Life Amid Abortion Debate" by Morgan Watkins and Joe Sonka. *Louisville Courier Journal*, March 2, 2022. https://www.courier-journal.com/story/news/politics/ky-general -assembly/2022/03/02/kentucky-lawmaker-danny-bentley-invokes-holocaust -jewish-women-sex-life-floor-speech/9350236002/.

All these extremist fever dreams came together on the desk of an obscure Texas judge: For background on Federal Judge Matthew Kacsmaryk, see "The Texas Judge Who Could Take Down the Abortion Pill" by Caroline Kitchener and Ann E. Marimow. *Washington Post*, February 25, 2023. https://www .washingtonpost.com/politics/2023/02/25/texas-judge-abortion-pill-decision/; "Oppose the Confirmation of Matthew Kacsmaryk to the U.S. District Court for the Northern District of Texas." The Leadership Conference on Civil and Human Rights, December 12, 2017. https://civilrights.org/resource/oppose-confirmation -matthew-kacsmaryk-u-s-district-court-northern-district-texas/; "Oregon Appeals Court Upholds Discrimination Ruling in Sweet Cakes Case, but Vacates Penalties" by Dirk VanderHart. Oregon Public Broadcasting, January 26, 2022. https://www.opb.org/article/2022/01/26/oregon-appeals-court-sweet-cakes -bakery-same-sex-discrimination-ruling; "The Controversial Article Matthew Kacsmaryk Did Not Disclose to the Senate" by Caroline Kitchener, Robert Barnes, and Ann E. Marimow. *Washington Post*, April 15, 2023. https://www .washingtonpost.com/politics/2023/04/15/matthew-kacsmaryk-law-review/.

CHAPTER 14: SPENDING POLITICAL CAPITAL

The battle over Obamacare was painful: For details on the impact of Obamacare, see "Pre-Existing Condition Prevalence for Individuals and

Families" by Gary Claxton, Cynthia Cox, Anthony Damico, Larry Levitt, and Karen Pollitz. KFF.org, October 4, 2019. https://www.kff.org/affordable-care-act/issue-brief/pre-existing-condition-prevalence-for-individuals-and-families/; "At Risk: Pre-Existing Conditions Could Affect 1 in 2 Americans." CMS.gov, Centers for Medicare and Medicaid Services. https://www.cms.gov/CCIIO/Resources/Forms-Reports-and-Other-Resources/preexisting; "Background: The Affordable Care Act's New Rules on Preventive Care." CMS.gov, Centers for Medicare and Medicaid Services, July 14, 2010. https://www.cms.gov/CCIIO/Resources/Fact-Sheets-and-FAQs/preventive-care-background.

CHAPTER 15: THE COACH'S JOURNEY

For decades, climatologists have tracked rising worldwide temperatures: For the Moynihan memo on climate change, see "Memorandum: The White House, Washington, September 17, 1969," by Daniel P. Moynihan, Richard Nixon Presidential Library and Museum, https://www.nixonlibrary.gov/sites/default/files/virtuallibrary/documents/jul10/56.pdf; for Senator Joe Biden's early climate change bill, see "Was Joe Biden a Climate Change Pioneer in Congress? History Says Yes," by John Kruzel, PolitiFact, May 8, 2019, https://www.politifact.com/factchecks/2019/may/08/joe-biden/was-joe-biden-climate-change-pioneer-congress-hist/; for the Hansen testimony about global warming, see "Thirty Years Warmer," by Madeline Ostrander, *Slate*, July 2, 2018, https://slate.com/technology/2018/07/james-hansens-1988-climate-change-warning-30-years-on.html.

A ballyhooed but complicated bipartisan climate-change bill designed by Democrats John Kerry and Joe Lieberman and Republican Lindsay Graham was collapsing: Background on cap-and-trade and the Kerry-Lieberman-Graham legislation: "As the World Burns" by Ryan Lizza. *New Yorker*, October 3, 2010. https://www.newyorker.com/magazine/2010/10/11/as-the-world-burns; and "McCain Slams 'Horrendous' Climate Bill" by Lisa Lerer. *Politico*, November 19, 2009. https://www.politico.com/story/2009/11/mccain-slams-horrendous-climate-bill-029747; "How Policy Got Done in 2022" by David Dayen. *American Prospect*, September 26, 2022. https://prospect.org/politics/how-policy-got-done-in-2022/; "Five Decades in the Making: Why It Took

Congress So Long to Act on Climate" by Coral Davenport and Lisa Friedman. *New York Times*, August 7, 2022. https://www.nytimes.com/2022/08/07/climate/senate-climate-law.html; "Democrats Are Shockingly Unprepared to Fight Climate Change" by Robinson Meyer. *The Atlantic*, November 15, 2017. https://www.theatlantic.com/science/archive/2017/11/there-is-no-democratic-plan-to-fight-climate-change/543981/.

Oregon's Spotted Owl was the advance guard of global climate change: For information about the impact of climate change on Oregonians, see "What Climate Change Means for Oregon." U.S. Environmental Protection Agency. https://19january2017snapshot.epa.gov/sites/production/files/2016-09/documents/climate-change-or.pdf; "Economic Impact of Oregon's Marine Fisheries." Oregon Department of Fish and Wildlife. https://www.dfw.state.or.us/agency/economic_impact.asp; "Oregon's Forest Sector Employment Totals 62,000 in 2021" by Anna Johnson. State of Oregon Employment Department, November 28, 2022. https://www.qualityinfo.org/-/oregon-s-forest-sector-employment-totals-62-000-in-2021-2.

Divided government has been the norm: For more about the history of divided governments in the U.S. and the need for compromise, see "Our History of Divided Government," *Americana Corner*, https://www.americanacorner.com/blog/history-divided-government; "House Dysfunction by the Numbers: 724 Votes, Only 27 Laws Enacted" by Annie Karnie. *New York Times*, December 19, 2023. https://www.nytimes.com/2023/12/19/us/politics/house-republicans-laws-year.html; "Transcript: Ezra Klein Interviews Jacob Grumbach." *New York Times*, December 6, 2022. https://www.nytimes.com/2022/12/06/podcasts/transcript-ezra-klein-interviews-jacob-grumbach.html.

It took 32 years from the Wright Brothers' first flight in Kitty Hawk, North Carolina: For background on theories of innovation, see "The Three Phases of Value Capture: Finding Competitive Advantage in the Information Age" by Rhonda Germany and Raman Muralidharan. *strategy+business*, January 1, 2001. https://www.strategy-business.com/article/10884; "Innovation" by Timothy Sandefur. *Econlib.* https://www.econlib.org/library/Enc/Innovation.html; *The Innovator's Dilemma: The Revolutionary Book That Will Change the*

Way You Do Business by Clayton M. Christensen (Harper Business, 2011); and *Prophet of Innovation: Joseph Schumpeter and Creative Destruction* by Thomas K. McCraw (Harvard University Press, 2008).

"The Senate's most powerful committee": For background on the U.S. Senate Finance Committee and my rise to the chair position, see "Tax Lobby Builds Ties to Chairman of Finance Panel" by Eric Lipton. *New York Times*, April 6, 2013. https://www.nytimes.com/2013/04/07/us/politics/tax-lobby-builds-ties-to-max -baucus.html; "A Brief History of the Senate Committee on Finance." United States Capitol Historical Society. https://capitolhistory.org/explore/historical -articles/a-brief-history-of-the-committee-on-finance/; "The Senate Finance Committee Just Got a Lot More Liberal, Now That Ron Wyden Is in Charge" by Danny Vinik. *New Republic*, February 20, 2014. https://newrepublic.com /article/116682/ron-wyden-senate-finance-chair-could-pull-committee-left; and "The Rise of Ron Wyden" by Brian Faler. *Politico*, February 11, 2014. https:// www.politico.com/story/2014/02/ron-wyden-finance-chairman-103352.

On May 5, 2017, I introduced the Clean Energy for America Act: For background on the Trump Administration's destructive climate policies and on my Clean Energy legislation, see "What Is the Trump Administration's Track Record on the Environment?" by Samantha Gross. Brookings, August 4, 2020. https://www.brookings.edu/articles/what-is-the-trump-administrations-track -record-on-the-environment; "US Elections 2020: A History of Trump's Climate Change Denial" by Akshit Sangomla. *Down to Earth*, November 3, 2020. https://www.downtoearth.org.in/news/climate-change/us-elections-2020-a -history-of-trump-s-climate-change-denial-74075; "Five Decades in the Making: Why It Took Congress So Long to Act on Climate" by Coral Davenport and Lisa Friedman. *New York Times*, August 7, 2022. https://www.nytimes .com/2022/08/07/climate/senate-climate-law.html; "U.S. Report Says Humans Cause Climate Change, Contradicting Top Trump Officials" by Lisa Friedman and Glenn Thrush. *New York Times*, November 3, 2017. https://www.nytimes .com/2017/11/03/climate/us-climate-report.html; "Wyden Unveils Clean Energy for America Act" by Rachel McCleery. United States Senate Committee on Finance, May 5, 2017. https://www.finance.senate.gov/ranking-members-news /wyden-unveils-clean-energy-for-america-act.

The stop-it-now school of environmentalism: For background on "punitive ecology" and the environmental movement's evolution and embrace of job creation, see *The Population Bomb* by Paul R. Ehrlich (Rivercity Press, 1971); "Putting People at the Heart of the Green Transition." WWF with IPPR, the Institute for Public Policy Research, October 2019. https://www.wwf.org.uk /sites/default/files/2019-10/green_transition_Essays.pdf.

The bill that President Biden signed on August 16, 2022… "reshapes industry across the country and the world": For data on the impact of the Inflation Reduction Act, see "How the Inflation Reduction Act Has Reshaped the U.S.—and the World" by Justin Worland. *Time*, August 11, 2023. https:// time.com/6304143/inflation-reduction-act-us-global-impact/; "The Inflation Reduction Act: Here's What's in It" by Justin Badlam, Jared Cox, Adi Kumar, Nehal Mehta, Sara O'Rourke, and Julia Silvis. McKinsey & Company, October 24, 2022. https://www.mckinsey.com/industries/public-sector/our-insights /the-inflation-reduction-act-heres-whats-in-it; "The Inflation Reduction Act: A Year in Review" by Trevor Higgins. Cap20, September 21, 2023. https://www .americanprogress.org/article/the-inflation-reduction-act-a-year-in-review/; "Forget FDR. Biden Is a Major President in His Own Right" by Walter Shapiro. *The New Republic*, August 22, 2022. https://newrepublic.com/article/167474 /joe-biden-fdr-polls-inflation-reduction-act; "The Astronomical Price of Insulin Hurts American Families." Rand, January 26, 2021. https://www.rand.org/pubs /articles/2021/the-astronomical-price-of-insulin-hurts-american-families.html.